I AM WHERE I COME FROM

June 2017

To Kimi,

I hope these stories inspire you
to remain strong in
your Navajo/Ho-chunk/Lakota
identity and to always follow
your dreams. Congratulations
to you Shiyazhi!

Love,
Mom

I AM WHERE I COME FROM

Native American College Students and Graduates Tell Their Life Stories

EDITED BY

Andrew Garrod, Robert Kilkenny, and Melanie Benson Taylor

WITH A FOREWORD BY

K. Tsianina Lomawaima

Cornell University Press
Ithaca and London

First published 2017 by Cornell University Press
First printing, Cornell Paperbacks, 2017

Printed in the United States of America

Library of Congress Cataloging-in-Publication Data

Names: Garrod, Andrew, 1937– editor. | Kilkenny, Robert, editor. | Taylor, Melanie Benson, 1976– editor. | Container of (work): Prince, Shannon. Seeking to be whole.
Title: I am where I come from : Native American college students and graduates tell their life stories / edited by Andrew Garrod, Robert Kilkenny, and Melanie Benson Taylor.
Other titles: First person, first peoples.
Description: Ithaca : Cornell University Press, 2017. | "The essays by N. Bruce Duthu, Davina Two Bears, and Bob Bennett originally appeared in the 1997 book, First Person, First Peoples: Native American College Graduates Tell Their Life Stories"—Foreword. | ·Includes bibliographical references.
Identifiers: LCCN 2016049570 (print) | LCCN 2016050595 (ebook) | ISBN 9781501706912 (cloth : alk. paper) | ISBN 9781501706929 (pbk. : alk. paper) | ISBN 9781501708015 (epub/mobi) | ISBN 9781501708022 (pdf)
Subjects: LCSH: Indians of North America—Education (Higher)—New Hampshire—Hanover. | Indian college students—New Hampshire—Hanover—Biography. | Minority college graduates—New Hampshire—Hanover—Biography. | Dartmouth College—Students—Biography.
Classification: LCC E97.65.N4 I24 2017 (print) | LCC E97.65.N4 (ebook) | DDC 378.1/9829707423—dc23
LC record available at https://lccn.loc.gov/2016049570

This book is dedicated to the Native students who have opened their lives with such generosity and grace and to the many others whose stories have yet to be told.

And to former Native students, friends, and teachers at Dartmouth and in the Marshall Islands:

Taylor Keen
Melissa Candelaria
Carnell Chosa
Diandra Benally
Saige Hoaglin
Cody Riggers
Casey Sovo
Paige Anderson
Peter Sabori
Sarah McGlaughlin
Casey Lozar
Nehomah Thundercloud
Colleen Larimore
Carmen Lopez
Eric Hogenson
Cheryl Two Bears
Jacqueline Begay
Hannah Sahn
Gilbert Littlewolf
Dwight Bero
Kodiak Burke
Cote Theriault
Aaluk Edwardson
Aza Erdrich
Shawn Attakai
Don Carlos Steele
Amado Sainz
Shawn Schmitt
Andre Cramblit
AG

Contents

Foreword

In his haunting, searingly beautiful memoir of early twentieth-century student life at St. Peter Claver's Indian Residential School—known to its captive boys as "Spanish"—Ojibwa educator and language scholar Basil Johnston wrote of shame, laughter, desolation, rebellion, camaraderie, and, eventually, escape. He concluded by quoting his friend Dominic: "We toughed it out, didn't we? They couldn't break us down, could they?"[1] When I interviewed my dad, Curtis Thorpe Carr (Creek) and about fifty other alumni of the Chilocco Indian Agricultural School, their memories of Indian school in the 1920s and 1930s—like Johnston's—mingled anger, joy, nostalgia, and anguish.[2] Bitter recollection intertwined with fond remembrance, as survivors of Canadian residential and US boarding schools made meaning of their lives. That is *not* to say that the institutions themselves were balanced, or equitable, or humane. They were not. They were schools that took schooling to extremes, and in the blast furnace of colonialism welded the worst aspects of schooling—rigidity, homogenization, abuse of power, mindless bureaucracy, demeaning labor, and rote "learning"—with racism, oppression, and dispossession to eliminate the Native.[3] They destroyed some, wounded others, but also forged resilient survivors.

The experiences, then, of Native peoples with colonial schools are diverse, complex, and filled with paradox. We must not forget: for Native peoples, most schools still are colonial. That's true in 2017, and well beyond, most likely. Indigenous self-determination in education has deep—centuries-deep—roots; but the beginnings of Indigenous self-determination in *schooling* in the United States date back only to the

1970s. Native-controlled schools, language programs, culturally responsive education, tribal charter schools, tribal community colleges are all exciting, dynamic developments on the schooling landscape; and they are all, in the long view a historian takes, quite recent. As a consequence, the powerful voices collected in this volume resonate historically, just as the ongoing legacies of colonial schooling and its violences resonate in Native communities and lives. The Native alumni of Dartmouth have experienced schooling in ways distinct from and yet similar to the Indian school days experienced by Basil Johnston and Curt Carr. They all "toughed it out," and also found occasion and cause for good times, satisfaction, and achievement. These powerful voices also resonate in our present day, each voice evoking echoes of those shut out from, or those who turned away from, academic accomplishment.

We could call *I Am Where I Come From* a qualitative study, based on the quality of the Native student and alumni voices that speak to us, but the contemporary context for its importance can also be measured quantitatively. For every one hundred Native students who begin ninth grade in the United States, forty-eight will graduate high school. Of those forty-eight, twenty will continue in some sort of higher education institution: technical college, community or tribal college, four-year college or university. One will graduate within six years with a four-year degree. Native America produces one MA for every twenty-five hundred people, and one PhD for every seven thousand.[4] Set in that context, Dartmouth's numbers resonate. Since 1970, Dartmouth has graduated more than seven hundred American Indian students from over two hundred tribes (preface to this volume). Viewed from the landscape of Indian country, each and every young person who makes it to college is a precious resource.

How do they make it to college? It's not a trivial question when the odds are so stacked against them. In a 2015 dissertation, Diné scholar Amanda Tachine weaves the stories of ten Diné (Navajo) students' journeys toward college into a "whole story rug," applying the traditional Navajo story of the Twin Warriors to describe students' "monsters"—sociocultural and personal barriers—and "weapons"—the sources of strength that guided them in life and toward college.[5] The pages that follow are replete with monsters and weapons in diverse journeys to, through, and beyond college. The monsters are big and scary. Addicted, abusive, or absent parents, especially fathers. Racism, sexism, and homophobia. Sexual assault. Alcoholism and depression. The loss of loved ones. Battles for identity and confidence and ease in being yourself.

Battles against anxiety, rage, and self-doubt. These intrepid survivors, however, also wield effective, life-nourishing weapons.

They are committed to others. Shannon Prince always remembers her responsibility to the people usually "stuck with the brooms and frying pans." Blythe George does "not strive to climb the heights merely to appreciate the view. I am trying to find a way to bring a piece of that skyline back to the ones I love to make their world better and brighter." They are rooted in home communities. AlexAnna Salmon writes: "*Igyararmiunguunga*—I belong to the Village of Igiugig," and John Around Him felt impelled to stay alive through his duty in Iraq by "profound affection for home." Their weapons are instruments of hope. Their weapons include success in school; the love and support of family; and personal pursuits such as running, poetry, music, and baseball. They find comfort in writing, sports, college clubs, and "Cheese Deluxe" sandwiches. They think about red-shale hills. They depend on committed teachers, counselors, coaches, grandparents, great-grandparents, mothers, fathers, friends, and NAD/Native Americans at Dartmouth. They learn the lessons of "living life in a posture of humility," of "loving your enemies and praying for those who despise you." And they all found or created a feeling of Dartmouth as home.

K. Tsianina Lomawaima

Preface

I Am Where I Come From: Native American Undergraduates and Graduates Tell Their Life Stories presents the personal narratives of Native American students who have studied at Dartmouth College, which is located in Hanover, New Hampshire. Between 2009 and 2015, the editors invited approximately thirty of these students to write about growing up in their home communities; their experiences attending college in New Hampshire; and, where relevant, their life after graduation. We asked them to focus in particular on the challenges and rewards of attending Dartmouth College. The contributors to this anthology, six men and seven women, are all current students at or graduates of Dartmouth College. These thirteen authors represent Native American tribes from across the United States and Canada, including the Cherokee, Yurok, Choctaw, Northern Cheyenne, Oglala Lakota, Navajo, and United Houma Nation tribes. The essays by N. Bruce Duthu, Davina Two Bears, and Bob Bennett originally appeared in the 1997 book *First Person, First Peoples: Native American College Graduates Tell Their Life Stories,* edited by Andrew Garrod and Colleen Larimore. Reprinted here—twenty years later—each of the three is accompanied by an essay that explores the personal and professional path the author has followed in the intervening years, thus offering us a developmental perspective on the contributor.

Our focus on Dartmouth College students and graduates is fitting, given the institution's historical connection to Native Americans. In the college's 1769 charter, England's King George III proclaimed the school as a place "for the education and instruction of Youth of the Indian Tribes in the Land in reading, writing, and all parts of Learning which shall appear necessary and expedient."[1] Dartmouth was established on the land of the Abenaki, which stretched from northern Massachusetts to the St. Lawrence River, and from Lake Champlain to Maine.[2] And, interestingly, a Mohegan Indian named Samson Occom, one of college founder Reverend Eleazar Wheelock's first students, was later instrumental in raising funds for the college in England.[3]

Despite these historical roots, Dartmouth's commitment to educating Native Americans was not solidified until the 1970s. In fact, in the two hundred years after its founding, the college enrolled only ninety-nine Native Americans—seventy-one between 1770 and 1865, and twenty-eight between 1865 and 1965—and only nineteen graduated.[4] Then, in 1970, Dartmouth's thirteenth president, John G. Kemeny, announced a concerted effort to return to the college's Native American roots. In his inauguration speech, Kemeny promised to enroll a "significantly greater" number of Native Americans than had attended Dartmouth since the college's founding,[5] and the early 1970s did bring many changes to Dartmouth's Native American student support system. In 1970, Kemeny established the Native American Program to help Native American students "flourish" at the college,[6] and students established Native Americans at Dartmouth, a student-run organization for all people interested in the college's Native community.[7] This was followed in 1972 with the birth of the college's Native American Studies Department, which initially offered courses on Native American ethnology, literature, and history,[8] and the opening of a Native American House at 18 North Park Street, which served as a residential, social, and cultural space for Native American students. In 1973, Dartmouth held its first annual powwow.[9]

Since 1970, Dartmouth has graduated more than seven hundred American Indian students from over two hundred tribes.[10] In the years 2011–2016, Native American enrollment at Dartmouth has remained at about 3 percent of the total student population, up from 2 percent in 2005.[11] The College of Arts and Sciences class of 2014 included forty-two Native Americans (4% of the incoming class), and the class of 2015 will graduate thirty-eight Native Americans (3% of the incoming class).[12] Native American students also comprise 4 percent of the three most recent incoming undergraduate classes, with thirty-nine, forty-six, and forty-seven enrolled in the classes of 2016, 2017, 2018, respectively.[13] Compared to national graduation figures for Native American students, these numbers are impressive: according to a 2014 report from the National Center for Education Statistics, 40.2 percent of Native Americans who enrolled in a four-year college in 2006 graduated within six years; this compares to a rate of 59.2 percent for all US college students.[14] Since

2006, an average of 83 percent of Native American students in each class graduated from Dartmouth within six years, compared to an average of 95 percent for all students.[15]

Dartmouth's on-campus support system for Native students has also expanded since 1970. The Native American Studies Department now offers more than twenty courses each academic year, and both a major and minor track.[16] The program will also begin a new off-campus program at the Institute of American Indian Arts in Santa Fe, New Mexico, in fall 2015. Between eight and eighteen students have graduated with a degree in Native American studies in each of the last five years,[17] the majority of whom have self-identified as Native American.[18] The Native American Program has also grown, and currently operates within Dartmouth's Office of Pluralism and Leadership. The program provides one-on-one advising sessions for undergraduate Native students, in collaboration with Dartmouth faculty and staff members.[19] It is run by an adviser, who also oversees the Native American House, which moved from the original location to a building constructed in 1995.[20]

While Dartmouth plays a prominent role in Native American education, it is not alone. Other prestigious American colleges and universities, such as Harvard and the College of William and Mary, were also founded with the express purpose of educating "the Indian." Today, over one hundred colleges have robust Native American studies programs, and many of Dartmouth's peer institutions, such as Stanford, Yale, Columbia, and the University of Pennsylvania, are actively recruiting and retaining larger cohorts of Native students. Just recently, the 2014 "Report on the John Evans Study Committee" interrogated one of the founders of Northwestern University—also a key player in the Sand Creek Massacre of Cheyenne and Arapaho Indians in 1864—and questioned whether the very financial founding of the institution can be yoked to Evans's Indian policies and atrocities (http://www.northwestern.edu/provost/committees/john-evans-study/study-committee-report.pdf). In the wake of this report, colleges and universities nationwide are reinvigorating their commitments to Native American issues and populations. In this expanding context, Dartmouth's history, location, and culture may still be considered unique, but not singular.

I Am Where I Come From is a qualitative exploration of the lives of thirteen brave and thoughtful Dartmouth students and graduates who reflect on the impact their Native American status has had on their identity formation and their lives. These compelling essays capture the phenomenology of being Native American in the United States today, and in doing so, engage, inspire, and move our readers. These personal stories are essentially memoirs, in which the authors reflect on their formative relationships and influences, life-changing events, and the role their Native heritage has played in shaping their personal identities, values, and choices.

A memoir serves an important purpose for the writer. Annie Dillard, author of *Pilgrim at Tinker Creek*, comments on writing her memoir, *An American Childhood:* "In the course of writing this memoir I've learned all sorts of things, quite inadvertently, about myself and various relationships." Her memoir, she says, is "about waking up"—about what it feels like to "notice that you've been set down in a going world."[21] Memoir, says William Zinsser, is "how we validate our lives," adding that a memoir often helps readers understand themselves, too: "Memoir writing puts lives in perspective, not only for the writer, but for the rest of us."[22]

For many of these Native American authors, the process of putting their experiences into words has acted as a catalyst for further reflection on their identities and life histories. In twenty-six years of encouraging this type of work, the editors have consistently observed that the process of autobiographical writing can have a profoundly transformative effect on the spiritual, moral, and emotional domains of a writer's life, and that a life is often changed by such deep introspection. We have found would-be contributors overwhelmingly open to making sense of their childhood and adolescent experiences, and of their young adulthood, which up to then had been inchoate and unintegrated. This opportunity to reflect can often reconcile the writers to traumas they have experienced, and bring emotional resolution and understanding to the primary relationships and vicissitudes in their lives. We have felt deeply privileged to guide our writers through deeper levels of self-understanding and to help them gain purchase on their personal world through self-analysis and articulation.

The editors encouraged the contributors to conduct the frankest possible examination of their lives, relationships, and the role identity played in shaping their attitudes and behaviors. In light of this, we offered each writer the option of anonymity; it is striking that not one of the thirteen availed themselves of this opportunity. Tribal affiliation clearly is such an important aspect of many of our writers' Native identity that all chose to write in their own name. A few authors used pseudonyms, but only to protect the identity of others featured in their essay. All the writers were asked to give a final stamp of approval to their chapter(s) of the book.

In assigning the essays, we initially encouraged the authors to follow broad guidelines as they reflected on how the formative aspects of their home culture, values, and identities had affected their transition to college. They were asked to think about classroom experiences at Dartmouth in the context of the intellectual stimulation offered by the college learning environment; about their interactions with the Native American Studies Department, Native American House, and fellow students; and about their friendships that crossed the lines of race, ethnicity, class, gender, and sexual orientation. We asked how their engagement in college life affected issues of identity (personal and ethnic), and whether they expected to return to their home community after graduation or at some later point in their life. To help our writers articulate their stories, we offered the following guiding questions:

- What gets you up in the morning? What is most important in your life? What do you live for? What is of transcendent value to you?
- Have there been critical incidents in your life (i.e., religious conversion, divorce of parents, death in the family, first love) after which nothing is quite the same—for good or ill, or for some mixture of these two?
- Explore the most important relationships in your life—within the family and outside it.
- What sort of a child were you? Did you have a particular role within your family?
- What were you like in your early years at school? Were you popular? If so, with whom? Were you a lonely child? Did any teacher pick you out as promising? Did you attend a school that was composed mostly of Native students, or was it more multiracial and multiethnic?
- Were you an early or late developer as you moved into adolescence, or did you move at about the normal pace? If you were an early developer, how do you think it affected the way people saw you?
- In high school, did you develop any particular skill or interest that made you stand out? Were your best friends of the same ethnicity as you? Discuss one or two of the most significant friendships you had in your later high-school years.
- When you were a child, was race/ethnicity discussed at home? If so, in what way? When were you aware that your heritage was a "minority heritage"? Have you been the victim of racism? If so, describe the first time. How did you feel? How did you react? How did you come to terms, if you did, with this racism?
- Why did you come to Dartmouth? What were you looking for? Was this environment much more or much less diverse than your home or

school environment? Has this been a supportive community for you? Have you been active in organizations that are concerned with issues of race and ethnicity? If so, how and why? If not, why not? Are most of your close friends Native American?

- Have you taken Native American courses while at Dartmouth? What did you gain from taking these courses? Were you active with Native Americans at Dartmouth (NAD)? How important was the existence of NAD to you in your life at Dartmouth? Do you feel you have connected powerfully with a faculty member or an administrator during your time at this college?
- Does being Native American help you understand racial/ethnic dynamics in this college and in this culture in a way that you might think whites do not?
- If you have a mixed heritage, do you identify with one component of your racial background more than the other? If so, which one, why, and what are the perspectives or insights on life that identity provides?
- What are some of the issues (tensions) that are discussed among the Native American population at Dartmouth? How do some of these issues relate to you and your life?
- What has been most rewarding/most challenging about your academic engagement at Dartmouth?
- As you consider moving on from your Dartmouth undergraduate days, how do you see yourself moving into the outside world? Do you think your sense of racial/ethnic identity has been strengthened in the last few years? What is the role of ethnic/racial identity within your total identity? (For some students, other aspects of identity may be more significant than race/ethnicity.)
- Do you anticipate working in the community that you came from after college or perhaps later in your life?

These questions were offered as prompts or probes. Many of our writers chose to engage with some of the questions and others found their own inspiration.

While the editors worked on a weekly basis with the writers, we made an effort to keep our assumptions about where the individual stories might go in view, but out of the way of the participants. Because the emphasis was on process—urging and helping the contributors to undertake that most complex of all writerly tasks, the location of voice—no editorial interventions were made during the generative stage. Although the parameters were necessarily established by the editors, we encouraged writers to develop their own themes and to make sense of their experiences in ways that gave them significant meaning in their own lives. All we asked was that they keep their thinking, feeling, and writing as honest as they could possibly manage. There was no assumption on either part that the story was "there," waiting to come out readily formed, as if from the head of Zeus; rather, we shared the belief that the story had to be "found"—uncovered piece by piece as patterns emerged and themes asserted themselves. Typically, a student would submit seven or eight pages to Andrew Garrod before each meeting, and we would discuss these pages when we met. Editor and writer also discussed how to proceed with the next portion of the narrative. A writer was frequently halfway through the process before he or she came to understand the essay's central concerns or themes.

The first drafts of these essays usually ranged from thirty to fifty pages, although one or two were considerably longer and sometimes one would be much shorter. After careful consultation and discussion over many months, occasionally even years, cutting and editing reduced and sharpened the texts to a manageable fifteen to twenty-five pages each. Variations in the tone, degree of self-analysis, and style of expression reflect our commitment to respect each author's story and life. Editors' changes to the text were in most cases minimal.

While the three editors discussed the shape of the book and its contents in detail, each of us played a different role. After a draft was reduced from its original length to approximately twenty-five pages, it was sent to Robert Kilkenny, who had not worked with the students or graduates and therefore could offer a more objective reaction to their essays. This was done to bring the essays to another level of psychological cohesion so that themes that seemed underdeveloped or mysteriously unaddressed in the stories could be brought to each writer's attention. Kilkenny suggested how and why a story would be better understood if some of these lacunae were explored more thoroughly. He also aimed to push the writers to the edge of their ability in pondering their own life stories. It was not unusual for a writer to balk, or to claim that they were genuinely unable to reflect further about an experience that was still raw and unresolved. Melanie Benson Taylor, who played a key part in the organization of the book, wrote the introduction and worked with some of the contributors in the final stages of reflection and revision.

We, the editors, are profoundly grateful to many student researchers and assistants, friends, and associates for the realization of this book.

Bruce Duthu, professor and former chair of the Native American Studies Department at Dartmouth and himself one of our contributors, was a tireless supporter of our project and suggested potential student contributors. Dody Riggs, a great friend and colleague on our anthology projects over many iterations, offered essential editorial suggestions as the manuscripts achieved their final forms. Andre Cramblit was ever quick to give us statistics on Native Americans in higher education and point us to important reference works. Given that the project has been six or seven years in the making, it is no surprise that we have many Dartmouth students, some of whom have become alumni/ae, to thank for organizational, administrative, and computer assistance. Karolina Krelinova, Trevor King, Tien-Tien Jong, Taylor Malmsheimer, Stephanie Abbott-Grobicki, Tendai Masangomai, Ramtin Rahmani, Dennis Zeveloff, Alex Johnson, Katherine Hanzalik, Marco Barragan, Roberto Lopez, Dayle Wang, and Andrew Weckstein all have helped improve the text markedly, keep the editors organized, and prepare the manuscript. We owe a very special thanks to Torrese Ouellette, who has been invaluable in making editorial suggestions and preparing the manuscript for publication. Andrew Nalani also has provided critical assistance. We are, in addition, grateful to the three anonymous reviewers for Cornell University Press.

It is not easy to open your life and your reflections on that life to public inspection. We wish to recognize all the contributors who have written with such courage and commitment to bring their stories into the public domain.

I AM WHERE I COME FROM

Coming Home   Melanie Benson Taylor

> Columbus landed in the second grade for me, and my teacher made me
> swallow the names of the boats one by one until in the bathtub of my summer
> vacation I opened my mouth and they came back out—Niña, Pinta, Santa
> Maria—and bobbed on the surface of the water like toys. I clapped my hand
> over my mouth once, Indian style, then looked up, for my mother, so she
> could pull the plug, stop all this, but when I opened my mouth again it was
> just blood and blood and blood.

Stephen Graham Jones, epigraph to Bleed Into Me

At some point during every Native American literature course I teach
at Dartmouth College, I ask students to read Blackfeet author Stephen
Graham Jones's extraordinary collection of short stories, *Bleed Into Me*
(2005), which opens with the arresting epigraph above. Jones identifies it
with the phrase "Overheard in group," suggesting that the speaker here
is engaging in a moment of therapeutic catharsis. For most traditional
Dartmouth students, it can be difficult to appreciate Jones's metaphor of
US education as a forceful internalization of imperial histories, or to grasp
the wrenching imagery of an Indian child regurgitating this knowledge in
a cascade of "blood and blood and blood," or to empathize with the tacit
relief of putting one's primal suffering into words and sharing it with a
supportive audience. But this is precisely what we encounter in Jones's
cathartic stories and so much of contemporary Native American literature
more broadly, as it attempts to give voice to the distinctive trauma of the
American Indian experience. Its pages unveil wounded children who look
futilely to the proverbial mother—family, tribe, tradition—to shore them
up, to end the recurring nightmare of being Indian in the United States,
yet find themselves unable to turn back the tide to a simpler, more innocent time before "Columbus landed" in both history and our own lives

and senses of self. Theirs are voices that testify to the subtle violence of having one's stories, cultures, and languages persistently overruled and overwritten; to the determination and difficulty of nonetheless moving forward and upward rather than peering painfully behind; and to the urge toward both an "Indian style" of self-protective silence and a confessional eruption of dark memories and pain.

In many ways, the United States is still learning to hear the dark tales of its Native residents, in part because "real" contemporary Indians have been rendered invisible by mythologies of extinction and the Hollywood romance of the noble savage. But Native Americans have played their own part as well in perpetuating notions of their anachronicity, often by clinging wistfully to stark, untenable distinctions between tribe and "others," home and "away," tradition and modernity. When *First Person, First Peoples* was published in 1997, the Native American voices it contained were a revelation, even as they, too, evinced the effects of living within and between such dichotomies. The writers, all former students of Dartmouth College in Hanover, New Hampshire, spoke with novel candor about the often painful experience of straddling two worlds: their home communities on the one hand, and the sometimes alienating world of higher education on the other. For those writers, this crisis found especially dramatic terrain at Dartmouth, one of very few institutions (along with Harvard and the College of William and Mary) founded specifically to educate Indian students, but delivering on the promise of its original charter in only sporadic and belated ways. After graduating only a handful of Native students in its first two centuries, the college rededicated itself to its founding mission in 1970 under the leadership of president John Kemeny. The Native American Program (NAP) was established to provide student support services to a dramatically increased Indian student body, and a Native American House (NAH) provided a space for students to live, gather, and share meals and ceremonies. The Admissions Office embarks on a vigorous yearly recruitment process, including a well-known "fly-in" program, to entice promising Indian students to join the next year's first-year class. Now Native Americans enroll at Dartmouth in rates sometimes four times higher than average for US colleges and universities.[1] Despite these seemingly enthusiastic gestures of inclusivity, American Indian students have often felt more like unwanted guests at the grand and sometimes threatening bazaar of knowledge and opportunity in which they find themselves. In *First Person, First Peoples*, the writers thus delineated Dartmouth with terrific ambivalence: as a place of both hope and estrangement for the Indians who have often felt more like its mascots than its scholars.

Nearly two decades later, that perception sometimes persists. Yet the writers in this follow-up volume quietly but consistently demonstrate that the apparent clash of cultures experienced by Natives in the academy is not quite as simple or straightforward as it seems. As historian (and member of the Native American studies faculty) Colin G. Calloway notes, "For many Indian students and their families in the West, Dartmouth is 'out there' in a remote northeastern corner of the country, far from the Indian communities they know—yet it is a school with a role in Indian country."[2] Indeed, a more capacious notion of "education" places Dartmouth in a remarkable position—as both a stronghold of Western knowledge and tradition as well as a rich site of Indian visibility and community that actually enriches one's quest for self-knowledge. In many ways, Dartmouth is indeed a cross-section of Indian country writ large, in all its expansive breadth and diversity: in any given year there may be over forty tribal nations represented from more than half the states in the nation and several Canadian provinces. For many of the nonreservation Native students who attend Dartmouth, it may be the first time they have had the opportunity to live and learn among so many Native peers and mentors. For those raised among their tribal communities, it is often their first introduction to the incredible diversity of American Indian cultures. The strength of the community is augmented by the exceptional size of its robust Native American Studies Program. I myself joined the program eagerly in 2009, after stints at other universities that typically offered only a handful of special-topics courses in Amerindian studies (often my own). I now know that this was mainly happenstance, as there are actually an increasing number of strong Indigenous studies programs at US and Canadian colleges and universities, not to mention at least thirty-four accredited, competitive tribal colleges throughout the nation.

For many Indian students, then, the experience of going away to college has become not just a departure but an unexpected homecoming. Nearly all the writers in *I Am Where I Come From* recall vividly the moment they learned of their acceptance to college, and most have indelible memories of the first time they set foot on the Dartmouth Green. While for some of these Native students Dartmouth itself functions as a transformative site, for others its role is far less seismic or less clear. On the one hand, as alumnus Bill Bray observed in his essay for *First Person, First Peoples*, Dartmouth is still "almost a mini-America": it "has alternately used, courted, tossed aside, enticed, mocked, ignored, and, occasionally, educated Native Americans."[3] And yet, on the other hand, many of the writers in *I Am Where I Come From* found flexible ways to orient and indeed empower themselves within such typically American spaces, ones that, in the twenty-first century, seem far more familiar than strange. No longer the simple epitome of a crisis in Indian-American relations, nor even any longer a unique space for Native students, Dartmouth appears instead as a waypoint on a protracted journey toward self-determination, one whose destination is not always clear or consistent.

Like Stephen Graham Jones's narrator, these authors often arrive at college already wearied by early experiences of discrimination, disparity, and despair. They have long felt the weight of being rendered different, "other," or invisible in a country that privileges a white, male, heteronormative ideal. They learn to see themselves as deficient, and to yearn for the trappings of normalcy and success; as Shannon Prince puts it in the opening essay here, "My white environment had shaped me. . . . Even my dreamscapes had been colonized." But as we see in Jones's metaphor of the child in the bathtub, one might eventually find one's true voice beneath the torrent of imposed dreams, histories, and pain. In part, *I Am Where I Come From* intends to open just such a space for Native American stories to emerge. In an earlier version of his story printed here, Hillary Abe recalled an assignment given by one of his high-school teachers to "tell . . . who you are. Who you *really* are. In this one paper," with the admission that "whatever we wrote would inherently indicate something about us—even if it wasn't our intention." The stories here function in much the same way: while the writers often seek to tell a particular kind of story, their words speak other truths as well. In the details lie an acknowledgment—perhaps unwitting—of a sense of connection and community that crosses tribal and cultural lines, opening their authors up to a more porous and capacious sense of what it means to be Native American in its most heterogeneous sense. This is the power of story and narrative, so integral to many Native traditions: with our words, we both construct and undo our senses of self, community, and home. To say *I Am Where I Come From*, as so many of these writers do, is to locate oneself not within a place so much as process—and it is one that never ceases.

In this way, the collection of voices here speak comparatively less about Dartmouth than the essayists in the predecessor volume, *First Person, First Peoples*. Indeed, what they share about their college experiences could be said of nearly any US college campus, where spectacles of privilege and overconsumption can be jarring new vistas to those arriving from the margins of society. Even what sets Dartmouth apart—its particular commitment to recruiting and cultivating a Native elite akin to W. E. B. DuBois's African American "Talented Tenth"—is something these authors apprehend with deep humility. While they consistently express their gratitude and sometimes awe at being selected for such an opportunity, they remain devoted to their overriding purpose: to make a difference in the lives of their families and tribes. What Louise Erdrich wrote in the foreword to *First Person, First Peoples* we might well observe again here: "Not a single narrative is about the wish to attain status, the ambition to make large amounts of money, or the desire to become famous. Instead, these students make a circular path, and even wind backwards down the generations, *come home*" (xi). The journey is not always simple or direct, and it can be filled with heartache as well as triumph. In its progress, Dartmouth serves as a waypoint, a pivot; these students are not unchanged by their experience here, but then, neither is Dartmouth.

Broken: Racial Mixture and Cultural Hybridity

"So how Indian are you?" is a question most Indians hear at least once in their lives. For those of us born with light skin and the features of our European ancestors, it might happen once a week. The question reflects an assumption about Indigenous identity that is unique for ethnic and racial minorities, and it is heavy with the vestiges of colonialism: "real" Indians are not assumed to exist anymore, and if they think they do, they must prove it. This expectation tends to go hand in hand with debates over Indian mascots, which can be interpreted as an honor to Native peoples only when one presumes that those people are dead; caricatures and anachronisms don't tend to glorify the living. The pressure to look and behave a certain way is something that Native Americans often deride, but just as frequently it can become a bewildering source of pride and inspiration. Put simply, there is something to be gained in the form of both cultural and economic capital from playing the kind of Indian that the dominant society expects. As Comanche critic and Smithsonian curator Paul Chaat Smith says, "Too much of Indian art settles for the protest, and the comforting, pastoral images that for the vast majority of us originate in the same place as they do for non-Indians. Our predetermined role is to remain within the images of ecology, of anger, of easy celebration."[4] Accepting this fate means embracing "the commodification of distorted, invented Indian values," the kind that fills trinket shops and tourist traps, and even well-meaning museum exhibits.[5] Smith laments this phenomenon, but he also understands it: "We dimly accept the role of spiritual masters and first environmentalists. . . . We take pride in Westerns which make us look gorgeous (which we are!). . . . We secretly wish we were more like the Indians in the movies" because "maybe it's better to be vilified and romanticized than completely ignored."[6]

Complicating this experience is the very real fact of cultural hybridity that typifies the genealogy of nearly every American subject, and is particularly corrosive for Native peoples seeking to shore up their fragile sense of belonging. How does one choose an identity from the array of options offered by one's eclectic family trees and experiences? Is it a betrayal to claim the white relatives whose ancestors may have had a hand in the decimation of one's tribal culture? And if so, how does one reject one's own grandparents, or even mothers or fathers? The density of this burden explains in part the preoccupation, throughout this anthology, with measuring identity. In particular, many of the writers worry that they are "not Indian enough," either for white standards or their culture's own. Blythe George's experience is typical for many young Natives: "My blue eyes were a source of confusion to me early on," she remembers, "and I stuck out like a sore thumb when sitting with the other Indian children." Similarly, Preston Wells recalls struggling as a young man to convince his peers that he is *not* white even if his skin tone might suggest otherwise. While it may at first seem bewildering that his greatest skeptics are also nonwhite—African, Hispanic, and Native American—it makes a perverse sort of sense given that such peers would have been well schooled in the racial politics of American life. In the United States, race is assumed to be visible, as it has frequently been (and with great peril) for African Americans, while contemporary Native identity can be a less tangible matrix of inheritance, culture, politics, and legal definitions. From within and without, then, young Indian people face inordinate pressure to display their indigeneity with incontrovertible authority. For many of the writers featured here, appearing less than "full-blood" induces a fear of being lesser, lacking, and somehow not whole.

Walking into any gathering of Native American students at Dartmouth would likely surprise those expecting to see ruddy-skinned warriors clothed anachronistically (and impractically) in beaded regalia and feathered headdresses; instead, one encounters the full range of skin tones, eye and hair color, and styles of modern dress. Degrees of Indian "blood" vary tremendously, as do connections to one's ancestral communities; but all identify proudly as Native Americans. And yet the politics of racial identification in the United States don't always square with such practice; even Native tribes themselves, many of whom rely on blood quantum measurements for their enrollment criteria, often appear confused about their own benchmarks for inclusion. Shannon Prince, whose heritage is Cherokee and African American, among others, is vigorous in her determination to embrace her multiple identities simultaneously and equally: "I pay no attention to the pseudoscientific idea of blood quantum (the idea that race is a biological, measurable reality), and am uninterested in dividing myself into fractions. I am completely, concurrently, and proudly all of my heritages." Prince's innocence about such unity inevitably falters under the scrutiny that intensifies as one becomes conscious of the world's adjudicating gaze: "Being multicultural is kind of like being a messy handwritten note," she muses: "You have a definite message, but people will read you as they see fit." The script for misreading is particularly pervasive for those with Indian blood: as the Ojibwe writer David Treuer puts it, most Americans betray their "exoticized foreknowledge" about what Indians are, often without ever meeting or interacting with one, as a result of popular culture's stereotype industry;[7] Hollywood Westerns, Halloween costumes, and Land O'Lakes butter cartons leave little room for the textures and complexities of reality. Naturally, such pressure escalates in an environment filled with ambitious young people anxiously observing and estimating one another.

For some, the perception of inadequacy can lead to "playing Indian," or overemphasizing the signal, and often stereotypical, features of indigeneity that others expect. For others, though, particularly those who grew up on reservations and among tight-knit tribal communities, remaining Indian despite obvious racial mixture requires no exaggeration or theatrics. Among our authors, Cinnamon Spear acknowledges that her light skin might leave others "confused," but experiences no such consternation herself: she identifies completely and exclusively with her tribal heritage: "*Just* Cheyenne." "Part this or part that . . . confused me," she recalls. "I thought either you *were* or you weren't. Parts didn't make sense to me. . . . Sure, you'd have those two kids in school who were black or white, but even *they* were Cheyenne." Importantly, Spear distinguishes indigeneity from race as a category of belonging: being Indian is about where you come from, who your people are, and whose traditions you own—not about the color of your skin or the texture of your hair. But even among fellow Natives, Spear's confident essentialism is not always easily understood or embraced.

Indeed, for a variety of reasons, Dartmouth has not always been a hospitable place for the Native students who arrive with already challenged notions of self and identity. Amplified pressures to embody a particular kind of indigeneity come not just from the non-Native community, but from within NAD (Native Americans at Dartmouth) as well. While some of our authors express frustration over the contingent of what Spear calls "box-checkers"—individuals with only remote connections to their Indian ancestry—others acknowledge that even growing up on the reservation might not certify one as "authentic" in the ways that seem to matter, both to whites and to Indians. More than anything, though, our writers all seem to agree that Dartmouth offered them a temporary, meaningful environment to question, challenge, and sharpen their own and others' sense of what it means to be a Native person in the United States, in all its inherent diversity and richness. Rather than claiming innate knowledge of even their own tribal identities, most are aware that identity is a fluid and mutable thing, particularly for Native peoples, and that challenge is considerably complicated but also enriched by the enormous diversity of tribal cultures represented within the NAD community. This sense of communion appears vital to the many multicultured, mixed-blood students seeking, in Prince's words, "to be whole." And yet for others, that very diversity continues to be challenging to one's sense of wholeness and belonging. Throughout this volume, the writers exhibit very different and often somewhat extreme attitudes toward their own identity and that of their peers, reminding us of the deeply fraught and painfully contingent nature of contemporary Indigenous personhood.

An Indian Education: Leaving and Finding Home at Dartmouth College

It is axiomatic that college is a place where young people go to "find themselves." For many Native Americans, that process is amplified by the complex demands of shoring up one's cultural identity as well, and some appear to do so—at least provisionally—at Dartmouth. Uncannily, several writers here share the memory of "love at first sight" on arrival; others recount the feeling of a "homecoming," an unforeseen impression of discovering one's culture, one's self, and one's community in this new and unlikely place. The signifiers of "home" are various: for some, like Jerry Watchman, it represents an imagined ideal, a comforting space of newness and difference glimmering with opportunity. For others, such as AlexAnna Salmon, the relative isolation and insularity of Dartmouth's rural New Hampshire setting make it unexpectedly familiar, much like the small village community she left behind in Igiugig, Alaska. Whether their Indigenous heritage constitutes a fraction or the entirety of their self-image, these Native students gravitate toward the opportunities for cultural knowledge and community that Dartmouth offers: they know that the college's unique institutional history ensures an ongoing pledge to Indigenous issues and a vibrant student community and academic programs. Many arrive intending immediately to major in Native American studies, floored by historical and cultural knowledge that they didn't even know they were missing or misunderstanding.

Watchman recalls having his "entire worldview shattered" within minutes of enrolling in Professor Calloway's American Indian History class and discovering the nuances of a past he thought he knew; the experience left him charged with "a desire to understand this history, this perspective that had been denied to me and to Native people everywhere." Such lessons might come in the form of complicated legal doctrines, or the intricacies of political theory, or the pages of Navajo poetry. All such knowledge has the power to impress on one the extraordinary miscellany of tribal experiences, as well as their ability to cross tribal borders; and sometimes the discoveries are profoundly personal. As Salmon recalls, "At one point I opened a book in the NAS library and looked directly at a photo of my great-great-grandfather, who was over one hundred years old at the time. I didn't even know he had been interviewed." Certainly, many are surprised to encounter such opportunities in an environment so removed from home. As Abe puts it, "I was disappointed that I had to go so far away from my Native community to study and learn the things that I hoped would empower me."

While much of this education takes place in the classroom, just as much occurs outside as well; there are ample opportunities to learn about tribal cultures distinct from one's own. For some, the process can be totalizing; in Spear's view, "Dartmouth is in the business of manufacturing Natives. These kids come to dinners and learn to make frybread and wojape. They learn how to smudge and pray, and they feel so sacred doing it. . . . They take Native American Studies courses on history and culture to arm themselves with an identity fed from books." Spear's point is less an indictment of Dartmouth per se than the widespread phenomenon of "playing Indian." Certainly, there are plenty of Americans who falsely assert Indigenous heritage for their own gain: contrary to popular belief, however, the benefit is rarely economic (the windfall of casino enterprises and tribal scholarships has been grossly overstated) but rather personal and spiritual. In the face of globalization's erosion of tight-knit cultural bonds and distinctions, and the ennui and emptiness associated with advanced capitalism, Native tribes' perceived connections to family, tradition, ecology, and spirituality are perennially seductive. But while Spear's critique targets the curious performers primarily, other writers here admit to their own seduction: learning how to be Indian is a viable project even for those born with all the apparent markers of cultural integrity. Taking refuge in Indigenous knowledge is often a panacea for those feelings of being "broken" and lost that afflict so many Native students.

The quest "to be whole" tends to take two divergent paths, then: one is an overdetermination of "Indian" identity, a flattening of vast tribal distinctions into a monolithic, pan-Indian archetype that can be just as misleading and destructive as that imposed from the outside. Or, conversely, one may instead embrace the abundant ways that Native experience intersects with those of other minority groups in the United States: while tribal cultures are individually distinctive, to be sure, they also bear important family resemblances to the struggles of marginalized groups more broadly. More often than not, the writers represented here are eager for such cross-cultural connection long before arriving at Dartmouth. The points of convergence are often racial or cultural: African American activist Malcolm X appears as an alluring ally in racial resistance for both Abe and Prince, and the Latina writer Sandra Cisneros, with her moving depictions of poverty and community, surprises Spear with a "Latino version of my own home." Even more canonical, white writers leave their mark: Spear gravitates toward J. D. Salinger's iconic *Catcher in the Rye*, as does John Around Him, who encountered the book in high-school English class and remembers instantly relating to the main character, Holden Caulfield, and his struggles with school, family, and loss. Such moments of literary identification and inspiration are cited with remarkable frequency in these narratives; they are reminders of the ways hardship cuts deeply across cultural lines, and they provide significant models of the power of storytelling to readers who often feel powerless and voiceless. Opportunities for kinship and catharsis via the written word continue at college, the place where many recall finding their own voices for the first time as well. Undoubtedly, participating in the composition of this volume is another significant step in that journey.

The organizing principle for this anthology is the common Native American heritage of its authors; and yet that thread proves to be the most tenuous of all, as the experience of indigeneity differs radically for each of them. While many experience a centripetal pull toward a cohesive Indian experience, the indications throughout these essays lean toward a richer, more illustrative panorama of difference. What tends to bind them together are not cultural practices or spiritual attitudes per se, but rather circumstances that have no exclusive province in Indian country: that is, first and foremost, poverty, and its attendant symptoms of violence, substance abuse, and both physical and mental illness. They write wrenchingly of late-night arguments that tear families apart, often literally, and of unspeakable abuses suffered as children and young adults. They confess openly their own struggles with alcohol and addiction, as well as bouts with severe depression and mental illness; they admit to suicidal fantasies or attempts to end their own lives. They curse their closest relatives and love them desperately, often at the same time; they want urgently to escape their pasts and home communities, even as they feel pulled incessantly back toward them. Yet many of the experiences we would be tempted to label particularly "Indian" are in effect socioeconomic ones, and these essays are especially adept, if not always explicitly or intentionally, at reminding us of the degree to which lower-class individuals (often but not always minorities) occupy similar forms of marginalization.

Education plays a critical role in such lives: many of the authors recall adoring school as young people, as it constituted a place of escape and a rare opportunity to thrive. Ma'Ko'Quah Jones remembers how she clung to the praise of her teachers, feeling not just clever but also cared for and, quite simply, *seen* in ways that she did not always experience at home. So many of these writers grew up acutely aware of the "low expectations" for Indian survival and excellence, whether on the reservation or in the classroom, and found themselves ever more determined to surmount those meager horizons. Dartmouth plays a critical role in this process: it represents the culmination of years of striving and achievement, even as it sets the stage for still more anxiety, isolation, and sometimes addiction. Several recall vividly their first moments on campus, eyeing with suspicion and envy their well-dressed peers buoyed by posh belongings and family members' supportive arms. Many juggled several on-campus jobs to defray their expenses, working late hours at the library or cafeteria rather than relaxing with friends in the basement of a Greek house. Indeed, while cultural differences inevitably come to matter, the first and most divisive wedge on any elite college campus is that of class, with all the disparities in preparation and posture that come along with it. In many ways, these essays will resonate deeply with any first-generation college student negotiating the disjunct between pride and excitement in having "made it out," and the terrible feelings of inadequacy and self-doubt that leave them to wonder: How will I measure up? Will I survive at all?

Full Circle: Returning and Remaking Home

While many Native students consider dropping out at some point during their college careers—indeed, the overall graduation rate for Native American college students is lower than that of any other ethnic group[8]—the writers here all managed to stay and complete their degrees. For many, the stakes are simply too great—not just for the individual students who matriculate but for the extended families and tribes whose fates often turn on the prospects of its brightest stars. Some, like Salmon, leave home with every intention of returning someday, armed with the intellectual equipment to improve the lives of her people. For her, there was simply no choice: she felt she "belonged" to her home village in ways that no outside perspective or job offer could change. Overall, there runs potently through these essays an assumed obligation and desire to "give back" in some way by bringing the resources of a Dartmouth education back to one's home community. This can be perceived as an invasive gesture by some, but our writers instead frame it as collaborative and conjunctural—a way of weaving together the worlds within and outside the reservation borders. Implicitly, they acknowledge and revise the stereotype of the "circle" as an Indigenous motif: rather than a closed, insular, or essentialist idea, theirs is a more expansive one generated by a thoughtful embrace of pluralism. The circle of friends, family, and community is quite simply enlarged by their widened orbit of experience and empathy.

While many of the writers do return to their tribal communities after graduation, ideas about "home" become more malleable and complicated. As Around Him admits, the experiences of attending Dartmouth, serving in the military during armed conflict in Iraq, and finding a loving mate allowed him to more candidly recall his childhood as an extraordinarily challenging and traumatic one, "filled with anxiety and low self-esteem." Spear, too, acknowledges the initial temptation for Native youth to flee these environments of hurt and struggle in their efforts at self-preservation. But while temporary reprieves are necessary and healing, and while Dartmouth often serves as a haven of rest and reflection, the compulsion to return home can be overwhelming. Salmon reimmersed herself in Igiugig with seamless commitment, bringing the tools of her Dartmouth education back to a traditional lifestyle that she finds incredibly fulfilling. Around Him and Abe harbor hopes of reinvigorating their tribal languages. On the shelves of the Igiugig gift shop, Salmon's Dartmouth thesis sits bound and ready for purchase—a testament to the extraordinary sacrifices of her tribe and family to make such an accomplishment possible; a symbol of knowledge and power manifest in the written word; and a tangible reminder of the great promise that may be brought home by a community's most ambitious, determined members.

It would be a mistake, however, to see this path as a linear delivery of knowledge back to the benighted reservation. On the contrary, most of these writers affirm that the process of education runs in both directions, and that they have been called on to teach Dartmouth just as much as Dartmouth has taught them. What constitutes scholarship in the academy has often been limited to library or archival research detached from the lived realities of the subjects under examination. Of course, the most robust intellectual work being done these days rises more directly from tangible sources, a principle that certainly governs the field of Native American studies and its commitment to the health and endurance of tribal sovereignty. But other disciplines may be less attuned to the complexities of contemporary Native cultures, and it often falls to Indian students to serve as cultural ambassadors in classrooms that lack a clear Indigenous perspective. On campus generally, the NAD community often welcomes outsiders to participate in cultural opportunities with guest speakers, performers, and artists, or to attend major events like the annual student-run Dartmouth Powwow held on the Dartmouth Green.

Such occasions for cross-cultural teaching are usually met with eagerness and pride; but just as often, they can be experienced as a burden, particularly when Native students feel pressured to somehow represent *all* of Indian country or, worse, to defend their communities from unfair criticism or misconceptions. Kalina Newmark recalls one such moment in a Native American studies class when "a student raised his hand and asked the professor why Native people could not get over their issues and conform to American standards. . . . My hands were shaking as I tried to explain to this student why Native people are in the situations they are today. I was astounded that people still believed in these harmful stereotypes, especially at a place like Dartmouth." I remember this moment vividly, too, because it took place in my own Native American Literature class; I was the professor who fielded the naive query. I remember wondering how many students were nodding in silent agreement, secretly sharing this student's uncharitable views. I wondered how anyone could read the disarming works of contemporary literature we were studying that term and still harbor such callous sentiments about the systemic instigators of poverty and oppression. And mostly, I wondered if it meant that I was failing at my job as a Native American studies professor if my students were still clinging to such outdated, injurious notions. What I understand better in retrospect is, appropriately, the power of hindsight: over time, both Kalina and I have come to appreciate that difficult moment for the teaching opportunity it presented, and I can only hope that the benefit of distance, reflection, and empathy have likewise altered the attitude of that questioning student, and the many others like him—at Dartmouth and elsewhere. As US citizens, and as Native peoples, it is both a responsibility and occasionally our burden to continue to learn as well as to teach. That process takes us far and long beyond the borders of any academic classroom.

Continuing Education: NADs Reflect on Their Journeys

And that brings us, fittingly, to the final voices of this volume, which circle back to the previous anthology in order to better reflect on the journeys our Native students have taken and will yet undergo. Three of the writers from *First Person, First Peoples*—Bruce Duthu, Robert Bennett, and Davina Two Bears—revisit their original essays, reprinted here as well, and provide an update on their experiences in the past eighteen years. All three have changed jobs multiple times, returned to school for advanced degrees, started and increased their families, and, along the way, have continuously revised and refined what it means to be Indian. In many ways, it is the very variety and complexity of these real-world experiences that leave them with a more intricate sense of the ways that "self" and "identity" both cohere and diverge. Indeed, rather than coming into clearer focus, indigeneity as a construct becomes more loosely defined. For Bob Bennett, a retired professional baseball player, the real education began after college; and even then, Bennett confesses, "I can tell you some stories about the Lakota I am today . . . [but] I still don't know much." A similar sentiment is implied by Duthu's essay, which evokes a Yogi Berra quip, "If you don't know where you are going, you might wind up someplace else." Indeed, as Duthu's story demonstrates, one's journey to self-knowledge needn't be mapped out in advance, and the route may not be well marked: "I'm not as anxious about winding up someplace else as I used to be," he decides. Two Bears writes in a comparable way about the unexpected turn her own life took after leaving college: "Life is never so straightforward. At first it seemed to be so, and everything was going on schedule. Graduate from Dartmouth, check. Get a job, check. Start graduate school, check. Marry your college boyfriend, check. Have kids, check,

check, check. Buy a house, check. Get divorced? No, that was never supposed to happen."

When Bennett's baseball career ended abruptly, he found solace and a new beginning by moving back home and embarking on a new career in law enforcement; simultaneously, he set himself on the path "to learn how to be an Indian." Duthu's wisdom also derives from the value of lived experience—his careers as a successful lawyer and Native American studies professor at Dartmouth, his happy marriage and children—as well as from his past. In particular, he credits his Houma grandfather with embodying a kind of humility that still offers Duthu a personal compass of grace. Similarly, Two Bears gained strength after her divorce by returning home and working on behalf of her tribe's archaeological efforts. After encountering numerous obstacles to her work, Two Bears's anxiety manifested itself in serious physical ailments: "I knew my growth was being stunted, and something had to change real fast, or I was going to wither away." This time, her survival instincts took her far away from home and from her comfort zone: she enrolled in a doctoral program at Indiana University so that she could become an archaeologist in her own right.

For these writers, it seems they will always find themselves moving fluidly—if not always painlessly—from their home communities to mainstream US institutions and back again. Unlike their younger selves, whose voices are echoed by many of the new writers in this volume, they have found a kind of peace in the journey. They are wiser now, aware of the ways that the world is "hard" for Indians: they encounter racism, often unspoken but nonetheless palpable; they experience loss and heartbreak; and they find themselves battling against not just non-Natives but their own people as well. Throughout it all, home remains a vital touchstone, but it is an increasingly mobile and amorphous one. It is less a place than a supple concept where "education" continues—even if it continues to take one away from family and tribe in order to return with new ideas, perspectives, opportunities, and hopes. Thus, the sense of "homecoming" that strikes so many Native students when they matriculate doesn't end when they leave the campus; and like the different paths that intersect on the green, the roads they travel before, during, and after their college years meet and diverge in countless ways. As editors, we have chosen to provide a loose framework and prefatory materials for encountering these voices, but not a formal conclusion; instead, we hope to allow these voices themselves to evoke a multiplicity of passages, a stunning variety of pathways through contemporary Native American experience.

It seems supremely fitting that the open-ended American story in the twenty-first century might be told in these stark, moving, and generous essays by the descendants of its earliest residents. The narratives are often dark, to be sure—there is what Stephen Graham Jones depicts as the "blood and blood and blood" of physical trauma, emotional suffering, and cultural attenuation. But such pain functions as catalyst, too, and becomes the lifeblood pumping stubbornly through veins that identify proudly as Indian against all odds, expectations, and blood quantum requirements. These writers move about and stake their claim on territories far more expansive than the literal or figurative reservation, or the Green of Dartmouth College. *I Am Where I Come From* is a cry heard both plainly and tacitly in the essays that follow, but the "where" of the writers' origins refuses to be corralled in a single space. For Native Americans in particular, that freedom and mobility is a stunning achievement.

PART I

BROKEN

Racial Mixture and Cultural Hybridity

1

Seeking to Be Whole   Shannon Joyce Prince

A particular memory from my teenage years stands out as one experience that shaped how I thought about race, racism, and responsibility. Ironically, it's a memory of the extremes a white woman took to make my family feel welcome in a predominantly white space. We were at the Greenbrier in White Sulphur Springs, West Virginia, a centuries-old resort staffed by many black employees, where my family and our friends are usually the only nonwhite patrons. A docent was explaining some of the resort's history to us, and she pointed to a lithograph of the resort back from the 1700s.

"You see," she said, beaming at my little sister, Ashley, and me, "if we were back in the colonial era, the two of you young ladies would be sitting on the porch drinking tea." My sister and I both tried desperately not to laugh. We knew that we definitely would not have been drinking tea on the porch of the Greenbrier in the 1700s. But the docent was so unwilling to face the human-rights abuses of the past—and the inequity of the present that still kept most nonwhites out of the Greenbrier, except as staff—that she wittingly or unwittingly engaged in historical revisionism. She completely lied.

That revisionism couldn't help but throw some light on the truths I hadn't been able to see before. The experience was compounded on that same trip when an African American bellman smiled at Ashley and me and asked, "Is everyone treating you well?"

"Oh, yes," we told him. "Everyone has treated us beautifully."

"I know they have," he said, and then his smile became more conspiratorial, "because we take care of our own." Even though I'm a mix of cultures, three of which the bellman probably wouldn't consider "his own," the way I experience race means that all of me feels a sense of solidarity with someone offering good-natured kinship. I realized the bellman was articulating the attitude of many nonwhite service workers I had encountered, especially those at my predominantly white, private college-preparatory school. They encouraged and supported us, their pride always evident. They did take care of their own, but what about us? I realized that minority individuals privileged enough to benefit from institutions like private schools or historic resorts had responsibilities to those men and women not given the same opportunities. The fact that in both contexts white people got to be the students and guests while nonwhite people were stuck with the brooms and frying pans wasn't an accident. It was an inequity. It was the direct result of the situation the docent had been too uncomfortable to acknowledge. My experience at the Greenbrier occurred when I was a teenager, but if I'm going to describe my journey with race, I'll need to go back much further.

Whenever I've been called on to define my heritage, I've never been perplexed about how to answer. My response has not changed since I was first able to speak, just as my ethnic identity has never shifted. When asked what I am, I smile and say, "I am African American, Cherokee (Aniyunwiya) Native American, Chinese (Cantonese) American, and English American." I excise nothing of myself. I claim the slave who was a mathematical genius; the storyteller, the quilt maker, and the wise healer; the bilingual railroad laborer and the farmer—regardless of the amount of melanin in any of their skins. I pay no attention to the pseudoscientific idea of blood quantum (the idea that race is a biological, measurable reality) and am uninterested in dividing myself into fractions. I am completely, concurrently, and proudly all of my heritages.

From the time I was able to think about such things, I have considered myself both quadricultural and ana-racial (my personal neologism for "without race.") I am zero (raceless) and hoop (part of peoples from the world over). I think my parents might have been a little more comfortable with my homogeneous white world had I been a little less comfortable in it, but I felt that four peoples had found space in my blood; thus, people of all bloods belonged in every space in general. I was comfortable at school not because I didn't know who I was but because I did. And I knew who I was because I came from a strong family.

When I was little, I didn't recognize my relationships with my relatives as being racialized. I adored and was close friends with my black/white/Cherokee great-grandfather, Papa, but it was my African American great-grandmother, Mamo Seal, whom I idolized. I was able to bond with Papa. With his gold skin, straight hair, and pale blue eyes that other nonwhites had been trained to worship, Papa was my playmate. We drove tractors together, walked through the woods, and played with the cows on his farm. I recognized that his startling azure eyes made him unique, and I admired his uniqueness, but I didn't value his irises over any others. In contrast, Mamo Seal inspired genuflection. To me, my African American great-grandmother was and remains an unparalleled beauty. Her most celebrated quality was her dark skin—hence her name. She was a feisty woman not entirely opposed to profanity. I usually sat across the room from her, not in her lap, and listened to her rather than chatting with her.

One of my fondest memories is of helping her to dress. I remember guiding a bright scarlet dress over her head, ringing her neck with crayon-bright glass beads, pulling stockings over her ebony calves, wondering if the baby-soft texture of her skin was somehow connected to its pure blackness. The world tried to teach me to see beauty as Papa, but Papa saw beauty as Mamo Seal, and so did I. When I was young, Mamo Seal (and Papa, too) were simply beautiful. As I grew older, their beauty was politicized. And in a world where Queen Elizabeth was on the curriculum but not Yaa Asantewaa, where girls dreamed of being Britney Spears but not India Arie, seeing Mamo Seal revered and having her to revere was one of many affirming examples set by my family.

For that reason, my constant proximity to whiteness didn't cause me to romanticize, normalize, or idealize it. It did cause me to expiate it, however. I was always around white people and white people were always nice to me. It didn't occur to me that maybe I was palatable to white people because I was a pigtailed, upper-middle-class little kid. I considered myself an empiricist, mainly because I was reluctant to condemn unjustly, and my experience had taught me that racism among whites was rare. If white people didn't discriminate against me as an individual, then they must not discriminate against nonwhites as a group.

I understand that there's a trope in horror movies where the protagonist will see someone she knows and begin happily interacting with him or her, only to discover that her acquaintance's body has been taken over by aliens or monsters. The protagonist feels shock, revulsion, panic, and horror. She doesn't know those she thought she did. She realizes the world isn't what she thought it was and discovers that her perspective was flawed—and that scares her. It scared me. But I didn't feel fear when a classmate told me they were moving to a public school that "was a good one without lots of minorities," or when a girl I knew described being afraid because "a big black guy" asked her to dance at a party, I felt horror. The mask had been ripped off to reveal the ugliness underneath.

Something I also understand about horror movies is that their viewers often warn protagonists not to walk into dangerous environments. "Don't go up those stairs!" they cry. "Don't open that door!" "Are you crazy? Don't go in there!" But what do you do when your whole world is "in there"?

What do you do if the stable where you take riding lessons, the golf course where you practice your swing, the incredible museums you regularly visit are all "in there"? What do you do if your people have spent the past few centuries literally dying for your right to go "in there"? What happens when the actions and passivity of your peers "in there" reveal that the majority of them have been "body snatched"? Sometimes I'd argue with myself that my glimpses of the beings behind the masks were only tricks of the light. I had to figure out what to do with my increasing awareness that my world wasn't what it had seemed.

In my predominantly white world, addressing racism meant you were oversensitive. It meant you waited eagerly to play the "race card" and enjoyed being a victim. It meant you "made everything about race." Nonwhite people were inherently seen as biased, as unable to determine objectively what was and was not racism. I noticed that the person who criticized racism was the problem. The person who perpetrated the racism was the victim.

When I entered upper school and began to acknowledge racism, I tried to address it, always voicing my concerns and suggestions with the utmost care. I would point out to the headmaster that if I didn't love our school, I wouldn't want the student body to be more diverse; it was only because I thought the school was wonderful that I wanted more nonwhite students to attend. When I approached the upper-school librarian about library books, some of them published in the past few years, that contained statements such as "abolitionists exaggerated the negative aspects of slavery," I would explain that my objection to the books being in our collection was a manifestation of my care for the library. I was (and remain) quiet and soft-spoken, and I rarely brought up the subject of racism. When I did, my concerns sometimes were met with the greatest respect, compassion, and, most important, positive action. I did not feel, however, as though I was always heard—such as when the principal continued to allow my teacher to wear Confederate-flag ties to school.

I was coming to realize that the same people who thought I was a cute five-foot-five teenage girl clutched their purses tighter when my six-foot-one father passed them on the street. The same students and teachers who enjoyed having one or two of me in a class didn't want to be in a neighborhood full of me after dark. It occurred to me that whereas any negative action a nonwhite person took was seen as confirming stereotypes, positive actions a nonwhite person took didn't erode them. The positive actions of nonwhite individuals only allowed them to be seen as exceptions to the rule. And it hurt so badly to realize that someone I loved, someone who loved me, was racist.

I started becoming aware of the way my white environment had shaped me. Before kindergarten, when I pictured falling in love with somebody, the image was always of a guy with brown skin. Somewhere along the way, completely unconsciously, it changed to that of a white guy. As a little girl, even before I began creative writing, I would make up stories in my imagination as I waited to fall asleep. It occurred to me one day that whenever I crafted stories, all but one or two characters would be white. Again, the practice was unconscious. I wasn't choosing to dream up predominantly white characters; it was just that the environments I imagined naturally reflected the one I inhabited. Such realizations surprised, fascinated, and disturbed me. I didn't mind white people playing a part in my imagination, but it bothered me that they dominated it. Even my dreamscapes had been colonized.

My parents couldn't have been happier when I became aware of white privilege. Although almost all our family and individual activities took place in predominantly white contexts, it was the school they had selected for my little sister, Ashley, and me, where we spent most of our waking hours, that concerned them the most. They had picked our school because it offered a world-class education, but they wondered if the extreme lack of diversity we experienced there was too high a cost to pay. They particularly worried about me, as Ashley never struck them as assimilated. While I had always taken pride in my heritage, it wasn't until I acknowledged the presence and prevalence of racism that they were able to exhale. My radicalization meant they could relax.

On paper my parents don't seem like the kind of people who would send their children to a predominantly white school in the first place. As a little child, my black, Cherokee, English mother had adored Malcolm X the way other girls fell in love with rock stars. She admired Martin Luther King Jr., but his patience and nonviolence wearied her. In college she became fluent in Swahili, eventually teaching courses in the language. She challenged her professors on everything from the maps they used that showed Africa as disproportionately small to their neglect and distortions of African history. Her activism (and kindness and beauty) eventually won her a proposal from the king of an African country—which she politely declined.

Instead she married one of her college classmates, my father, a black Chinese man so disgusted with America's racism that he was well into his twenties before he could bring himself to say the Pledge of Allegiance. He cited prejudice in the arena of employment as a primary incentive for owning his own business. My father was baffled at how he could be given the key to the city and still get pulled over for driving while black. He occasionally entertained my little sister and me with the true story of how racist policemen once nearly arrested him for "robbing" his own parents' house.

My parents searched for schools for me when I was still a baby. In fact, my mother may have still been pregnant when they started. They visited one school where nonwhite children only a few years old spoke a variety of languages with great fluency, but, as my mother explained, "There was no joy in their eyes." At the school they ultimately settled on (when I was still under a year old), the one my sister and I would attend from kindergarten through twelfth grade, they saw a scholarly and warm faculty teaching enthusiastic students in state-of-the-art classrooms and theaters. Little kids were playing with sheep and chickens in the campus petting zoo. Older students relaxed in beautiful, colorful gardens. Everyone looked engaged, inspired, and happy. But almost everyone was white. The black and brown people around the school were cafeteria ladies and maintenance men, as well as nannies and housekeepers picking up their charges in the carpool line. That fact concerned my parents.

So they tried to compensate, and I believe they succeeded. Their efforts remind me of the "culture camps" to which white American parents send their transracially adopted children from Korea and China. During the summers, my mother taught my sister and me the nonwhite history that our school's curriculum only gave a nod to. She brewed us Cherokee pine-needle tea to build up our immune systems when the moderate Houston winter began. My father taught us how gentrification was affecting the city, and our grandmother introduced us to the work of her college professor, John Biggers, one of the greatest African American painters of the twentieth century.

Looking back, I find some of their tactics amusing. I remember the book of hand games my parents gave my sister and me. Most African American girls learn the clapping and rhyming games from their black friends; my sister and I had to read about them. We had books praising the beauty of skin tones described as peanut butter, warm mocha, and sweet licorice, although we were far more likely to see those shades on the people on our book pages than on those around us. Ashley could perform West African dance. I could weave on a loom. But neither of us could claim to have black or Native American friends for the better parts of our childhoods. As I said, my parents weren't really worried about Ashley's racial self-esteem. They were concerned, however, that despite my love for my cultures, I denied the prevalence of racial injustice.

I think my parents were confused. How could I be secure in my racial identity if I didn't understand the important role racism played in the world? It seems that my immediate and extended families and I debated the point endlessly when I was little. It wasn't that the discussion began with my relatives trying to convince me of the reality of white supremacy. The conversations usually started with a very real, very painful humiliation suffered by one of us the previous week, a tale retold cathartically. But what my relatives saw as prejudice, I was more likely to excuse as simple rudeness.

My sister and I would sit in our maternal grandmother, Dear's, lap, while my parents sat on either side of her wooden desk. My Creole step-grandfather would sit at the end of the sofa. My aunt Linda and my adopted African American aunt Gwen would frequently stand, animated by passion.

"Wednesday," I remember Gwen saying once, "we were asking for directions. We were in this white neighborhood, driving around looking for this restaurant, and we just could not find it. So we pulled over and asked these two white people if they knew where the restaurant was. The woman said, 'I don't, but Greg does.' And meanwhile the man was just looking around, looking at the ground. And the woman kept saying, 'Greg, you know where it is. You *know* you know where it is. Why won't you tell them?' And the man just wouldn't tell us because he didn't want us in that neighborhood."

"That's how they are sometimes," said Dear mildly.

"They do the same thing to me," added my dad. "I got a phony speeding ticket for just driving through a white neighborhood, trying to pick the girls up from school. Sometimes they just don't want us around."

"Why are your people like that?" Aunt Linda teased Grandfather.

"I'm not one of them!" he said, emphatically.

"It's not fair to judge all of a race by one person," I reasoned. "Maybe Greg was just mean." What I saw as isolated incidents—though in retrospect, continuous isolated incidents—the adults in my family saw as part of a larger pattern.

"I'm around white people all the time," I said. "My classmates and their parents and my teachers aren't like that." This was true.

But sometimes I wonder if my belief that racism was rare might have been reinforced by my environment. If white people were so bad, then why would my parents choose to be surrounded by them, in the neighborhoods where we lived, the schools they sent us to, and so on? What was I supposed to do—believe that my parents and grandparents and aunts and uncles were right in thinking that it was rare for white people to be truly free of racism, and still comfortably spend all my time learning and playing with them? Did they want me to live the life they designed for me without fully believing in it? Would that calm them down?

Don't get me wrong. As a little girl I sincerely believed that racism just didn't happen all that often and that bigots were as rare as hens' teeth. My belief that most people were full of sunshine and rainbows was genuine—it wasn't a coping mechanism. But I wonder what my life would have been like had I not believed those things.

I remember the arguments my dad and I would have about racism. I found it hard to believe him when he talked about the prevalence of white ignorance. But, as I said, I was an empiricist, and my dad declined to offer me proof until I was old enough not to need it. I was in my late teens before he would tell me how, after a few too many glasses of wine at parents' night, white fathers would tell him jovially, "You know, I really like black people!" Or how white mothers would flirt with him, their overtures oddly racialized. One woman told my dad, "You're so cute, like that man in *How Stella Got Her Groove Back*." Seriously. He didn't want to hurt me by challenging my view of the world, so he didn't offer any examples to bolster his assertions. And in the absence of those assertions, I simply didn't believe him. I don't always find my dad correct on racial issues, but now that I'm older I see him as more credible—not because he has changed, but because I have.

As a little girl, when I heard my parents discussing white people, I immediately thought about the white people I knew. Did my best friend who used to put my hair in Dutch braids when I put hers in French braids think I was anti-intellectual? Did the teacher who sent me a calligraphic thank-you note for letting her exhibit my seashell collection in our homeroom secretly believe most of my peoples preferred welfare to work? As I grew up, I did indeed find that a friend's parent who had hugged and kissed me and treated me with warmth for years requested that I ask a black guy friend or cousin to the girl's choice cotillion "so I wouldn't make anyone uncomfortable," and that the friend I could talk about everything with into the wee hours of the morning believed that blacks and Hispanics had a predilection for gang violence. But looking back, I wonder if it ever occurred to my parents that if I couldn't have friendships with my classmates at an early age uncomplicated by politics, I would have nobody else to give my friendship to. I don't believe that ignorance is blissful or even beneficial; it's just that there are no easy answers. There's no simple way to be four races in a homogeneously white space.

What my family wanted, of course, was for me to use the best education available in the state of Texas to create a great future not just for myself but for my peoples. That expectation was not without precedent. Dear had used the bachelor's degree she earned, at a time when few women of any color went to college, to teach black, Hispanic, and white students for almost half a century in Houston's poorest public schools. She had helped integrate the Houston Independent School District and pilot one of the city's first Head Start programs. She had used her education to further her commitment to racial and social justice. Grandfather had only a fifth-grade education. When his father was crippled in an accident, he had to leave school to pick sugarcane. Still, he is an autodidact who became fluent in several languages. When he began his produce/Cajun foods shop, he used his Spanish skills to provide fair-paying, respectful work for immigrant laborers. My father taught young minority men and women how to be entrepreneurs, and my mother, who, during the beginning of her marriage, worked as a child therapist, often cared for families with diverse backgrounds who were on welfare. My family had a history of using their knowledge and talents to benefit minority (and white) people who didn't have the same opportunities. I too loved volunteering, although my passions were not focused on ameliorating racism but on endangered animals and poverty.

My mother says that when my sister and I were babies, the first time we were rained on after we had begun talking was wondrous to us. "What's this?" we had asked, tiny hands outstretched, long-lashed eyes looking upward. The ability to use language to discuss rain heightened our experience of being rained on. Similarly, my awareness of the prevalence of racism during upper school came at about the same time I began creative writing. Thus, my poetry, creative nonfiction, and fiction were often about institutional prejudice, white imperialist feminism, indigenous sovereignty, and Orientalism. As a young girl, I didn't speak much in general, and spoke seldom about racism in particular. As a teen, however, I wrote profusely, frequently addressing prejudice.

Like many African and African American, Native American, and Chinese people, I believed that I belonged to a community made up of ancestors, living peers, and future generations not yet conceived. As a good citizen of that community, I was responsible for all three groups. Writing for me wasn't so much about the Western end of self-expression but a commitment to those who had gone before and those yet to come. It was my way of speaking for those living, dead, and yet to be who could not speak for themselves. Many Chinese people believe in hungry ghosts; thus the idea that the ancestors must be fed and revered by the living. Writing allowed me to execute this responsibility. When I heard about prejudice against either my own peoples, or Amazonian Indians who were being evicted from their lands, or women in poor countries being forcibly sterilized, I sometimes felt that I couldn't get a moment's peace until I addressed the issue in my writing. It was as though my ancestors were tugging at me. I knew my aims as a writer were to be an oracle, not an entertainer.

So, strangely, it was at my predominantly white school where I forged my revolutionary ethos. Since I was a multicultural girl in a white space, I used my situation to try to bring things to my peers' and teachers' attention that they wouldn't ordinarily notice. My quest to speak truth to power was facilitated by being in one of power's centers. And I was humbled when, over time, I became a resource for my teachers on nonwhite issues.

After I graduated from upper school, I went to Dartmouth, a predominantly white college in New Hampshire, the second-whitest state in the country. At my old school, melanin in an adult person's skin most likely meant they were a menial laborer, whereas in Hanover, the town where Dartmouth is located, melanin was a status symbol, as it automatically meant you were an Ivy League student or professor. Nonwhite people had no other roles in the town. Many nonwhite students felt uncomfortable in such a white space, even to the point of leaving the college. I was stunned by their reactions.

"I've never seen so much diversity in my life," I would say, shocked. Although Houston is an extremely diverse city, the parts of it in which I lived and moved were far whiter than Hanover and Dartmouth. With an Ibo professor and friends from Nepal and Albania, I felt as though I was on Disney's "It's a Small World" ride.

My boyfriend during freshman year was from Ghana. In contrast to the ever-present white guy of my little-kid cotillion dreams, my boyfriend was a proud Ashanti who paired the three European tongues he was fluent in with three West African languages. We were friends whose hours spent talking, watching indie films, and listening to Ghanaian music segued into romance.

My relationship with my boyfriend seems, in ways spoken and unspoken, to have affected my relationship with my parents, especially my father. I remember, as a little girl, pointing to an ad in *Town and Country* magazine with a picture of a JFK Jr. look-alike and saying I wanted to marry a man who looked like him. My father wondered aloud why I would want to marry a guy from a race different from his. While the model's debonair smile and old-fashioned taste in clothing reminded me of my father, all my dad could see was the model's lack of melanin. But just as my parents couldn't fully believe I was secure in my heritage until I could acknowledge the reality of racism, my love for a young Ashanti man affirmed to them my love for my background, and perhaps my esteem for our family.

My relationship with my boyfriend was about neither race generally nor our particular cultures specifically. We would have loved each other had we been Maori, Mayan, or Scottish. Nevertheless, much of our journey toward each other was inspired by an interest in each other's heritages. He was intrigued by my existence in the diaspora; I was enchanted by his homeland. Both before and after becoming my significant other, my boyfriend was one of my first black friends, and we looked on each other like long-lost cousins catching up after a centuries-long separation, exploring the bounds of nature and nurture. He and I both saw our love, and our friendship, as a sort of homecoming.

Despite the fact that qualities such as integrity, compassion, and piety rather than ethnicity are what attract me to guys, my two other college boyfriends, one American and one Jamaican, were both black. Race was not a conscious factor for me in choosing to be with them, but the happy coincidence vindicated me in a "See, I haven't been maimed by my environment" way.

My friendships, like my romantic relationships, reflected the diversity in my environment. Furthermore, once I wasn't restricted to the option of having white (or occasionally Asian) friends or none at all, I could be choosier about my relationships. As a child I used to grade white peoples' antiracist literacy on a curve. I still have friends I love from lower, middle, and upper school who will try to excuse the Confederacy or rant about the wrongs of affirmative action, but at Dartmouth I stopped befriending people like that. The white people I made friends with at college, whether they were savvy about racial issues or were largely unaware about the extent of discrimination against nonwhites, were uniformly people I felt I could be safe with. They didn't inadvertently say racist things. They didn't deny nonwhite perceptions of reality or history.

Fortunately, despite all the diversity at Dartmouth, I wasn't as naive as I once was. I recognized that just because Dartmouth was more diverse than what I was used to didn't mean that various racial and ethnic groups were equitably represented. The fact that elderly white women at church gave me directions to their homes and urged me not to hesitate if I needed anything didn't cause me to discount the fact that several nonwhite guys on campus described being harassed by the police.

Still, I felt comfortable at Dartmouth, not primarily because it was more diverse than what I was used to, but because, outside of my political concern with fair representation, I still didn't notice the color of the people around me. Today I care about the inequity that leads to homogeneously white spaces, but for better or worse, on a daily basis I still don't notice race in my environment. Because this is such a fundamental part of my nature, I think I would have felt the same at Dartmouth even if I had been raised in primarily nonwhite spaces. By contrast, many of my peers were uncomfortable at Dartmouth. Whiteness wasn't invisible to them. These students had known something I never had: the experience of growing up in places where they were the rule rather than the exception.

So at Dartmouth I saw both how much I had and how much I had missed. As a Cherokee girl whose prep-school education meant I spoke three European languages, I looked wistfully at a Diné girl whose upbringing on a reservation meant she was fluent in her people's tongue. Who was the privileged one? Who was underprivileged? Her school hadn't taught advanced math. No one in my family spoke Tsalagi. Both of us had mastered one world and sought to succeed in a second. Like many—maybe even all—the nonwhite students at Dartmouth, we were seeking to be whole.

And for me, being a whole African American, Cherokee, Chinese, English woman meant that there were two things I needed to do. First, I had to seek to rectify the inequity I had witnessed in my past. Second, I wanted to take advantage of being in a diverse community for the first time in my life in order to learn more about and protect my peoples' spiritual and cultural ways of life. For me, Dartmouth represented more than the opportunity to get an extraordinary education. It was a chance to participate in communities I wasn't able to be part of previously. No more learning hand games from how-to books.

I immediately thought about these goals when I heard of Dartmouth's First-Year Summer Research project. Why not use my education to address the inequity I had seen in my past by researching the experiences of poor minority workers at my privileged white school? Why not ask them what it meant to be a modern-day Atlas, not the archaic Greek mythological figure who literally bore the skies on his shoulders, but one of the many impoverished people of color whose labors hold up a world run by the white and elite? I felt that as a creative writer, the best thing I could do to show my appreciation to the minority service workers who supported me during my time at school was to interview as many of them as possible about race and class issues, and from their interviews write creative nonfiction oral histories. Thus my project "Atlas Speaks," a portfolio of oral histories crafted from the words of minority service workers, was born. The project was based on my interest in race and space. Who was allowed where, and did they come through the front or back door? Along with race and space, I was interested in voice.

I remember one interview with a worker who had been employed at the school for decades. She told me the story of her journey from stay-at-home mom to becoming one of the school's employees, of being called by her first name by little children, of her camaraderie with her colleagues and the paucity of black teachers, and how much she valued "her babies"—the students, white and nonwhite, that she cared for. She told me of suffering from institutional disrespect and engaging in guerilla advocacy for minority students.

"I can't tell you how much I appreciate you doing this interview," I said, as we wound down our conversation, well past the allotted hour. She looked at me and smiled.

"You are what we fought for," she said. Her tone suggested a subtext: *So you must fight for us.* The role of storytellers in the battle for social equity was affirmed for me once more.

It was my hope that by naming the issues, planning improvements, defining realities, and articulating hopes, by acknowledging the truth of conditions at my school, I could help it become a space of diversity and appreciation. I tried to communicate to the school's employees, "This is your space. This centuries-old school, its rose-brick buildings, its tennis courts and libraries and art exhibits and outdoor bayou classroom are your spaces." They tended it lovingly, labored in it diligently, and cared for it loyally— and they had the right to be esteemed highly and compensated fairly.

But I also wanted to say to them, referring to the white paper on which I had written their stories, "This too is your space. You have a right to

a place on paper, in essays. You have a right to a forum and to give testimony. You have the right not to remain silent. Anything you say just
might set you or someone else free." I had reached the point in my storytelling where, instead of accepting a nearly homogeneously white cast of
characters, I could put the spotlight on nonwhites.

My cultural goals at college weren't like a checklist. It's not as if I said,
"Well, I've done some activist ethnography, now I'm finished fighting for
social justice." "Atlas Speaks" was part of my journey, not a task completed
or a battle won. And it was while recognizing that fact that I began working on my second aim: joining my peoples' communities and becoming
better at serving and practicing my cultures.

There were communities available on campus for students of all the cultures in my heritage. I just had to find my space. But having lots of cultures
in you can be like having lots of kids: you have to find time to devote to
each one. I spoke English, French, and Spanish, but should I try to learn
a language from one of my nonwhite cultures? Tsalagi? A West African
language such as Yoruba? Cantonese? Which one? All three? Would such a
course of action make me more culturally competent, or just crazy? Should
I join a group pertaining to each ethnic heritage? When I graduated,
should I join alumni associations pertaining to each one too? And if I didn't,
would that mean that I was prioritizing some of my cultures over others?

I ended up organizing my time more organically. I went to black-
student meetings and participated in Students for Africa. I helped hire the
first professor of Asian American literature in the English Department
and attended Asian cultural events. During sophomore summer, I lived in
the African American affinity house. I wrote political articles, celebrated
a range of holidays, and protested when I was called to. But there was one
community I was hesitant to join.

"It's your space," said Dr. Brewer, a Dartmouth Cherokee scholar, when
I discussed the matter with him in his office. "You have a good instinct for
the sensitivities around issues of Native American identity," he continued.
"It's your space."

"It" was the affinity house for Native Americans at Dartmouth, or
NADs. I was a NAD, but a secret one. While I practiced Cherokee traditions quietly and privately, I'd only entered the house once by my junior
year at Dartmouth. Since I didn't know how to dance, during the college
powwows I would volunteer at the T-shirt booth, which put me meta-
phorically and literally on the sidelines.

"I've never gone to NAD meetings because I thought they were for
people who had been raised in Native American communities. I didn't

want to intrude on space that wasn't mine," I explained. And there was something else: I never referred to myself as being "part" something or the other because I knew I was not a fractured person. When my ascendants forged their cross-cultural connections, they did not break their descendants. I'm not like a plate that lies on the floor in pieces, something less than whole, diminished, disinherited. But what if in the NAD house I was seen as a broken cookie? Being multicultural is kind of like being a messy handwritten note. You have a definite message, but people will read you as they see fit; they will possibly misinterpret you or find you ambiguous. I was concerned that by being many, I would be deemed not enough. And I felt that NADs who had been raised traditionally had the right to make that judgment. I just didn't want to subject myself to it.

I said earlier that I don't notice the race of the people around me. And I guess that's true, as I spent the majority of my life in predominantly white environments. What has changed, though, is that every now and then I become keenly aware of my own heritage. I feel especially at home in the francophone African community in Paris. I feel proud walking through the streets of Chinatown. African Americans, Asians, and whites are easily accepting of my plurality on the rare occasions when it comes up. For example, no Asian has ever looked at me askance for celebrating the Chinese New Year. But because racial authenticity is such a fraught question in the Native American community, when I was considering entering the NAD community, I was particularly conscious of race(s), the community's and my own.

And then there was my appearance. I don't like to describe myself in terms of the stereotyped features attributed to each of my cultures, but I think I look African American, whatever that means. I also think I look like all of my peoples. Some people recognize Asian or Native American features in me. Others don't. Most days I'm assumed to be African American. Often I am asked, "What are you?" If you made a spectrum of people with Sami on one end and Dinkas on the other, I would have the brown color pretty much in the middle. My bust-length hair is the last auburn on the spectrum before black. My eyes are brown. People of various races mistake me for being Asian Indian or of another Southeast Asian culture.

But despite all this, Dr. Brewer was unequivocal: "It's your space." And when I attended my first NAD meeting, I was welcomed. No one questioned whether I belonged in the house on that first Thursday evening, while cooking frybread in the kitchen on Saturdays to sell at fund-raisers, or in discussions about the racism behind Dartmouth's unofficial mascot, "the Dartmouth Indian."

I joined the Native Americans at Dartmouth group the day after I spoke to Dr. Brewer, and I welcomed the sense of communion. I learned how to peyote stitch and passed on the knowledge of Cherokee medicine I had been taught by elderly relatives. I round-danced, discussed decolonizing academia, and was introduced to the wonderful world of Pendleton blankets. But it wasn't until my senior year, when I had gathered with some other Native American students in one of the dormitory basements with a Tuscarora professor, that I had an epiphany. As we talked about Europeans in America, Native Americans in the ivory tower, and what it meant to walk in two worlds, I realized that most of the Native Americans in the room had questioned what it means to be, to be accepted as, and to be located as a Native American.

"I heard the term 'blood quantum' for the first time and it confused me," said a slender Diné boy. "I went home and asked my mom, 'How much Indian am I?'" He mimicked his mother rolling her eyes and smiling. "'You're as Indian as you feel,' she told me."

"I didn't know all the stuff about Indians living in harmony with nature until I went to school," another boy added. "And I grew up on a reservation. The way we were described in books was so far from what I knew. I thought: *Is that what we did historically? Really?*"

I was surprised. Even students who were so-called full-blooded Indians, students who were fluent in Native American languages and had grown up on reservations, had been made to doubt their indigenousness and to wonder if they fit the definitions constructed by both non-Natives and fellow Indians. Other students discussed the issue of "ghost NADs," Native American students who left the NAD community either because they personally were rejected for not being "Indian enough" or because they were offended by the judgments others made.

Finally, I spoke. "That's what kept me away from the NAD community for a long time. I thought maybe I shouldn't be there since I wasn't traditionally raised. But fortunately no one ever rejected me."

"Oh, Shannon!" exclaimed a sophomore student in dismay. I had never told anyone but Dr. Brewer about my concerns in joining NAD. I think the sophomore had just thought I was especially shy. The professor looked at me in sympathy as we all affirmed to each other what Dr. Brewer had told me months ago. That we were in the right space.

Since that time, I've heard or read about the same discussions occurring among blacks, Arabs, Asian Indians, and East Asians. I recognize their concern that the culture they identify with will find them lacking, that after a lifetime of being a minority in white spaces, they might not belong in the spaces of their own peoples either.

When people ask me, "What are you?" I'm neither offended by being queried nor perplexed about how to answer. My response, like my ethnic identity, has never shifted, but just because I don't falter doesn't mean I'm not wary of being doubted or challenged. I know I'll never be the first thing that comes to mind when people picture a preparatory-school student, Greenbrier guest, or a Native American at Dartmouth, but through maturing and my experiences in college, and particularly as a NAD, I have learned that it's not just important to know who you are; you also have to affirm where you belong. That's why I joined the Native Women's Dance Society in my senior year at Dartmouth and learned to dance "fancy shawl." When powwow came that spring, I entered the circle—my space, and the space of my people—as an African American, Cherokee Native American, Chinese American, and English American. And I danced.

After graduating magna cum laude from Dartmouth College with Highest Honors in a Senior Fellowship, Shannon became a Lombard Fellow in Mongolia and a Reynolds Scholar in Australia. She then earned her master's degree in English at Harvard University. Shannon is currently pursuing a law degree at Yale University and a PhD at Harvard. Her legal studies focus on human rights theory and practice with a particular focus on Indigenous peoples. Her doctorate work focuses on African and African American studies. Shannon's writing has been published in several places including *Black Agenda Report*, *Houston Literary Review*, *Indian Country Today*, *Amandala*, and *African-American News & Issues*.

2

Bringing Back a Piece of the Sky   Blythe George

A moment spent in Indian country will show you that everyone is related to somebody "important." Growing up, I had always heard the name Spott along with allusions to tribal grandeur, but, quite honestly, looking at me wouldn't make you think I was one of those people. My Gramma Clair was dark, and the darkness of her skin, her hair, and her beautiful almond eyes was what struck me most as a child. I am on the other side of the spectrum phenotypically, a carbon copy of my half-Yurok mom, and both of us take after "Red," my full-blooded Irish Grampa. Mom has dark-auburn hair and dark eyes, and she says her light skin is negated by her "mean look." I have the same reddish hair and freckly skin, but as a result of having one grandparent on each side with blue eyes, I wound up with a pair of my own. My brother has dark brown hair, and dark eyes like my dad and mom, while I look like an Irish girl.

I am the daughter of Anthony "Tony" George and Eileen "Benny" Ragain, and older sister by fourteen months of Taylor George and by eighteen years of Drake Horn. I am the granddaughter of Clarann Childs and Clovis "Red" Ragain, and Tom "Pop" George and Cynthia "Cindy" Killam. My mom and her mother are members of the Yurok Tribe of Northern California, as am I. Through Clair I am descended from Robert Spott, one of the last Yurok cultural leaders, who worked closely with the cultural anthropologist A. L. Kroeber to document Yurok and other Northern California tribal practices, many of which were included in the books *Yurok Narratives* and *Yurok Myths*. But it wasn't until recently that I could give you this much information about my ancestry.

My blue eyes were a source of confusion to me early on, and I stuck out like a sore thumb when sitting with the other Indian children. I remember getting a book about cats for my eighth birthday, and after reading it cover to cover, I explained to my parents how they could end up with a blue-eyed child despite their both having brown eyes, based on the dominant/ recessive trait chart of black and white cats. From very early on, I loved school for so many reasons, and I was good at it. As I advanced through the grades, the other Indians did not think it was cool that I liked school and did so well. On top of that, I talked a lot and didn't listen respectfully as a good little Yurok should. So not only was I was loud and opinionated, I didn't look anything like the other kids, unless you knew what to look for. As time went on, it was obvious that being Yurok was difficult for me because I chafed at the expectations of my Native peers.

For a long time I didn't want to take on the Yurok mantle openly because I associated so many negative things with the dark skin of my peers. I had assumptions about "drunken Indians" who didn't succeed in life, and I had other plans. I loved school and was fortunate to have been blessed with a good work ethic and intelligence. I had college on my mind from the time I was eight years old and decided I wanted to be a lawyer. I was lucky to have parents who were honest with themselves about our situation, and my mom pushed my brother and me from an early age to want more than what they had been able to give us. We lived in a home full of love, but little else. Lack of money was always a problem, and my parents argued and hit each other while arguing about money for as long as I can remember. Little did I know that this experience of poverty, domestic violence, and, later, substance abuse would bind me tighter to my Yurok peers than any other bond of skin or culture could. School was, and is, my sanctuary from the instability of home, and yet it is in this instability that I have found the largest part of my Yurok identity.

When I think back, it's not the bad parts of my childhood that I recall most often. I remember laughing with my family until my cheeks hurt, walking long trails together where it felt like we were in another world. We watched many sunsets over the ocean and picked berries until my hands, face, and pockets were stained purple. We played with dogs, cats, rats, and even opossums! Every time I come back home to McKinleyville, California, it's not the lack of technology, roads, or civilization that stands out to me but a profound appreciation for every part of that coastline, those redwoods, the unending ocean, and every trail in between, because each is marked by a memory shared with my family.

Our family of four was as strong as fire-tested steel, but undergoing the pain of fire was most definitely how we gained that strength. I love my family, and we were a happy one, but the happiness we shared was unstable, to say the least. Even before things began to deteriorate during my teen years, our good times were always sprinkled with bad. If money was tighter than usual or one of them had a bad day, my parents would devolve into a "knock-down drag-out," as they called it, while my brother and I would run outside to get as far away from the yelling and scream- ing as we could. I remember trying to lose myself in a novel to get away from their voices and cries, but those brief escapes were inevitably cut short by the loud noises echoing through walls, sounding like someone was hurt because the words had turned into punches. But no matter how bad the fights would get or who had a black eye the next day at breakfast, our family would spring back as if nothing had happened, or at least as if it wouldn't happen again. For us, laughter was never far off. I was hugged, kissed, and loved like only the most fortunate of children can claim. My parents never laid a hand on me or my brother, but that doesn't mean their actions toward each other didn't leave a lasting impression.

My parents hit each other, said hurtful words, played mind games, and manipulated each other into becoming their worst selves. I love my father, and he was a great provider for my family with the hard-earned wages of a lumber worker. Yet I can never truly forgive him for hitting my mom. Instead of acknowledging the stress of poverty and a hard job, or whatever else in life was vexing him, my dad channeled his rage onto mom. My dad was only twenty-two and my mom twenty-one when I was born, so I can't blame them for not having the skills to cope with their anger in more mature ways. But I also can't say that their choices didn't have an impact on my brother and me. Even though my parents didn't want us involved in their fights, and I'm thankful for that, I did try to put myself between them as soon as I was big enough, and when I was older I even tried to hold them back from one another, only to be cast off because I shouldn't have been there in the first place. But I would still jump in the next time because I was damned if I was going to "let" the two people I loved most in this world hurt each other.

In my opinion, the frequent domestic violence in our home was directly related to the stress of poverty. The worry of not having enough was all too common at our house. My mom's constant urgings—"Do bet- ter, want more, get more. Not this. Never this."—was the backdrop to my conscious self. My parents were saddled with the constant stress of living paycheck to paycheck, which took its toll in the form of these violent outbursts. Despite this pressure, my parents found ways to compensate. They managed to scrape enough money together to take my brother and me on a trip nearly every year. One of my favorite memories is the Easter we spent in Sacramento, where we fed peanuts to squirrels and accidently went in the back entrance of the California State Capitol Building. I remember asking my mom how the Easter Bunny would find us, and she promised that he would know we were on vacation. And he did—we woke up Easter morning to car seats FULL of the Easter Bunny's bounty. These traveling experiences were so far removed from our daily stresses and instability, and they are some of my fondest memories.

No matter how often they fought, how loudly my parents argued, or what was found broken when all was said and done, we always managed to put these things behind us and laugh again. However, this ability to move on did not last forever, and the trauma our family would experience in the ensuing years made the domestic violence of my childhood seem tame. I can trace this change back to one afternoon when I was twelve years old.

We had recently been evicted from the house where I spent most of my childhood, a small two-bedroom located on a half acre of land, where my brother and I spent nearly every afternoon running around with the dogs. I don't know what prompted that eviction, but it was the first of many times my family would have to make such a move. This time we ended up living with my grampa, in the house where my mom grew up. My mother soon told us that my father had been fired from his job. Dad had worked at the same lumber mill for most of my life, and while he was good at his job, he had always been known as a "shit-starter," a man who was always fighting with someone. One of these altercations boiled over into a midnight standoff between my dad and a coworker. Neither was injured, but the confrontation got my father fired from his job of thirteen years. That firing started a slide into dysfunction that would inevitably be the end of my family as we knew it.

When I was younger, I remember him as one big kid who played with my brother and me better than any other father could. He taught us to build a fire, shoot BB guns, climb mountains, and build an entire carnival out of K'Nex, to name just a few things. I remember, too, the time I came home to my pet rat being transported across our living room by zip line after my father had spent the day building a Ferris wheel and pulley lines out of the Lego-like materials. He tried to be the best father he could be for fifteen years, but my father has made choices in the last decade that fundamentally changed both him and his relationship with my family.

After he lost his lumber-mill job, Dad bounced from job to job and my mom started to work, but they never earned enough to pay the bills. We moved every year after that first eviction, but by the time I was fourteen, things seemed to be changing for the better. Dad found a job at the local dump that was within walking distance of our new house, which we had moved into just two days before I started high school. We had spent the previous month homeless, living in a local campground with all of our animals. But now we finally had a house and Dad had a good job, so things were going to be okay—or so I thought. Soon after he started the new job, my dad stopped coming home at night, or he would stop by briefly, then leave again to search for "things" at the dump. TVs, video games, fans, speakers, and many other things Dad had brought home from the dump now decorated our house, but from the beginning, my mom knew something was off, and it was only out of sheer denial that my brother and I didn't admit it as well.

My dad had struggled with drug abuse since a hard childhood sent him to work with undesirable drug growers in the rural mountains of Northern California. When they met many years earlier, my mom had managed to clean up her "mountain man," and his drug abuse faded into the background. But after years of his own family's poverty, compounded by his inability to provide for his family any longer and the availability of drugs at his new job, my dad became addicted to methamphetamine. This drug has become the scourge of communities around the nation, and McKinleyville was no different. Although Mom had known from day one, it took years for us as a family to admit that drugs were the source of the changes in Dad.

My parents' fights became louder and more violent as Dad's moods became more erratic, due to his drug use. I remember dreading the sound of his voice denying everything to my mom, but at least if I could hear him I knew he was safe. There were many nights that I fell asleep waiting for him to come home, and would wake up only to find that he hadn't re-turned. It was an ache that sat heavily in all our hearts and put tremendous strain on each of us, but somehow our denial about what was really going on kicked in each time Dad inevitably returned home. He always man-aged to spin some yarn to explain his absence and account for his unkempt appearance. We would welcome him back just out of the sheer relief that he came back at all.

The cycle of addiction is a family disease, and denial lets it remain un-treated for so long. When my dad would come back, we could somehow still manage to laugh together again, but those times became increasingly rare as his nights away became routine, and the stress of not knowing if he'd ever return became second nature. Our family unit, which had survived so many troubles before, was crumbling because one of its pillars was gone. It would be years before we could recover from those years of Dad's addiction.

I recall the last Thanksgiving and Christmas my brother and I spent with my dad. He had been on one of his benders for days before each holiday, and he was "unpleasant" to be with as he came down from the drugs. But we forged ahead for each other, not wanting to be the one who "ruined" the holiday. There wasn't a lick of furniture in our current house because we had gone through so many moves, but it was easily the most beautiful one we had ever lived in. We went to a Chinese buffet on Thanksgiving because we couldn't afford to buy the traditional food; besides which, my mom had to work and my dad was too strung out to cook. That year's Christmas was the first one we had no gifts to open—or even a tree to keep gifts under.

Because we had grown up poor, not having gifts or a turkey wasn't actually a big deal for my brother and me, but our sheer lack of joy hurt so much. I think we were all just tired of trying to be happy, of trying to smile when there was something so obviously wrong yet so impossible to fix. While denial made it possible for me to smile despite my pain, it also put us in a state of limbo that wore us down. There was only one thing that could free us from those chains—the truth.

I remember perching at the top of the stairs as my parents conversed in hushed tones in the living room below. It was usually not hard to hear the words they flung at each other. We were all so jaded by then that it seemed weird my parents were obviously hiding something. My brother was in his room, trying not to listen, but as the older sibling I could never do that. I had to be ready to launch myself into the melee if something went wrong, so I was listening dutifully. I could hear every word as my dad admitted that my mom was right—he had been using methamphetamine for the last two years, and he was now hopelessly addicted. They eventually called us downstairs to tell us, and I remember how forlorn he looked. He had taken to wearing Under Armour underwear beneath his clothing since he spent so many nights outdoors, and I remember thinking how thin he looked in a shirt that hugged every bone, his dark eyes so sad above his hollowed cheeks. It was not the first time I had seen my dad cry, but it was the first time I did not feel bad for him. I just felt relieved that we couldn't deny his drug use any more. I was also very angry. How could he do this to us? How could he throw it all away? How could he pick some nasty white powder over his family? The profound selfishness that was part of my father's drug addiction is something I have never understood or let go of my hatred for, despite having decided to forgive him for my own peace of mind. Maybe that would be different had his coming clean led to anything, but it didn't.

Dad went to rehab, but within months he fell off the wagon. The last time he lived with us, my parents were in a loving mood when I left the house to go visit a friend. They were rarely so amorous, and it was that loving mood that made the next morning so bewildering. Since Dad had returned from rehab he was always home when I woke up, and it was nice to get back to that normalcy. So when I woke up that morning and he was obviously gone, it was confusing. My mom had no explanation. Dad had gotten up in the middle of the night, tried to start a fight, and left soon afterward. It was now over. He never slept at our house again. After that night, we went two weeks with nary a sound nor sight of Dad. My brother and I accidentally ran into him in the forest behind the local grocery store. It hurt to know that he wasn't looking for us, but it was a relief to see him alive and uninjured. Since his addiction had begun, that was all we could ask for.

My father's addiction was the formative influence of my childhood. It is the source of my humanity and the driving force behind my aspiration to relieve poverty in communities like the one I grew up in. There is no reason any child should see their parent consumed by the monster of addiction, a plague that changes the very person who gave you your own moral fiber and taught you the difference between right and wrong. No child should have to see every semblance of the family they have known shattered by one snort of white powder, or stare into the dead eyes of a drug speaking with the voice of your father. Poverty is one thing, violence is another, but nothing made me want to leave home more than my father's addiction. So I applied to college on the other side of the country, wanting to get as far away from McKinleyville as fast as I could.

I was in luck—Dartmouth College fell in love with me just as much as I did with it from the moment of my visit to the campus via the Native Fly-In Program. I applied for early decision, and knew that I would hear the results on a particular Wednesday in December of my senior year. I was so nervous that I was nauseated for two days straight. The letter was supposed to arrive by e-mail at lunchtime that day, and my physics teacher let me use his computer to check. One of the best moments of my life was when the letter popped up on the screen with a huge "CONGRATULATIONS!!!" at the top. I ran through the hallways of my high school telling everyone—I will never forget that day.

After receiving my Dartmouth acceptance, I waited for weeks to hear whether I would be awarded a Gates Millennium Scholarship that would cover all my expenses for both undergraduate and graduate education. My mom picked me up from school, and as she drove me to work at the local grocery store she casually mentioned that the mail had come. The way she said it told me that the award letter had arrived. I was overjoyed when I ripped open the huge envelope and read the letter confirming my award. I could see the tears rolling down my mom's face under her ever-present Oakleys. She had told me my whole life that hard work and dedication in the classroom would pay off, and I was holding in my hands the proof of that. I had a full ride to my first-choice college. No matter what had happened to us in the years before, we had made it! I say "we" because my future was never just for me. From the moment in third grade when I decided to become a lawyer I always had a desire to provide for my family—to be able to give my mom not only the things she needed but the things she wanted. I wanted to relieve the stress that had dogged her, and to free her mind from the worries she had become too accustomed to bearing. My commitment to provide for her and my brother only grew when my father left us, and I could not have predicted how much my college acceptance would intensify it.

I hate the fact that my father chose to become an addict, but coping with that stress gave me the strength to face any fire. It also taught me humility and empathy for others in similar circumstances. Having experienced the pain of addiction against a backdrop of poverty and domestic violence, I felt intense pressure to honor the opportunity to help others that my education had given me. This deep sense of commitment matched my desire for higher education. Earning an advanced degree and doing high-quality research will allow me to address poverty by contributing to well-informed social policy, and that is how I want to use my life experience to better the life of others. I can't take the scourge of addiction away from someone, but if I can help make sure that there are quality jobs, housing, and schools for every family and child, maybe there will be one less family that goes through what mine did. This goal has driven me since before I could fully articulate it, all the way back to that last summer before I went to Dartmouth.

From the time I was accepted at Dartmouth until I left for school, my family's level of happiness did a complete turnaround. When I applied, my mom, my brother, and I were all living under the same roof, but the stress of my father's addiction and his eventual departure had driven us apart. The three of us being together only emphasized the fact that one of us was missing, so it was uncomfortable, to say the least, and we all began doing our own thing—separately. The pain that void caused had driven me to dream of a life three thousand miles away. A few months passed, and my mom settled down with someone named Kevin. I hated that, because it was a further reminder that our nuclear family no longer existed, and no matter what my father had done, the smallest part of me hoped that we would one day be reunited as a family. But Kevin was there to stay, and I had to accept it sooner than I expected. Time was ticking down before I was to leave for school, and we all started to spend more time together—including Kevin. I couldn't help but be won over by Kevin, who reminded me of my dad in so many little ways. As we got into the rhythm of a new dynamic, something happened that pushed us all back together in a way we never could have predicted.

The week after my eighteenth birthday, my mom asked my brother and me if she could take us out to dinner. We never went out for dinner, so I assumed that maybe my birthday or upcoming college departure was a reason for a nice night out, but my brother guessed from the get-go that something bigger was up. Before the food even came, Mom and Kevin, who were sitting across the booth from my brother and me, wore a look of both happiness and trepidation as they said, "We wanted to tell you guys that we are pregnant." They looked into each other's eyes with love as they said it, but my brother and I were stunned. It is hilarious in retrospect, given that my mom was confessing to her son and daughter that *she* was pregnant, as if we were the parents who would discipline the "irresponsible" couple.

I had come to tolerate Kevin, but my anger at my missing father now reared its head. I was stunned, but congratulated Mom and Kevin as much as I could. Here I was sitting next to my only sibling, getting ready to leave for college in a matter of months, and my mom is telling me I'm about to have another sibling! I'm ashamed to admit how angry and sad I was when I first heard the news, but it had nothing to do with the new relationship between Kevin and my mom, exemplified by this new baby. It was the painful finality of losing the family we had been before. With this news, the George family ceased to exist, and a part of me had to mourn that loss. I had begun going to church during this time to help me grapple with the recent changes in my family, so I spent that night praying and reflecting on what had happened. I awoke the next morning happy beyond words, despite my grief the previous night. I knew that no matter what we had lost in the previous years, there was nothing but good to be gained from Mom and Kevin's news. In fact, it was a chance for a new family—that baby stopped our drifting and brought us even closer together than we had been in all the eighteen years before. My baby brother Drake has changed my life like no other person!

While I loved nearly every minute I spent in college, with every step forward I was also looking over my shoulder at the home and family I loved. My mom understood this and made sure not to let it hold me back. She often told me to fly with eagles, and she reminds me to keep flying every time my obligations to home turn my thoughts in the wrong direction, which is the greatest gift she could ever give me. My mom pushed me to want things I couldn't even fathom, and because of her I have seen and known worlds she never will. However, that freedom is sometimes a heavy burden to bear, loving my family like I do, but it is the freedom a phoenix needs to become an eagle. And now I truly am an eagle because of my mother's love and support.

Nevertheless, I did fly back to the nest, both literally and figuratively, as often as I could. I called my mom every day—"for her sake," I'd tell my friends, but it was as much for me as it was for her . . . to hear her voice, her day's news, the weather, and updates on Drake's progress. I loved every minute I spent with my new friends and eventual family at Dartmouth, but a part of my heart was always a little homesick from the minute I crossed through the security gate at my local airport until I crossed back.

When a kid like me leaves home to attend college three thousand miles away, it feels like I am abandoning everything I love for the sake of my own success. That guilt can be like a millstone around your neck if you forget why you've left in the first place—to one day return and make life better for your family and community members. While I bear this responsibility with pride, this deep sense of obligation affects students from disadvantaged backgrounds more than others, yet there are few resources available to support these students as they make their way.

In my community and other minority communities, thinking and acting for oneself isn't as highly valued as it is in the Western, individualistic, capitalist sense. I will never consider my success complete until it includes the success of my mom, my brothers, and the rest of the Yurok community. I do not strive to climb the heights merely to appreciate the view. I am trying to find a way to bring a piece of that skyline back to the ones I love to make their world better and brighter. And after going to Dartmouth and meeting my fellow Native Americans at Dartmouth (NADs), I know that I am not the only one who thinks this way.

Soon after arriving at Dartmouth, the need to fulfill this sense of duty arose. At first I was merely grappling with how I could still be the "Big Sis" from three thousand miles away, as I could not be my best self at college if I felt I wasn't honoring my obligations to my family, despite the distance. After expressing in an essay how I felt about my obligations, my freshman writing instructor, Nancy Crumbine, pulled me aside and gave me one of the best pieces of advice I ever got at Dartmouth. She explained that she had told her son something similar to what my mom had told me: no matter what happened in the next four years, I had to honor my commitment to myself just as highly as my commitment to my family. There were going to be times when I wanted to run back home to help and provide guidance as my older-sister sensibilities told me I should, but I couldn't listen to that voice every time. I had to realize that my family would make it without me, and that by being committed to bettering myself in college I was doing more for my family than I ever could at home. I came to realize that this inner conflict will probably always be present in me, and that's a burden I must bear in order to soar with eagles.

I actually spent most of my first two years at Dartmouth outside the NAD community. I had great friends from my other affiliations, and while I knew many of the NADs in my class year, I couldn't get past my old feelings of Native inadequacy. I went to the NAD event during orientation, and while I saw several faces that I remembered from the fly-in the summer before, I couldn't help but feel both too white and not Indian enough. I was an off-reservation kid and didn't know enough culturally to fully represent the Yurok tribe. That is one of the first and most important distinctions in the NAD community. My family had attended powwows while I was growing up, and my dad had taught us to camp on the Salmon River where the Karuk tribe resides, but I had never participated in my culture's dances, and I chafed at that feeling of inferiority. I wasn't comfortable enough in my identity to hang with Native classmates, and I didn't feel that pressure when with my non-NAD friends. Thus my relationships outside the Native community flourished in my first two college years, but I should have known that I wouldn't stay away from NAD forever.

During my freshman fall I was lucky enough to take a class called Class in the Classroom with Jay Davis, which fundamentally changed my career path, and therefore my life. Up to that point, I had thought I would honor my duty to my community through law or medicine, the things that my wide-eyed childhood self had dreamed of. That was all predicated on the fact that I thought those were the fields where I could effect the most change. But this class showed me that there was something much more immediate and personal that needed attention: the US public school system. I learned that so many kids born into families like mine didn't have the opportunity to go to a good public school that had plenty of resources and quality teachers. Nor did their parents have the jobs or skills to support them in and out of the classroom. While there were many reasons for this, the result was that these kids were robbed of a future simply because they were born in a specific family or neighborhood, or on a particular reservation.

As I continued to learn about joblessness and poverty in US minority communities through my sociology major, I yearned for the chance to see the problems of my home community through my new, "Dartmouth-educated" eyes. I was granted a Partners in Community Service fellowship through the Tucker Foundation, and used the funds to craft a rotating internship that was sponsored by the Northern California Indian Development Council. For the majority of my internship, I worked at a charter high school on my tribe's reservation. I served as a teacher's assistant, tutor, warm-bodied chaperone, and whatever else they needed in the small school of thirty students, who were primarily Yurok, although several other local tribes were also represented. Nearly every student came from a family living below the poverty line. As I learned more about the families that these students went home to each day, I was surprised at how natural it all felt.

Growing up, I had always been keenly aware that my family's dysfunction was different from the lives of my friends, particularly my white, middle-class, AP-track peers, and this obvious juxtaposition made our secrets seem even more shameful. Yet it soon became apparent that if I had grown up on the reservation, my family would have been just one of many with such problems. While I could see the possible camaraderie born of such circumstances, I was shocked at how this "normalization" of delinquency seemed to rob the students of their motivation. They were united in their shared lack of resources, and this deprivation had morphed into a representation of the Yurok culture. No matter how I ached at the effect this had on student achievement, I could understand the inclination to gain comfort through shared experiences. Having to deal with such family problems on my own as a child had been incredibly hard, so I admired the way the students shared their experiences in solidarity with one another, processing them and healing together. I shared my own background with them, as well as my ability to succeed despite those obstacles, and it was in this sharing that I felt my Yurok identity was affirmed as never before. I differed in skin and eye color from many of the students, yet I could relate to them because I knew what it was like to see one's parents hit each other, or to be evicted, or to lose a family member to addiction. These experiences were the same, despite what my exterior showed, and it was through this shared experience of concentrated disadvantage that I found my Yurok identity. Despite growing up sixty miles away, I knew the poverty and deprivation of reservation life inside and out.

It was with this renewed identity that I returned to Dartmouth for my sophomore summer, and began to serve as the undergraduate adviser at the Native American House. I hardly knew anybody there, but I had an absolute blast that first term with all the NADs of my class year and I was able to ease my way into the NAD way of life. If students came to my room at the end of the second-floor hallway, they would find me ready to help with their concerns, big and small. It was hard at first, but I loved my job and used it to become part of the community. By this time I knew I was truly Yurok, and that was enough. It didn't matter what others thought, or that I still felt a pressure to overcompensate culturally to make up for my light features.

One of the ways I secured this new sense of belonging was by taking several Native American studies (NAS) courses during my last two years at Dartmouth. Through the instruction of people like Colin Calloway and Bruce Duthu, I learned more about my place within the history and future of Indian country, and how I needed to arm myself with a degree to protect this heritage, like generations before had armed themselves for war. This responsibility was affirmed as I learned more about the homes of my Native peers, who came from families and communities like mine. We were collectively few and far between at Dartmouth, and the camaraderie among those in the NAS Department was integral to my decision to pursue a graduate degree. Although I had always aspired to a law degree, my new interest in poverty research was just as important to our community and, as Bruce put it, "There was a time when we didn't have enough Native lawyers, but it is no longer that time." Words like those freed me to pursue a new goal in academia, where I would embrace the experiences of impoverished communities like the one I called home, experiences that could shed light on the generational transmission of poverty and, more important, on how to alleviate it.

Becoming a Native scholar was a twofold process for me. First, I had to be strong enough to claim my own identity regardless of what I looked like. Second, I had to learn how my own life timeline fit within the span of North America's colonization. This objective came to fruition one night while I prepared the historical section of my senior fellowship thesis. I had been working with a visiting scholar who specialized in the colonization of California, a history that is obscure even to those who live in the state, and

I had several books to read on the subject. I was moved to tears as I read them because I finally understood where I came from.

Where I grew up, there is a small mass of land under the bridge that spans Humboldt Bay, called Indian Island. In 1860, it was the site of one of the worst massacres in the state's history. Women, children, and elders of the Wiyot tribe were slaughtered in the night by a group of white settlers, who attacked knowing that the tribe's men would be away hunting. I had grown up knowing about this incident, but at no point in my entire education in McKinleyville was I told how common such genocide actually was. In fact, there are countless clearings along the coastline and mountains where I grew up that bear the legacy of such butchery.

According to this scholar's work and several other accounts, the common practice for removing the Yurok, Hoopa, Wiyot, and other area tribes was inhumane, to say the least. At dawn, Native villages would be surrounded by state militiamen, who would open fire on the sleeping settlements. After exhausting their bullets, they would finish off any survivors with a hatchet or sword. Those who did survive were sold into slavery at the very same time the nation was waging a war to end slavery farther eastward. These tactics were incredibly efficient: in 1849, when gold was discovered in California, there were an estimated 150,000 Natives in the state. By 1851, only two years later, nearly 100,000 of them were dead, and by 1910, at most 15,000 still survived. My own tribe had gotten down to four hundred members, including my great-grandparents.

Knowing that the blood of genocide survivors flows through my veins fills me with honor, but also a deep sense of loss. My grandmother was born in 1929, and she never learned to speak Yurok because her father "beat it out of her," fearing the reception it would get her in a country that only decades earlier had hunted down tribal members like game. I cannot begrudge her decision to leave the tribal lands, considering the historical context, but I can't help but mourn the tribal knowledge and cultural resources lost as a result of this genocide. We have already lost so much that I feel it is my duty to let everyone know I am Yurok, that my maternal line has looked out over the Pacific Ocean for time eternal, and that we are still here to live and prosper, despite state-sanctioned efforts to make us do otherwise. And, more important, I can use my platform as a Yurok scholar to honor this history and tell the story of those who remain, despite having faced great adversity. This sense of Yurok belonging was earned not only through my experience growing up, but also through finally learning how that experience was tied to those who came before me. I could not have accomplished the latter without the help of my NAS mentors.

The day of my graduation is forever embedded in my memory. My undergraduate career was over. My friends and I would scatter back to where we all had come from, and Dartmouth would soon be a distant memory (or so I thought). I met my family after the ceremony, and they were surprised at my melancholy. They were so happy for me, and while I appreciated graduating more in the days that followed, that day I was caught up in mourning the end of things rather than the beginning. We walked over to the NAD lunch after the graduation ceremony, and a huge weight was lifted off my shoulders. The tent was full of people who looked like my Native peers, each gathered in a little pod full of whoops and family laughter. We came from all around the country, but it felt like one big family reunion. I have always said that NAD celebrations made me feel like I was at home because no matter where you were, someone always looked like someone you were related to. And here we were, a bunch of Indians at an Ivy League school on a hot summer day. The tent echoed with the boisterous voices of proud parents, grandparents, happy babies, and endless congratulatory remarks. My family seemed especially happy—after days of meeting people who were so different from us, I think it was a relief to feel we were not the only people from a modest background—here there were all kinds! We all received our Pendleton blankets and then said good-bye to each other and to the NAS professors who had provided such important guidance. I was still wiping away tears at the end of the day, but I could not have asked for a better way to end my four college years.

I hope that readers of my story will take away one thing. A lot of messed up things can happen in life, and it can be all too easy to focus on the negative parts. But if you realize that those same experiences give you your strength, specifically the ability to persevere, you can use the skills they gave you to overcome any other challenges you might face. What happened yesterday doesn't matter, only how you learn from it to make today and tomorrow better. I've come so far, but my journey is far from over. I'm still climbing toward that sky, and when I catch it, I will be bringing a piece of it back home.

Blythe Katelyn George is a member of the Yurok Tribe, located in Klamath, California. She was born on July 9, 1990, to Anthony George and Eileen Ragain, and is the proud oldest of three, including Taylor George and Drake Horn. She grew up in McKinleyville,

California, and graduated from McKinleyville High School in 2008. She participated in Future Farmers of America during all four years of high school, and earned an American Farmer Degree.

Blythe is a member of the Dartmouth Class of 2012, having attended the college with a Gates Millennium Scholarship. She earned a Beinecke Fellowship in her junior year and completed a Senior Fellowship on Native student achievement in traditional and alternative schools. She graduated with a degree in sociology and was a member of the Palaeopitus Senior Society.

After working as an academic adviser at the Klamath River Early College of the Redwoods and a data consultant for the Humboldt County P-16 Council the year after her graduation, Blythe enrolled in graduate school. She is now a PhD candidate in sociology and social policy at Harvard University. Since beginning this degree, she has been awarded a National Science Foundation fellowship for her work extending theories of concentrated disadvantage and neighborhood effects from urban sociology to rural reservations. She will use these tools to describe how those living on the Yurok and Hoopa reservations experience unemployment, poverty, and crime, with the hope of building a more comprehensive theory of these phenomena to develop policy aimed at improving these places. After completing her degree, she hopes to work on designing more effective social policies in Washington, DC.

3

Chahta hattak sia, "I Am a Choctaw Man"   Preston Wells

I am the son of a pecan-farmer cowboy and a mother who has a heart for the people. I am the grandson of preaching evangelists who found life in speaking in tongues and helping others. I am a descendent of Texas Rangers who defended the Republic. I come from Mississippi Choctaws who found a new home in Indian Territory. My identity is split in two: these sides have been fighting for centuries and have continued to battle inside of me. On one side stands a courageous group of immigrants trying to defend a land they stole from the native dwellers; on the other is a nation of people who have lost their way of life. My father always told me the two aren't that different because both were only trying to protect their families. I have been trying to see the common ground, the shared intentions, so that I can find peace within myself.

My skin tells the story of my father's fathers, the pride of building a nation in the New World and making something out of nothing, but my heart beats knowing that this land has never been a New World, and it pumps blood the color of our new homelands in Oklahoma. I have been searching for wholeness my entire life. Tired of the fighting, I have been trying to reach a place where all parts of my identity fit together like the states on a map, maintaining their boundaries but still existing as one. But my identity remains split. Moreover, I am a bisexual man of deep faith who, on attending Dartmouth College, has struggled to find peace while sitting in a church. This story contains many narratives told from different perspectives and identities. Yes, I am a Choctaw man, but I am also a Texan. I am a Christian man, but I am also bisexual. I tell this story from these angles and several others to show the obstacles I have faced in my life, but also how I overcame them. In these stories

I find triumph, hope, and love; with them I hope to build a better self in my life after Dartmouth.

"Just say it, Preston. You're white." My parents missed me so much when I was away at college that they didn't mind me staying up late and being loud with my friends when I came home. But this time, the television was the only thing in the room making a sound, as Patrick and Bryant waited for my answer. In southeast Oklahoma, skin color often is the loudest voice in a room; if you don't have dark skin, you're white. I explained, again: "I am Native and Texan, but I do not identify as a 'white boy.'" Patrick eased onto the edge of his seat, resting his arms on his knees and clenching his hands together. I felt the weight of his dark brown eyes and arched eyebrows as he stared at me. What he wanted so badly I could not give him, so I just sat there, sinking deeper into the couch, wondering when they would stop interrogating me. "Preston, just tell him you're white so he'll stop," Bryant said; but this was an identity I did not ascribe to.

"White boy" was what they used to call me in high school, on the basketball floor in particular, where everyone else on the team was "black." Not everyone was *just* black, though; Patrick is black, Mexican, Native, and white; Bryant is black, white, and Native; and several teammates shared a similar mixed heritage. But one thing remained certain: I was the only white boy. The three of us had grown up together, enrolled in the same classes at school, and wore the same uniforms on the ball fields. In high school, when Bryant showed me his Choctaw membership card and I saw the low blood quantum, I never once said he wasn't Choctaw. When Patrick said he didn't know much Spanish, I never denounced his Mexican identity. Therefore I didn't understand how they could use my skin color against me. I had overcome my white skin when I came to college, yet they just couldn't let it go. Eventually, I just said it: "OK, my father's white, so technically, I am white too. But I don't identify as white." I don't know why they wanted to hear it so badly. Maybe they wanted to use it against me and continue to call out my privilege, or to act like my family was ostracizing them because we were white and they were not.

When I started having friends over to our house in middle school, they always spoke of my family as the "white" family because we had a nice house in a good neighborhood; they even related my being white to my parents not allowing bad language and making sure I had my homework done each night. They knew my mother worked for the tribe; they knew her dark skin like they knew the name of our cat. I know my skin is not as dark as my mother's. I know my wavy brown hair forms a duck tail if

I grow it out too much. I know that opposing basketball teams scouted me as "the only white boy on the team." But no one ever asked me how I see myself; nobody listened when I explained that I've never felt white or believed I was a "white boy." All Patrick and Bryant saw in my living room that night was white skin and privilege; it mattered not that I was learning the Choctaw language, or that I was majoring in Native American studies, or that I had started a Native activist group at Dartmouth. It mattered not that the sole reason my family had lived in Choctaw County for over one hundred years was because my Mississippi Choctaw ancestors had immigrated there. What they couldn't accept is that I am who I say I am—*Chahta hattak sia*. I am a Choctaw man.

I didn't grow up speaking the Choctaw language or going to ceremonies; the closest thing to tribal regalia I had growing up was a "Re-Elect Chief Greg Pyle" T-shirt. When my mother took my sister and me to the many community events and dinners, the chief and tribal council did not wear traditional Choctaw shirts. I also can't recall hearing any Choctaw spoken or eating any *banaha* or *tanchi labbona*.[1] When I was growing up, the most Indian I ever felt was when I went hunting with my father. He taught me how to shoot a gun and told me, "You're the Indian, you track the deer." But I didn't know if Little People were hiding behind the trees or other secrets of the woods, and I was at a loss for words when I took a deer's life. These things were not handed down to me. It's not that I didn't want to have these things; it's just that not many of us Choctaws did have them, at least not in my family. My ancestors gave me only one secret to keep. It is not a family ritual, a ghost story, or ancient medicine. It is not the beautiful Chahta Anumpa—the Choctaw language—that I am now learning to speak or the stories behind the diamonds on my Choctaw shirt. They only taught me how to be proud of who I am and where I come from. Without this pride there would be no journey, no story to tell. Pride is what makes me Choctaw. Pride cannot be bred out or lost in language, and pride will make my children and my children's children Choctaw.

No one has the right to tell your story for you. No one can dictate your identity so they will feel more comfortable. For the past 522 years, somebody has been trying to kill off my people's ways, trying to take the very language from my lips. For the past 522 years, someone has been coming into my home and telling me I'm living the wrong way and that my stories aren't true. For the past 522 years, I have been defending my existence. Others have been trying so hard to get me to conform, cut out my tongue, whitewash my heritage, and have called me a "white boy."

The Potato Hills of Tvshka Homma tell a different story.[2] They stand under the Choctaw sun, just as they rise inside of me. The old waters that flow in the Tombigbee also run through the Muddy Boggy.[3] The secrets have been hiding for generations in these hills and waters, just waiting for someone to pick them up.

I was born and raised in Hugo, Oklahoma, which sits in District 8 of the Choctaw Nation of Oklahoma, about twelve miles from the Red River, which is the border with Texas. Although Hugo sits within the Choctaw Nation, it sometimes forgets that. Too often it is a place where only black and white exist. Too often Natives are marginalized as the people who get all the free stuff and are trying to destroy the local economy with the casinos. My family has a farm just off the highway, where my father takes care of cattle and a pecan orchard—a way of life he learned from his father and grandpa. There's an old farmhouse and a couple of barns on the land, along with a house where my father's help used to live—what he calls "the Mexican house." My father has been a cowboy every day of his life—he wears a cowboy hat and boots, a bandana, and denim, speaks with a Texas drawl, and knows his way around a gun, tall tales, and dead truths.

Once he got to Oklahoma, my dad married the first Indian woman he danced with, my mother. She grew up not too far from Hugo, on the other side of Muddy Boggy River in a place called Unger. Her father was a carpenter during the day and an evangelist preacher at night. Her mother cleaned, cooked, and took care of their eight kids. She too was an evangelist, and she made sure the family went to all the revivals held throughout the countryside. My grandma was half Choctaw, and she passed her brown skin on to my mother, whose face is warm and dotted with freckles. My mother began working for the nation not long after graduating from high school, and she has been doing so for the past thirty years. She says she fell in love with my father "because he was a good lookin' cowboy and he knew how to dance." She was the shy and spiritual Indian woman; he was the "work-is-everything" dancing cowboy.

Although I don't believe in blood quantum, that doesn't mean that it hasn't hurt me.[4] In fact, for me it has been the worst thing about being Native. We are the only people in this country who are defined by and divided into fractions, as if we are animals being sold with papers. It dehumanizes us. When a tribe uses blood quantum to describe its members, it sets up a hierarchical caste system among its own people. Those with more Native blood are seen as more Native, as if they were blessed by the Creator to have been born "full blood." Those of us with less Native blood are often looked down on by our own people. Of course, not all tribes handle the blood issue this way, but the Choctaws did when I was growing up. Although to be a tribal member the amount of blood you have doesn't matter, to run for office in the Choctaw Nation of Oklahoma one must be one-quarter Choctaw. I am embarrassed that we still abide by these laws in the twenty-first century, which means that, although I will earn an Ivy League degree in Native American studies, and likely a master's degree and a PhD, I will never be able to be a councilman or chief of my tribe.

In truth, I didn't want to come to Dartmouth. "I think you'll like it there," my mother said. I read through the application and noticed that there was no supplement, meaning I didn't have to provide any extraneous information or write any more essays. I even had a fee waiver for the application, so I figured I had nothing to lose. I'm still unsure why my mother was so adamant about me applying to Dartmouth; maybe she felt I would be safer there, or be more likely to stay true to my roots. Either way, she knew where I'd go to college before I did.

Dartmouth was the first school I heard back from, and that's probably what lured me in. I immediately began searching their website and reading articles to get a sense of the Hanover community and campus life. What interested me most were the many Native programs Dartmouth had to offer. I could learn how to dance in the powwows, I could take classes in Native American studies, and I could sing on a drum. I knew I wanted to strengthen my Native identity, and no other college I applied to offered such experiences. I wanted to feel confident about who I was as a Native man, I wanted my walk to match my talk. Dartmouth became my only choice. But I was concerned that, despite my desire to find my roots, I was not Native enough. Was I already too removed from my history? Was my white skin an impassable boundary?

Soon after I got into Dartmouth, I traveled to Hanover for my first visit. I didn't know what to expect: Would the Natives there only see me as a *nv hollo* (white person)? But from the moment I stepped off the Dartmouth Coach, I felt at home. The green trees and the white buildings with their dark shutters greeted me like a heartfelt handshake. The Native American House immediately became like a second home to me, as I was able to stay there during my visit. Shortly after I got off the bus I met a man I will never forget: Ryan Red Corn. My host had mentioned that we would attend a panel discussion featuring three Indigenous artists; two (one of whom was Red Corn) would become profoundly influential role models to me over the coming years.

If you're a Native attending Dartmouth, chances are you've crossed paths with Ryan, a frequent visitor and mentor. He's a short white guy with a big mole on his right cheek, and wavy dishwater-blond hair. He generally wears a baseball cap and graphic tees, appearing to be a heavy-metal guitarist or powwow junkie. But beneath his white skin is something I could never have imagined: he's an Osage through and through. His history, identity, language, and culture emerge as soon as you talk to him. The fact that Ryan was whiter than I am quelled my own fears. If a man could have skin as white as snow and still be fully comfortable in his Native identity, I wondered what was stopping me from doing the same thing. All my worries about not being Native enough were pushed aside, and I was ready to begin my new journey as a fully recognizable Choctaw man.

My great-grandpa, whom we called Granddad, was a full-blood Mississippi Choctaw. I am told he stood five feet ten inches tall when he was young, and had dark-brown skin and a beautiful face with dark-brown eyes. Granddad married a white woman, I'm sure for good reasons, perhaps because he didn't want his kids to be as dark as he was. I don't know how much racial inequality he experienced, but I do know he had to travel by cattle car to get to Indian Territory. Maybe he didn't want his kids to feel like chattel or animals, as he did, and maybe he didn't want white people to look down on him. Granddad also withheld Chahta Anumpa from his children. Whenever he spoke to his friends and cousins, my grandmother begged him to teach her the language, but he would not. "They'll look down upon you," he would say. My family members tell me that my ancestors hid in the woods when the government came to relocate the Choctaws to their new homelands. They feared for their lives, and they wished to stay in their ancestral lands and continue living the life they had known for thousands of years.

During my freshman fall, while trying to reclaim my Choctaw heritage, I kept coming back to my granddad and couldn't get him out of my mind. Why did he withhold the language? Why had he married a white woman? One night I dreamed the scariest dream of my life: I was hiding in a traditional Choctaw *chukka* (home) when I heard the voices of soldiers screaming at me to come out. I was all alone, so I shuffled up against the wall and got lower to the ground. The voices were getting closer, joined by dogs barking viciously. I knew they would surely find me if I didn't leave the chukka. I began running into the woods, looking for anything that would shelter me from the soldiers on my trail. I was constantly looking behind me as I ran for my life, and when I finally woke up I was in a cold sweat, crying. For the first time in my life, I knew the fear my ancestors had felt almost two centuries before, and I finally understood why Granddad left me to teach myself the *Chahta aiimma* (ways of life). He didn't want me ever to experience the kind of fear his family felt when running from white soldiers, or not knowing if they could make it in a new place. But in a way I could not escape these things: I decided to go to a college in New Hampshire, far away from my home and family, where few people would understand who I was as a Choctaw and would often judge me for being "too white." Like my ancestors fleeing into the woods to escape the white soldiers, I too found myself searching for shelter in a new place—shelter that would protect me from ignorant peers and ensure that I could return home safely. In a way, white patriarchy made my skin white and it made my CDIB read 7/64.[5]

Later in my freshman year, I got a text message from my cousin Curtis asking me to contact him right away. We hadn't spoken in over a year, and I called him immediately. Curtis had always been quick to anger, never shying away from fistfights and confrontations with authority figures, but when he answered his voice was trembling, not from anger but from fear. Once he realized whom he was talking to, he sobbed. I hopped on my bike, one hand holding the phone and the other gripping a handlebar. My cowboy boots pressed against the pedals. "I need you to come pray for me," he begged. He must have been too messed up on drugs or alcohol to realize that I was a thousand miles away from him. He confessed, "I haven't been doing good, Preston." I imagined him covering his crying eyes and suddenly felt older, although he's the older cousin. It was a Sunday morning, and several people passed me on the sidewalk on their way to church. "I miss you," he muttered. I had never heard these words come from his mouth, and they sunk into me like the rocks we used to throw into country ponds. But the alcohol and drugs Curtis abused always sank him lower, and now they'd made him hit rock bottom. "I don't want my kid to know me like this," he said, still crying. He was only twenty years old, but he had gotten a girl back home pregnant.

What should I do when a grown man cries? I felt like my mother, because in an instant I become a consoler. Curtis broke through the tough skin he himself had taught me to wear, and I was taken away by his lonely, trembling voice. Before leaving my room that morning to head to church, I had placed my Bible inside of my jacket, covering my heart. I laughed when I did this, because it made me feel it could stop a bullet, like in the movies. I knew now that it couldn't. I remembered fishing with Curtis; once he reeled one in, and it was barely hooked in the eye. He made sure it was high on the bank so it didn't hop back into the water. I now held on to Curtis, like that fish on the bank, so he wouldn't slip away. "Just pray for me here," he said. I was taken back to the way our grandpa used to pray when Curtis and I sat together in the old wooden pews. Papa Odell wore a white button-up shirt, Wranglers, and cowboy boots. "Heavenly Father, Alpha and Omega, Beginning and End," he started out. We were just kids then, but his words were like dusty books on a shelf—I knew they had value so I kept them. Now I began pulling them out, putting them into a prayer that I hoped wasn't just words: *God keep him on the banks for good, he can't go back into the water.* With each word that passed through my lips, I prayed I would not lose him.

When I think about Curtis, I am at a loss for words, as I clearly could have been just like him, just like so many of the young men growing up in Choctaw County. If I hadn't gone to church camp during my seventh-grade summer, I would've started drinking and likely doing drugs. If my mom weren't as strong as she is, I probably would have grown up without a father, as Curtis had. All I feel for my cousin is love and empathy, because I know I once wasn't too far from where he was on that Sunday.

Curtis knew that I had been in a preacher phase before coming to Dartmouth. I believed that God was calling me to be a preacher, just like my grandfathers and uncles before me. I remember my mother once saying to me, "Preston, don't be mad." When my mother utters these words, which she does often, it always means she has signed me up for something without my permission. She continued: "Well, they were looking for someone to preach this Easter Sunday, and I know you want to be a preacher, so I told them you would do it." For the first time I wasn't upset that my mother had signed me up for something. I was locked deep into sharing the message and my testimony with others. This was what I wanted to do with my life; so I began preparing my message. I chose various Bible verses and other things my family had taught me, and mixed them in with some of my grandfather's wisdom to prepare something worth hearing. I walked into the old church house on Unger Road that Easter morning, not knowing what I was getting into. It was the same church where I had heard my Papa Odell and Granny Gleades preach; it was the place where I first felt the Holy Ghost; it was where my inner foundation was built. Now it was I standing at the front of the room with a Bible in hand, preaching. I walked up to the podium and started by asking everyone to forgive me: "This is my first time." I'll never forget preaching there that day; it was like the script was flipped. It was no longer the older generation giving the message, and the pews were no longer filled with screaming kids. Everyone had aged; *I* had aged. I was no longer the young kid playing Pokémon in the back of the church or the skater with long curling hair; I was a preacher, dressed in a white button-up shirt, Levis, and cowboy boots—just like my grandfather. As I preached, I could hear my aunts saying "amen" and "hallelujah." I saw my cousins sitting in the back of the room with tears in their eyes. Then, there were my mother and father . . . I was humbled, honored, and thankful.

A person can run from their identity only for so long before that identity catches up with them and demands that they confront it. From my grandparents, I learned about the Holy Spirit, the most important thing in my faith. It never abandoned you, you could always call on it to guide you, and it was always praying for you. When I remember my church experiences in my younger years, I primarily think about love and family, and about the Resurrection and the life it gives. My cousin used to say, "Jesus not only died for me, He died as me." When my grandparents passed away, we began attending a Southern Baptist church. This is where the love was silenced. The preacher was much more concerned with preaching about sin and how other religions were tools of the devil. This is when homosexuality became a topic of concern for me.

I knew from a young age that I wasn't straight. I remember going to my best friend's birthday party when I was twelve. Only a few boys went to the party, two of whom were twins and a year older than Conner and me. As the dusk began to settle in, we walked along the rocks and shoreline looking for arrowheads and empty beer cans. We talked and laughed while skipping rocks across the water. Somehow, one of the twins got his shorts wet and needed to change. We walked back to the cabin and I was in the room as he took his shorts off. I had never seen anyone wear boxer briefs, but I liked what I saw. They were tighter than the boxers I generally wore and made everything looked bigger. I walked out of the cabin to hide my excitement.

I didn't think much of the incident, other than that I was sexually aroused; it would not be the last time a boy would turn me on. For a time I was interested in wrestling, and I would go to my friend David's house to practice the moves. He was into wrestling too, so we'd wrestle and play around on the bed in his dad's room. While it may have looked like wrestling, in my mind it was more sexual than that. We also were boys going through puberty, and wrestling was one way we explored the changes our bodies were going through. It wasn't uncommon for us to act out sexual positions we had seen watching porn. At this time I also had a girlfriend, and I'd call her while at David's house. I guess it was becoming pretty clear that I was bisexual.

During my seventh-grade year, I went on a hunting trip with my dad, David, and his dad. We traveled to San Saba, Texas, a family place that sits next to the Colorado River. It was a six-hour drive, although the way my dad drives it seemed like eight. David and I were sitting in the backseat of my dad's four-door white Chevrolet pickup. We made a stop in Hico, Texas, to get gas and snacks. I recall that David got a doughnut with sprinkles on it. As we began driving the last eighty miles, David kept trying to get my attention. I knew what he wanted, but I felt I was at a crossroad. I started thinking about my Christianity and what God would want me to do, and I felt He was telling me, "If you can resist this now, you won't ever have to worry about homosexuality again. Your life will be perfect." David moved closer and closer to me. As much as I wanted to resist, I began petting him heavily underneath his shorts. He did the same to me for the remainder of our drive.

The next day, something was different. I don't know what happened to David, but any time I tried to touch or play with him after that, he rejected my advances. He began calling me "fag" and "gay boy." I was confused; hadn't he taken part in the same things I did? How could I be a fag while he was not? That was the last time I messed around with a guy before I got to college. I had thought David was the only person I could be open with about my sexuality, but it turned out I couldn't be with him either.

Growing up in the church, I had always been taught that masturbation and homosexuality were sins, so I felt guilty every time I pleasured myself and became depressed. However, it was also how I discovered poetry. It became a routine for me: I'd go to my bedroom at night, masturbate to porn or my own imagination, and then I'd pull out a purple notebook and write poetry. It was the only way I could cope with the feelings of guilt. I wrote about feeling guilty, but I also wrote about seeking forgiveness for my sins. Even though writing poetry was brought on by my sins, I felt most spiritual after finishing a poem. In less than three years I had written over sixty poems.

As time went by, my preferences didn't change. I still liked boys, but I didn't try to make a move on anyone. For one thing, I was always afraid that if I outed myself with another guy, there was the danger he would not reciprocate and would tell everyone I was gay. Also, in Oklahoma, being anything other than straight is not acceptable. Still, throughout my middle- and high-school years I was called a "fag" on a daily basis. This made me run even farther away from my sexual identity. It was demeaning when people used the word to describe me; it made me feel I was a lesser being.

All of my questions about my Native identity, my whiteness, and my sexuality intensified when I was diagnosed with bipolar disorder during the winter term of my junior year at Dartmouth. Students starting college are taught how to make the transition into their new home by watching others and imitating their behavior, and by simply spending more time there. What is not taught, however, is how to go back home. After church one Sunday morning in my hometown, a lady came up to me and asked how I liked Dartmouth. After telling her how much I enjoyed it, she simply said, "I bet it's a culture shock coming back here." I didn't know what to say. Before leaving for college, I told everyone that I'd be back: "I'm getting my education so I can use it back here." But the more time I spent at Dartmouth, the more I felt that Dartmouth was educating me out of this idea. Dartmouth taught me how to produce—to produce a lot and at a fast rate. There isn't time to express emotions; one must dam up their feelings if they are to survive. I became so good at hiding that it was almost a game for me. The only problem is that no one ever wins this game.

I had been on campus at Dartmouth for a year straight before spending my off term in Oklahoma in the winter of my junior year. I had secured an internship with Ryan Red Corn in Pawhuska in the Osage Nation. Despite the important work I would be doing, I wasn't ready to be back in a slow-paced environment. In addition, the girl I had been dating for two years wasn't very supportive during this time. I had always been the comforter in the relationship, and when I started having bad days, she wasn't able to help me. I can remember her saying, "Preston doesn't have bad days." The biggest difference between us was the fact that she came from a very wealthy family. She was Native but did not identify strongly with her roots. A white family had adopted her mother before the ICWA (Indian Child Welfare Act) was passed, and the only thing her mother had told her about her heritage was that people living on the reservation were apathetic and had addictive personalities.[6] Because of this, she wasn't comfortable with my Native identity; I often felt she wanted me to be a white boy. Because of her influence on me, and Dartmouth's, I felt pressured to be white, find a big important job in the city, and make lots of money. Enter depression and bad days.

I made it through the week in Pawhuska, and on the weekend I could either go home or visit my sister. I wasn't producing and therefore felt useless. I wasn't leading or interacting, I couldn't contribute to the graphic-design work that went on at the company, and I had nowhere else to go. Toward the end of February, I traveled to California to visit graduate schools and see my girlfriend. It was the last time I saw her while we were still together. When I got back to Oklahoma, I couldn't make myself return to Pawhuska. I felt my life was now at a crossroad.

The night I arrived in Tulsa, where my sister lived, the Freedom Budget dropped at Dartmouth. It was a document with over ninety demands to the administration on issues such as race, gender, sexuality, socioeconomic status, and ableism. I was enthralled; finally there was something demanding equal rights for so many of my identities. I didn't sleep that night, or the next night, or the one after that. In fact, I stayed awake for four straight days. I didn't know it yet, but I was soon to be diagnosed with bipolar disorder, and I was in a manic phase. I thought I was a prophet; I began seeing things, having visions, and prophesying to my mother about what was going to happen to our family. The mania drove me to a point where I did not care what others thought of me. It brought down all my barriers, and I became unashamed and even blunt about who I was. I had hidden my sexuality for too long and it was finally coming out, whether I liked it or not. When I came out to my girlfriend, she first cried uncontrollably, then broke up with me on the spot. I guess she thought I could no longer be trusted, that I would cheat on her.

I was too manic to be upset. After staying up for two nights, though, I decided that I needed to get some rest. On a late weekday night, my sister sent me to a local Walgreens for a sleep agent, something to calm my stomach, and gummy bears. I drove to the pharmacy, but when I got there it was closed. I found another one nearby; on the way there I started believing I could read the street signs with a newfound knowledge of the cardinal directions. I saw a homeless person walking down the street; it was at that moment that I began to think about picking someone up that night. I entered the Walgreens with one purpose: to get my medicine so I could go to sleep. As I walked into the store, I noticed a man sitting in a wheelchair. His head was cocked back, spit surrounded his lips, and there was a wet spot near his groin. I walked past him to the pharmacy, found the medicines I wanted, and asked the pharmacist if there would be any problem taking them together. She said no, and I went to the candy aisle for the gummy bears. As I picked them up, the man in the wheelchair turned toward me and asked something I couldn't understand. After asking him to repeat himself twice, I heard him ask, "Are you good with directions?" I responded, "I didn't use to be, but I think I'm learning now." Each time he spoke, he had to repeat himself so I could understand. He said, "I need to get to Fifteenth and Pine." My sister had lived in Tulsa only for a couple of months, and I didn't know much about the neighborhood. I later learned that Fifteenth and Pine wasn't a great place to be at night. It was probably ten o'clock, and this man needed a ride home, so I told him I had a free ride from a taxi service and would call them to pick him up. I called the service to ask for a pickup, and they said it would be at least twenty minutes. I told the man I would wait with him until they arrived. "It would be faster if you just took me," he said. If I hadn't been sleep deprived and on a manic streak, I doubt I would have responded to the man. Instead I pushed him to my car and the journey began.

As we were driving, he kept telling me over and over again: "Go back the way you came." I stopped to get him something at McDonald's, and then he started telling me about his neighborhood. "A lot of people say there's bad people who live there, but I know the people there, they're good people." I told him, "There are good and bad people in every neighborhood." I had been away from my sister's house for about thirty minutes by now, and she called, sounding worried.

I dropped him off at the first house on the left in a gated community. I reached out my hand to shake his. "What's your name?" I asked. "I'm William." I told him my name and said how nice it was to meet him. The last thing he told me was—again—to go back the way I came, but I tried to exit the gated community a different way. I soon realized I couldn't get out that way, so I drove back by his house and turned right. I decided to use my GPS to get back to my sister's house. Well, I didn't go back the way I came; in fact, I went in the opposite direction. That night I slept for six hours, but I stayed awake the next night. The following day I was checked into a mental hospital.

I had strayed so far away from who I was that it finally caught up with me. For some reason I kept on thinking about William; what did he mean when he told me to go back the way I came? I now believe that he meant I should return to my roots, that my home was my foundation and where I could make myself whole again. My grandparents had always told me that God works in mysterious ways and that you never know when He might visit you. I believe that William was some sort of messenger. In the following months I had countless anxiety attacks and depressing days, and I woke up crying many times. I thought about not returning to Dartmouth, that Dartmouth didn't understand or know me.

After taking medication for several months, I began to consider stopping it. I just wanted to feel like "me" again. But then I came to realize that I have been living without medication for my entire life; not the medical kind, but the spiritual medicine that transcends time and space. Even though I don't know my Native language, I have been talking through broken syllables in a sequence that only I can understand. I haven't had ceremony in my life since the moment I was born, yet I always pray when my eyes open in the morning, seeking a better day. I have stitched together the stories of my ancestors to make myself whole. I have discovered a new awakening in the patterned planting of pecan trees in my father's orchard. Behind the shadows of trees, I see myself walking into a new light. Strength and courage come with the four-step war dance that I move to and am disciplined to honor. A smile stretches across my face as I slap the mosquito off my mother's shoulder while we dance together in a line. As I smoke the tobacco harvested by my ancestors, I send up prayers with the smoke so that my gods will continue to bless me.

I now realize that blood cannot be changed. It enters into a family and cannot escape. I am Choctaw, Texan, white, and Oklahoman; I am tied to a land, sold and uprooted. My tongue is strained from trying to speak a language that has been dying for the past two centuries, but I still call these syllables home. History still flows when creeks and rivers run dry, like my bloodlines. Stories are the sun rising each morning to cast shadows of promise on every word spoken. I keep coming back to these stories: the story of how my grandfather was hauled in cattle cars to Indian Territory, or the story of the old country church, where hands became medicine and prayers became conversations with the Holy Ghost. The riverbanks of the Colorado, where the Republic of Texas still floats on the water, the beer cans and fishing lines that tie me down, and the mesquite smoke that carries the night. I remember the most beautiful woman I have ever met, who spoke in English but laughed in Choctaw, who wished to learn the ancient but handed me prayers instead. She made a woman just like her, my mother—the freckles that dot her brown face shine on our history like membership cards. Her hands clap to the old hymns and return to the old ways. If only you could see, hear, touch, and feel these stories I have given you. But you do. Hear and feel. You do touch. You laugh and see—because my voice is a story that spreads like fire in the valleys. Catch on.

Preston Wells graduated from Dartmouth College with a bachelor of arts in Native American studies in 2015. During his time at Dartmouth, he founded a Native activist media group called Savage Media, whose work can be found on YouTube. His junior fall, he helped start a chapter of a Native American fraternity on campus called Phi Sigma Nu. He also spent time in Dakota Wells, a folk band that included his best friend. At Dartmouth, Preston devoted much of his time to finding a space for Native voices to express their feelings, opinions, and beliefs. After Dartmouth, Preston plans to become fluent in the Choctaw language, embark on adventures, and get a dog. He is interested in both higher education and counseling, and may pursue these fields in the future. Since writing this story, Preston was given a Choctaw name, and now goes by Wakaya.

PART II

AN INDIAN EDUCATION

Leaving and Finding Home
at Dartmouth College

4

Nihalgai Bahane', A Fourth-World Story   Jerry Watchman

Yá'át'ééh, shi éí Ha'asidi yinishé. Tódich'íi'nii nishłíí dóó Tódich'íi'nii
báshishchiin. Áádóó Bilagaana dashicheii dóó 'Áshąąhi dashinálí.
Chihootsoídi shíghaan dóó naadiintaa' shinaahai.

*Hello, my name is Watchman. I am of the Bitter Water people, Born for the Bitter
Water people. My maternal grandfather is Anglo-American and my paternal
grandfather is of the Salt people. I am from Saint Michaels, Arizona, and I am
twenty-three years old.*

My given name is Jeremiah Watchman. Most know me as Jerry, and
I am a runner. When I was quite young I learned to introduce myself in
Diné Bizaad (the Navajo language) in much the same way my ancestors,
the Ni'hookaa Diyan Diné (Holy Earth People), have over the course of
boundless generations. Indeed, since our arrival in this world—Nihalgai
(the Glittering World)—and long before our words, our knowledge, and
our life ways were exposed to Western peoples and ideas. I feel I grew up
very much on the periphery of the Diné, geographically and socially as
Saint Michaels is near many of the invisible boundaries of Diné Bikeyah
(the Navajo Nation), Arizona, and New Mexico, respectively. My early life
was one I scarcely recall. Nevertheless, I can remember that I was often
found on the outskirts even among my peers and family for reasons ranging
from my status as a mixed-blooded Diné to the tattered, ill-fitting clothes
I often wore as a child. These were symbols of the steady poverty in which
I was born. These factors, as well as an often silent and abusive home life,
left me feeling quite alone and unwelcome in my own skin very early on.

Throughout much of my life, I have often sat in the silence of others
collecting memories, random details, facts—all in the hope of one day
building something with it all or to find meaning in the past. I have fallen

far short of establishing meaning and truth from my past, but what I do have are memories, stories, dreamings, and it is from there I will begin.

My parents were married in March 1984 in what remains the largest wedding ever held at Our Lady of the Blessed Sacrament Catholic Church in Fort Defiance, Arizona. Mom was pregnant with my eldest brother at the time; however, the wedding photos show no evidence of this. Shimá (Mom) looked exquisite in her wedding gown, while my grandparents looked quite young still and full of anticipation for their daughter and the journey that lay ahead. Shizhe'e (Dad) wore a white suit that day and stood tall and unsmiling in most, if not all, of the pictures, testament to the training and temperament of a United States Marine. *I wonder what was on his mind?*

My parent's relationship went sour soon after their marriage as my dad began drinking heavily and abusing my mom in what seems to have been a cruel and emotionless hobby. Mom was still pregnant with me the day she moved out of my father's home. He had been away for several days on a drinking binge, and my mother, pushed to her mind's edge, couldn't handle him or his abuse any longer. When asked about this time in her life, she refers to herself as his punching bag. That morning she loaded my second-eldest brother into the stroller, grabbed the diaper bag, and walked, with my eldest brother in tow, down a red clay hill toward my grandparents' home, a distance of just over two miles to the north. In a different time, a Diné woman could divorce her husband by simply leaving his possessions outside of the *boghaan* (homes designed by our ancestors symbolizing the universe) for him to collect and be on his way. All things associated with marriage and family belong to women as testament to the matriarchy inherent in Diné culture.

Shimá returned the same afternoon with Shicheii (my maternal grandfather), her brothers (in Navajo kinship, the distinction of brothers and cousins does not exist), and their trucks to pack and load what of our lives we would need. She left only that which was my father's in the trailer and departed. I asked her about this day many years later out of curiosity for this time in our family's history, and her answer was simple, dark: *I regret marrying your father. I don't regret having my boys. You were the best thing to happen to me. I regret having to raise you alone because it was so damn hard. I had to leave that day or I would probably be dead.*

My dad would come over, often inebriated, pleading with Shimá to take him back and return to the trailer on the hill; however, she never would. We lived in my mother's childhood home with my grandparents for a few months, until they moved to another home, in Chihootsoí (Saint

Michaels, Arizona), less than ten miles away, with my uncle, who was still a teenager at the time. On their departure, Shicheii left the keys to the trailer and told her to make it a home for her children. I was born as my parents underwent a tedious divorce; thereafter I only saw my father occasionally. He remarried in March 1990. My stepmother and sister are among the blessings in my life.

I recall waking up early one morning to a very loud knock on the front door. I peered out the window to a blackened sky not knowing the time or who the late visitor was. I heard Mom in the hall walking toward the door. She answered, "Who is it?" A familiar but distant voice replied only one word, "Me." I heard my mother let out a very long sigh as the bolt clicked and the doorknob turned. By this time I was out of bed and looking down the dimly lit hallway knowing my father had come. I walked slowly out of the bedroom, stopping just short of Mom. I looked up at my father's shadowed face as I began to smell a familiar but uncomforting scent emanating from him: a crude mixture of booze, tobacco, and self-loathing.

My mother continued to look at him with a detached expression for several long seconds. Finally breaking the long silence, she said, "Why do you always come here when you do this? This isn't your house. Why don't you go home to your wife and let her put up with you?" As I stood there hearing her say this I continued to look at my father curiously. It seemed he was swaying slowly from side to side and could barely say a word without stammering. He looked down at me and said after several seconds, "Why are you up?" I looked up at him and said, "I heard you knocking and it woke me up." As soon as I finished saying this I felt myself falling backward and a loud voice come after me saying, "Don't you talk back to me, boy!"

As I lay in the hallway in pain, crying and afraid, I looked over at my mother as she started to scream at my father, "You son a bitch! Get the hell out my house!" The yelling continued and reached crescendo until the familiar sound of fist to face split the din. I continued to sit staring frozen, fearful at what was in front of me. My brother then appeared, half carrying, half dragging me into our dark bedroom. The door was closed and locked. My brothers and I sat on the bed as time passed and all we heard were the callous screams and shouts echoing in from outside. It was some time before the house was quiet once more. I looked at the still faces of my brothers as they had fallen asleep where they sat, scared and tired. After several minutes, their faces became nothing more than silhouettes as a steady darkness blanketed the small room, replacing fear with soft dreams.

It was over.

Quietly, I climbed off the bed and walked to the door. As I pressed my ear against the cool wood, I could hear what sounded like sobs coming from down the hall. It was frightening to look out into the silent chaos that lingered—it seemed unreal. As I slipped quickly into the hallway, I saw a twisted silhouette sitting just outside the bathroom and I moved slowly toward it. Once closer, I saw my mother's battered face in the dim light cascading from the bathroom. There was blood trickling slowly down the side of her swollen face and low sobs coming from her bruised mouth. Kneeling beside her, I felt at fault for her now frail state. "I'm sorry, Mom. I shouldn't have said anything." There was a still silence after I spoke. She looked up at me, tenderly saying between compressed sobs, "This will never be your fault. Don't ever think it was. I'm sorry you had to see that."

Several minutes passed until my mom pulled herself off the floor and went into the restroom, closing the door softly behind her as she attempted to smile although her face was swollen. I turned down the hall as the sound of water falling from the bathroom faucet echoed down the hallway. I edged slowly toward the living room. Looking into the dimly lit room, I could see my father teetering slowly on the couch until he slumped to the side and snoring began to fill the empty silence. I knew I would never understand my father as this man, nor would I be able to accept him in my life. It is a dismal moment, which lives vividly in my mind to this day. I fell asleep in my mom's arms behind a locked bedroom door as the sun began to creep slowly into being over the horizon, becoming the dawn.

When I woke late the next morning, it felt as if everything that happened just hours before was nothing more than a dream, a nightmare. It wasn't until I walked into the kitchen where my mom sat at the table, dark eyed and silent, that I knew it was no dream. I sat down next to her and looked into the living room at the empty couch and the spot where my father had lain, inebriated and empty in the dark hours of morning. I said nothing.

I didn't see my father again for several months. During this time he was able to find help for his substance-abuse issues, entered a treatment program, and began the slow process of putting his life and actions into perspective. In the wake of these events, I learned to accept my father into my life again knowing the pain he had caused in the past would haunt my vision of him for the rest of my life. I wanted to build another vision of him as a man, a father I could communicate with and one day look up to without looking back in anger first. Today, our relationship has improved substantially. We talk often, mostly about simple things and the occasional discussion about life. More often than not, we laugh together, as humor has found a home in our relationship to bond and heal. We are more like old friends whose love has been conditioned by memory.

In the sixth grade, I joined the cross-country team as a way to become more active and healthy as well as to make friends. The first few months of running were sheer hell as I struggled to control my breathing and to motivate myself every day. While running was not easy at first, I soon understood how intricately it was ingrained in my spirit as a dream began to develop where I was running steadily through a mountain path lined with trees and the scent of pine, cedar, and forthcoming rain. This dreaming has followed me for many years: the trail farther, the path higher, sharper. In myriad ways, my dream has allowed me to *know* the beauty of running. It is an ancient act I was born for. Even now, I find myself waking at dawn to run in the early morning light in the way of my ancestors to welcome the new day and show my gratitude for being alive in my quest for wholeness.

At the same time, I found myself struggling with school for the first time in my life. I felt apathetic about assignments and became uninterested in classes, often finding myself reading books from the library or creating far-off adventures in my mind rather than paying attention or taking notes. My perception of school during this time had become one influenced by low expectations from teachers. Homework assignments often ranged from doing crossword puzzles or simple vocabulary sets to the banal task of drawing book reports with colored pencils and crayons. My apathy grew to such an extent that I looked forward to only four parts of my school day: Diné Bizaad, piano class, English, and cross-country practice.

Despite my disappointment with a majority of my classes, I genuinely enjoyed learning how to play the piano. It was challenging and fun learning to read musical notes and to play. In my mind, playing felt like creating life with each keystroke, summoning color from each sound as it drifted gracefully through space and time. I found a sense of power, control: an outlet to nurture my imagination and allow my mind to maneuver in new ways. Shimasaní (my maternal grandmother) especially enjoyed listening to me play and never missed my recitals. She even bought a keyboard for me to play for her. Like running, I had found a place in which I was entirely present, balanced, capable.

I was twelve when I started having fainting spells while running. It became a common occurrence to wake up drenched in sweat with a small crowd of teammates or coaches hovering over me with looks of horror and worry. A teammate of mine once said I looked like "the Energizer bunny unplugged" whenever this would happen. The fainting spells caused no more than a few scrapes and bruises at first, and I remained very dedicated to running.

I enrolled in Saint Michael High School in August 2003, taking sophomore classes primarily, and was heavily involved in cross-country and numerous extracurricular activities early on. My second-eldest brother and I slept on the couch at my grandparents' house for most of the next four years to make an easier commute, though I hardly remember being there very often. At school, my brother and I shared many of the same classes and ran on the cross-country team. Throughout high school, running became part of my identity and friendships, and served as a place of healing after the fainting episodes rose in frequency, becoming such a cause for concern that I was banned from running after collapsing during competition one afternoon in October 2004.

The temporary running hiatus brought about a slew of visits to a cardiac specialist in Albuquerque, New Mexico, culminating in the implantation of a heart monitor and a period of deep academic focus to preoccupy me otherwise. Despite the precautions I was under, after a few months I grew restless and began sneaking out to run at dawn, albeit casually, while my family remained fast asleep. I am not myself if I am not running every day.

Over time, the heart monitor was removed, the ban lifted, and I was free to roam the desert in my Asics once again. All the while, I remained dedicated to school, athletics, and extracurricular activities with relative ease, culminating with winning the men's state cross-country championship in November 2006.

By April 2007 I had been admitted to several universities across the country and was awarded the Gates Millennium Scholarship, transforming my collegiate dream to reality. I was home one afternoon reading *Atlas Shrugged* for Economics when the telephone rang: *Hello, I'm calling on behalf of the Native American Program at Dartmouth College. Congratulations on your acceptance to Dartmouth! I'm sure your family and friends are very proud of you. I'm calling to ask if you would like to come to Dartmouth for a few days for Dimensions, the admitted-student visit. Before you ask, it's going to be fun, and no, you won't be the only Navajo . . .*

A few weeks later I embarked on a short tour of East Coast colleges, visiting schools I had been accepted into. Over the course of my visits I realized I wanted a place where I could be myself and feel challenged and inspired. I wanted to be in an environment where I felt welcomed and whole. Dartmouth College was the last stop on my tour despite my wanting to go home after several odd and discouraging visits at other schools. I learned of Dartmouth in 2005 when I attended College Horizons, a summer program designed to prepare Indigenous students for the college and scholarship application process. While there, I was fortunate to meet a Dartmouth admissions officer who was an effervescent Hāadis/Diné woman, who told me that Dartmouth was founded to educate Native students and also wore the shiny distinction of being Ivy League. On seeing the campus for the first time, I fell in love with the school. Dartmouth was everything I imagined a college to be and more. I was home.

Growing up on Diné Bikeyah gave me the opportunity to live and breathe my culture, while instilling an unwavering sense of origin and place. Although I wasn't raised in a family bound to the intricacies of our Diné heritage, I was able to connect to the language, values, and stories through classes taught in school and through ceremonies. However, I realized that, beyond the dismal paragraph or two Native people are allocated in US history books, there was so much about the Native experience that I was ignorant of, which has influenced my upbringing profoundly. *How could this be? Why?*

On my first day of classes Professor Colin Calloway opened his lecture saying, "American history is, more often than not, one dimensional. The history of this country is portrayed as one of discovery, independence, progress, and an occasional war or two. But what is often missing from this history are the peoples and cultures that were alive and well long before any European knew of the continent, or corn for that matter." My note-taking ended somewhere soon after as I sat dumbfounded for the next hour and a half overcome with fascination, anger, rage, and a helplessness akin to being punched in the throat while my entire worldview was shattered with mere words by an intelligent Scotsman two thousand miles from my home. In its place I was left with a desire to understand this history, this perspective that had been denied to me and to Native people everywhere as a means to contain and destroy. No one had ever done that to me before. Needless to say, I chose Native American studies as my major on my very first day.

Soon after my arrival at Dartmouth I was raped by another student I believed to have been a new friend. I remember the night like this: somewhere in the corner of consciousness something is suddenly out of place and my eyes open, blurred. I'm in my room and I see him. Naked.

A long pause follows as I try to comprehend what is happening and I feel him. Naked. I realize what is happening and I am asking him to stop, *please* stop, *please*. He says to me, *Shut up, you stupid fuck. You want this.* I'm pinned down and I can't move, but I begin to beg, plead, *please* stop, *please*. There is a pause, a window of hope, and his face contorts into a grin, manic, intense, and I feel his fists slam against my face over and over and over. I sense tears forming in the corners of my eyes and slowly, I slip away in pain, out of control or sensibility. I feel him once again. Naked. I recede into the darkness, where memory has no place or meaning and no one can hurt me anymore.

I woke in intense pain and confusion the next afternoon. It was not until I saw myself in the mirror that I began to blame myself for what happened. I stood in the shower scrubbing my skin raw while shame overtook me and my mind raced trying to find an answer to what had happened. My heart raced harder than I had ever known as fear, panic, and an internal silence consumed me. I told myself I would never speak of the rape to anyone. I had been at Dartmouth fourteen days.

In wake of this, I was unable to show others my true self. I was a freshman and I just wanted to fit in. I felt like I couldn't be anything less than *perfect* around other people because if I wasn't, then they would know I was tainted, wrecked on the inside. It was exhausting, playing pretend, but I persisted to protect myself from the unknown. The man who raped me was a senior at the time, and I saw him frequently. Usually, I would just lower my head and walk away feeling less and less alive as my heart began pounding. Inside I was screaming, furious at him, but I was angrier with myself for sinking into a deep silence I could not overcome. It seemed the more I saw him, the more I would begin to fade until one day I would disappear completely, removed from memory and being.

My upbringing did little to nothing as far as informing or preparing me for the social sphere I would encounter at Dartmouth. To many, it is one heavily influenced by the prominence of Greek life on campus, liberal intake of Keystone Light and the occasional ignorant soul sporting an Indian-head T-shirt (Dartmouth's former pseudo-mascot, in the name of tradition, of course). Before I left for college, alcohol and drug abuse was, and continues to be, a very real presence in my family. In spite of this, I soon found alcohol to be a social lubricant and held room parties frequently. Mostly, I was terrified to be alone or to find out what people would think of me if they could see the ruptured spirit I shielded within. Regardless, I made it through my first year at Dartmouth and wanted nothing more than to be home, to be myself again.

I looked down as the desert stretched infinitely below while the plane descended toward a screeching halt at the Albuquerque airport ten months after and eighty pounds heavier than when I left home for a mentally and emotionally taxing freshman year. I walked out of the terminal toward my mom and grandparents, who sat waiting patiently for me to appear. I waved at them from a short distance away, but they did not respond to my greeting. I stood in front of my mom until she realized I was right in front of her even though she was looking around me. I believe she was expecting a thin, lively son to come bouncing toward her; instead she found a dark specter with shoulder-length hair and a belly standing in his place.

The first morning I was home, I attempted to run a few miles on a trail I had run so many times before and soon found myself overwhelmed after running a short distance and began to walk, gasping for breath behind lungs tainted by tar and shame from a habit of smoking to calm my nerves. When I returned home I cried in the shower, thinking about what had brought me to this place, to the point of struggling to do something so ingrained in my identity. I had become unrecognizable to myself, let alone my family, in just a matter of months. I dedicated the summer to running and somehow found a healing space for my thoughts.

I returned to Dartmouth for sophomore year in good form as I was running and reading anything I could get my hands on in an effort to reclaim my mind and body from the trauma I felt daily. My assailant had graduated by this time, and it made being at Dartmouth much more bearable, although the memory of him and that night continued to haunt me. Deep down I knew something was still crooked, gone even, and I was self-conscious, emotionless in everything I attempted to do. Men can't be raped. No one would believe me if I told anyone what happened, and so my secret remained hidden in my silence.

In October 2008 I became a brother of the Kappa Kappa Kappa fraternity and hated everything about myself. Tri-Kap (as it is informally known) was always a welcoming place to my friends and me as freshmen, and the few brothers I had met were very outgoing and personable whenever I saw them on campus. It was good to have new friends and a place to feel comfortable and have fun, but to also find people who would like me for who I was and who I wanted so much to be: imperfect, whole. While my time as a pledge was challenging and asked me to go far outside of my limited comfort zone, over time it helped me see I could share my time with people, relax, and have no regrets. Slowly, I began to trust people again and knew there was always a home, a family far from Diné Bikeyah, and for that I will always be grateful to my brotherhood.

March 2009. I'm staring out of my dorm window at pockets of snow. I haven't slept or eaten in six days. I have felt this way before, exhausted, starved, and unhinged. This time I know that if I don't reach out to someone, anyone, I will do anything to kill the void I am drowning in. I'm scared. I send an e-mail to my friend asking if he would meet me sometime later in the day. My head spins thick with distorted thoughts. I need someone I can trust. More than anything, I need to voice how outside of myself I feel. It's the only way. I stare at the computer waiting for a response. I don't know anyone else who is right to turn to, but this will have to do. I succumbed to a hopelessness I can no longer calm. I can't sleep for more than a few hours most nights. Some days I stay in my room with the lights off, lying in bed, powerless, unable to control my thoughts. I feel removed from everything: school, friends, running, life. I get by hiding behind a veil of laughter and fake smiles around others. The only relief from the disillusion crawling beneath my skin comes when I'm trashed, drunk until memory has no place or meaning and no one can hurt me anymore. I stayed up all night until, finally, my friend responds: *Sure thing, man. I've got class and work today but I can meet around seven.* I write back: *Please.*

The words are hard to find at first, but I start by trying to explain the hollowness, its immense weight. As I speak, I wonder how psychotic I sound and I'm convinced he will get up and leave as I'm mid-sentence. Anything is possible at this point, but I don't dare bring up the rape. He won't understand. No one will. I've thought about it again and again: I'm not looking for punishments or blame. I am desperately trying to remain here, to have a sense of wholeness once more, and I fear for my life.

Instead, he is sitting there listening intently as I rant on about my insecurities, my conditional stupidity as a Dartmouth student. More important, I tell him my own self-loathing is the only thing keeping me alive. He's quiet, thinking, internalizing every sound I've made, and says, *Jerry, I'm not going to lie to you and say that I didn't know something was wrong. A lot of people are worried about you. You know, NADs* [Native Americans at Dartmouth]—*we're family, and we notice when someone is in trouble or struggling with things. People talk when someone starts going out all the time. Drinking too much. Skipping class. Acting differently. It worries people and people are worried about you. I'm worried about you. I've seen what you can do and what you're capable of. You belong here. I knew this when you first got here because of how you would watch out for people and make sure they got home after a rough night or would volunteer to help our community. Even how much you love to run. It's all there. But lately, lately, you've become the person people have to look out for, take home at the end of the night. It's hard not to notice those things, you know. You are wanted here. You belong here.*

I thought about what he had said and I knew I was in over my head. I started to cry. I look at him and say, behind tear-filled eyes: *I don't know what I'm doing anymore. I don't even know who I am. I just want to feel like myself again. I just can't. I don't know how.* A strange sense of relief came over me as I spoke, and for the first time in over a year, I felt life stir, motion back in place, if only just. He stayed with me until the tears stopped, and I calmed down enough to realize what I was missing, other than sleep and sustenance, was a sense of compassion, understanding. I'm not sure if I ever thanked my friend for saving my life that day, but I am grateful he was there when I needed a friend, a brother most, and I am obliged to him every day since.

Sophomore summer comes and I want to leave Dartmouth, transfer maybe, or just float away on the Connecticut River. I try seeking help from the college counselors, but I'm too distracted, outside of myself every time I sit in front of the counselors with the fake smiles and treacherous pens somehow mocking my thoughts. I don't trust them and I stop going. The hollowness is crawling in me once again, coming like waves, steady, overwhelming: a day or two unable to get out of bed here, a week of insomnia and malnutrition there. Then I'm able to run again, to breathe . . . until the vicious cycle takes hold of me once more.

I have nothing left. Moral imperatives are a joke and so is the philosophy term paper I am to write about them. I find a quick solution: copy-paste-*whatever*. Wikipedia will say what I can't and more. Plagiarism, as I would learn, is a simple application for suspension. Letting go of Dartmouth in this way is as painless as cutting hair. After my suspension from school, I was drifting for a few weeks, attempting to understand what had just happened, searching for a trace of hope in myself. It is not hard to see there is nothing in front of me except the towering wall of anger I have tried so hard to ignore. During the day I sleep, dreamless. At night I go outside and walk, thinking, waiting for something beneath the starlight. All I find is that I want for nothing but to be home where I make sense.

My grandmother was never a very emotional person, but her generosity and kindness were what made her my favorite person in the world. She also never missed a thing. Ever present, observant in my memory. She became ill soon after I returned home due to complications from a lifetime of alcoholism and liver cirrhosis. She was in and out of the hospital, but I could never bring myself to visit her there. It hurt too much seeing her strung out and in pain. This wasn't the grandma I knew and loved. Instead, I did the only thing I could think of and burned sage and cedar throughout the house to ward off the voices of destruction, which brought her to this state. I would say small prayers asking her to come home. I needed her still.

I did what I could to help when she was home, though she relied heavily on my mom, aunt, and brother for her care. Mostly, I tried to stay out of the way. Some nights, I woke up to sounds of her discomfort and went to her room to check on her. I would help her to the restroom or get a glass of water. More often than not, I sat at the foot of the bed and told her where I ran that day, what I saw, or read to her late into the night trying to give the characters voices so she could follow along or until she was able to find sleep once more. It is the closest I have ever felt with her and I was able to find some strength to begin the process of healing and, slowly, of tearing down the wall towering over my life.

By June 2010 I returned to Dartmouth with a sense of power and control after receiving intensive therapy and some very helpful antidepressants. Getting up in the morning was not as dreadful as I remembered, communicating with others no longer terrified me, and I had a sense of focus and determination built by the love and compassion of my family to guide me. Running is an integral part of my life once again, and I'm able to share my love for it with my Tri-Kap brothers as we run a half-marathon for charity. I felt I had all I needed to survive far from home for the very first time, and it was a relief to feel close to myself again. I believe the greatest aid in my return came from counseling to manage my depression as well as the help of the Native American Program as I transitioned back to Dartmouth.

July. I just finished a linguistic exam and my phone rang. My mom is crying, unable to speak. Grandma is gone. I stayed on the line with her for several minutes while sobs from others in the hospital room echo in the background. I walk outside trying to understand what I just heard—it can't be true. I spoke to my grandma just the night before and she seemed healthy and happy. She said she had a good day and felt better than she had in a very long time. Now, I believe she said this to subtly say she was ready for her next journey, but at the time I felt as if I had been thrown from a building and was caught midair, gasping for oxygen. My grandmother was sixty-seven.

Four days after her funeral, I lay sleeping once again in my apartment at school while Shimasaní came to me in a dream. She looked thin, healthy standing in front of me, nothing like the ailing woman who had hugged me good-bye just a month and a half before as I returned to school. There was a fire burning softly between us, and the sun was warm and high above, and I recognize where we stood, Biih Bitood (Deer Springs). It is a place up in the mountains my family is intimately tied to as it is the place where we bury the afterbirth of our newborns to tie them to Nahasdzáán—the Earth—where we plant our crops, hold ceremonies, and bury our loved ones. Generations of my relatives are held there. It is said a group of Tódich'íi'nii returned to this place after Hwéeldi—the Long Walk in the 1860s. It is the most beautiful place I know. Shimasaní is standing before me. She is wearing a beautifully woven biil (rug dress) adorned with images of corn stalks and negative space representing rain clouds and mountains. A thin strand of yoołgai, white shell, hangs around her neck, and we talk for a while.

We talked about our family and about when we used to dance together when I was a little boy. She thanked me for giving her eulogy, asking me to repeat Nezahualcoyotl's simple words, which I used at her funeral, and so I did:

Cuix oc nelli nemohua o a in tlalticpac! Yhui. Ohuaye.
Annochipa tlalticpac
Zan achica ye nican
Ohuaye ohuaye
Tel ca chalchihuitl no xamani, no teocuitlatl in tlapani, oo quetzalli poztequi
Yahui ohuaye
Anochipa tlalticpac zan achica ye nican
Ohuaya ohuaya.[1]

She liked the poem a lot. She asked me to thank my mom for all she had done to keep her alive. I asked if it hurt to leave. She said it doesn't matter in the greater scheme of things. I asked how long she would be gone. She only replied, "I'm everywhere." I asked where she was going and she said, "Below, son. To where we are meant to be after this world has shared itself with us." I told her I would miss her every day. She said I didn't have to because she was always with me. The sun was fading over the high sandstone hills and she began walking north, to an old place. As she motions away, she runs her fingers through her long, black hair one time and stands still for a moment. Finally, she looks over her shoulder and says, "Don't give up on yourself. We'll talk again, Ha'asidi." I want to cry as she fades away, but watch as her shadow departs, gradually losing its human form until the silhouette of tł'iishtsoh, the bull snake, appears, our clan guardian, then vanishes, becoming one with the velvety night and flickers of starlight. A smile came across my face. I woke the next morning knowing this was much more than a dream.

By January, I became subject to depression once again, although this time it wasn't as charged or physically inhibiting thanks to the antidepressants I regularly took. I'm able to keep a routine, but I have no motivation and feel outside of myself most of the time. As a result, I'm not able to perform as well academically as I had during the previous term, and the grade from one of my classes was enough to warrant suspension once again. However, a successful appeal and support from my counselor allowed me to take medical leave from Dartmouth for a while so I might come to a place of comfort and self-assurance once again.

During the year I was away from college, I worked as an intern in myriad professions ranging from the Navajo Supreme Court to a brokerage firm on Wall Street, while receiving therapy periodically. I attempted to return to school for the following fall term. The school, however, felt I was not ready to return to academic life just yet. In spite of this news, I was informed by my dean of a treatment center specializing in depression in Tucson, Arizona. Receiving intensive treatment was the best way to prove I was ready not only to return to academic life but, more important, to get my life back in order. At first I felt ambushed by this information, but I realized it was offered out of care, and so I maintained an open mind about the opportunity. If anything, I looked forward to being in the desert once again, close to home.

I entered treatment in September 2011 optimistic, but uncertain of what I would get from the experience. If anything, I felt happy and safe for the first time in months. Two weeks after I arrived, I was leading an evening group discussion and thinking of what to talk about when it was my turn to share or pass. I could think of nothing, but after hearing the hurt and pain in the stories others shared in the room, I realized I was not alone anymore; I had a voice, which had been silenced for years, and I had nothing to lose. I had watched idly as my life sank right in front of me and anger nearly destroyed me. I had lost touch with the truth and beauty in my life, lost faith in what I am capable of, what I *could* be capable of. It was time for me to speak of what had happened to me. I was afraid at first, but the more I spoke about the rape, the more the wall inside of me began to fall, and so I shared everything until I could speak no more. I felt free, exhausted.

I was awake well into the early morning hours thinking and writing a letter to the man who raped me four years and three days prior. Afterward, I slept with a sense of comfort, peace I had not felt since high school.

I rose early to run, to greet the sun as myself once more and to begin letting go, to forgive myself and take in the world around me. I'm not sure if I will ever experience this type of freedom again, but I remember this morning vividly as I stared, watching dawn become day and finding myself a part of life again.

I sat with my therapy group, who, by this time, had become more like family to me, and shared everything about the rape once again. However, this time I allowed myself to cry and show my anger for the first time. I felt my voice, my life, begin to return after years of fear and shame. I was no longer afraid. After I finished the story, I asked if I could read what I had written the night prior. It went like this:

Dear Asshole,

I know you by no other name. I hate you for what you have done to me. I know who you are. I know where you're from. You were my friend and I trusted you. You were the first friend I had at Dartmouth and you ruined me. You destroyed my belief, my faith, my trust in myself. In its place, my life has been a wreck ever since the night you raped me. I do not forgive you for what you have done. I cannot. I never will.

I will, however, tell you this: this is my life. I take it back from you now and hope you get everything in life you deserve. This is my life and I will protect it, honor it until it is no more. This is my life, and you have no power over it and all that I want. This is my life, without you. This is my life. This is my life and you are no more in it. This is my life.

From that day forth I began my recovery knowing it would not be easy or quick or without its pitfalls. I did, however, know I would be ready for whatever may come and I would have to be patient, willing to relearn to live in myself and in my voice once more.

I returned to Dartmouth for the following winter term with a much deeper appreciation and hope for myself and for my future. I realized my family, my language, and my people are my highest priorities as they have influenced and aided me through everything I am and everything I will ever become. It is because of this I dream of one day becoming a teacher, like Shimasaní, maybe even a writer or a lawyer or a PhD or a Wall Street banker—maybe all of these things. Of this, I am not certain; however, I know one thing: I will be running.

In my life, running is a simple act of ceremony for the world, requiring only simple things: steady movement to acknowledge the good brought forth by the dawn to silence the evil and chaos in the world; steady breath to let life flow through my being and nourish the equal pieces of life and destruction within; and a good pair of Asics.

There have been destructive forces in this world for as long as my people can remember and likely even longer. The destruction almost overtook me two thousand miles from home, but it was the good I found in myself, the faith I found in others, and in the small truths of life, which saved me. The good came from a place deep within, which remains forever in the stories, songs, and prayers of my people, the Diné. It lives eternally in the dawn, changing, growing, moving to balance the ebb and flow of creation. To find the good, I had to surrender to the voice within and to the ceremony of *being*. I will do this until I receive my degree from Dartmouth College. I will do this wherever I go. I will do this until my life rests with my ancestors high in the mountains of Diné Bikeyah and my spirit ventures back to the world below to rejoin them at the heart of sa'ah naagháí bik'eh hózhó—beauty, harmony, wholeness.

This is my life—it is beautiful and it isn't.

Hozhogoo nááhásdlįį'
Hozhogoo nááhásdlįį'
Hozhogoo nááhásdlįį'
Hozhogoo nááhásdlįį'

Jerry Watchman grew up on the Navajo Nation in the town of Saint Michaels and studied Native American studies at Dartmouth College. He is a humble member of the Kappa Kappa Kappa Society and remembers the first time he accidentally stumbled upon the Orzoco Room at Dartmouth in the fall of 2007. The subsequent six hours spent in awe that rainy afternoon were worth it. He currently runs in Denver, Colorado.

5

Bracelets Upon My Soul   Ma'Ko'Quah Jones

Can poisoned fruit spring forth pure seed?
Are infected people who once sought salvation in death,
able to give life to something
without passing on the curse?
My past is a chessboard of only black squares.
Each move was either related to death or pain,
I saw no other colors.
Checkmate was my life.
Today my dreams fill my hands.
I can tangibly touch them,
I can feel them with my fingertips
and the resulting phenomenal happiness
lets me know I'm still alive.
But the scars on my arms have yet to fade.
Fossils left behind only to remind me how I once
reveled in violence upon myself
as a means of entertainment,
or injuries so deep that no human body
is capable of healing from?
Who knows?
My child will one day ask me about them,
a fear I hold on to until that day comes.
How can you explain a "why" that you still
ask yourself to this day?
I can only hope that my child can see my heart above my scars,
and also love them for what they truly are . . .
bracelets upon my soul.

The remnants of my past are visible on my forearms, the physical representations of deep emotional pain. At age nineteen, after years of suffering on the inside, I began to inflict violence on my physical body as a way to control my unseen internal pain. In short, I became a cutter. I wasn't trying to kill myself; it was just about the pain. For a time I sought other ways to hurt myself. I remember moving my arms along the serrated edge of a knife, which I thought would make a larger wound than the razors I usually used. Later in life, I read about the psychology of the self-mutilator. You can tell something about the cutter by observing what direction they cut on which body part, whether the cuts were visible or not, and how deeply they cut. On my own arms I see visible scars on top of scars across my wrists, in multiple directions and various depths. I remember cuts that didn't bleed so I had to recut in the same spot inside the previous cut. But in these moments, I held the reins to my pain. For the first time in my life, I controlled when and how I hurt, and I couldn't stop.

Strangers would stare at my cuts, their eyes filled with pity, which was exactly what I wanted. I wanted people to see how much I was suffering, and I wanted them to suffer from looking at me because that meant I wasn't alone in my suffering. I wanted to scar their minds the way I scarred my arms. I wanted my pain to be unforgettable.

My cutting behavior spanned three years. People still look at my scars and feel sorrow or shame for me, but I am not ashamed of them, nor do I feel guilty. Instead, I am proud of them. Very few people see the beauty in these scars and understand what they represent. But to me, they are artifacts of my hard journey, and I am proud that I am alive to show them off. I have since decorated my scars with tattoos that are strength symbols from my husband's and my own tribal cultures. The design is a bear's paw, which represents my role as a mother with the strength to protect my cubs. The paw is in the shape of a Celtic knot, which represents my husband's strength and his love. The tattoos remind me that my past is nothing to be ashamed of. Even though my scars represent the pain of my past, they also represent my survival. I am where I come from, a place of unbearable suffering.

As a child in Oklahoma, I often questioned whether my life was normal. My immediate family consisted of my mother, older sister, two younger brothers, and my stepfather whom I call "Dad" because he was the only father I knew. My family was always very poor. Almost daily, I heard conversations about where our food would come from, which utilities might be shut off, and whose house we could go to in order to bathe. I have many memories of being homeless and sleeping in the back of my dad's truck, or between two Dumpsters at a nearby park, in the fireworks stand where my parents worked in the summer, or at a religious homeless shelter. As a child, I didn't know any different and eventually normalized our way of life.

I had the responsibilities that come with being the oldest sibling, even though I was not. My daily chores included waking up early to rouse my stepfather so he could get to work on time, then waking my brothers so they would be ready for school. I loved school, and reveled in the fact that it was the one place I could truly be myself—a hard worker who was appreciated and honored. I dreaded going home each day, since my sister and I had to clean the house before my parents came home to avoid their harsh tempers, which exploded if they walked into a dirty house. If I over-slept, causing everyone to be late, or didn't clean properly, or showed what my mother considered a bad attitude, I believed it was nobody's fault but my own. I would get "beat," which meant "gettin' whipped" with a belt, my parents' hands, a fly swatter, or anything that was within reach at the time.

Even though I feared physical abuse, for me, the verbal abuse was the most hurtful. While my parents carried out their punishment, they would tell me how selfish and irresponsible I was, and that I didn't deserve any-thing good. These disparaging words from my parents overshadowed any of my academic achievements. Although I consistently ranked at the top of my class and was often recognized for my academic achievements, none of this success made up for the hurtful things that my parents had taught me to believe about myself. Eventually, any praise I received fell on deaf ears.

As a child, I found learning came easily. In the classroom, I felt in con-trol and had a sense of pride. I was never the popular kid at school. I was more quiet and shy, but did my best to appear to be a happy, outgoing child. My sister, on the other hand, was tracked as a troubled student because of a possible learning disability and emotional problems. This angered my mother, who didn't like our family to receive any negative at-tention. I became an overachiever to help overcome the stain of my sister's academic struggles. I later realized that my academic achievements did not matter to my mother; although she wore the face of a proud parent in public, when out of the sight of others she still saw me as inferior. In a world where I felt powerless, I found a source of strength and wisdom in the classroom. In fact, my education has served to help heal my wounds.

While in eighth grade, I first contemplated taking my own life. Up until then, I had been able to maintain a facade of normalcy, but that year, many unexpected events made me sort of "give up" on life. During a counseling session with a group of friends, I inadvertently disclosed the fact that my grandfather had been sexually abusing me for almost a decade. My counselor's immediate reaction let me know right away that this admission would be life changing for me. She told me she had to report the abuse. Once I revealed the secret of eight years to my parents, my dad wanted to beat up my grandfather, and my mother had an emotional breakdown. When my mother told my grandmother about my grandfather's indiscretions, her lack of surprise confirmed that she knew all along what was happening to me. This explained why she favored my sister, decided to stay in motels with my sister while I was alone in her house with my grandfather, and treated me harshly, no matter what I did to try and please her.

We decided to press charges, and my parents accompanied me to the police station, where I had to recount what little memory I had of my grandfather's abuse. A therapist later explained that I had blocked out most of the horrifying childhood memories. I do remember nights when my grandfather would let me stay up late with him, which made me feel special and grown up. I reveled in the ability to watch *Star Trek* and late-night infomercials while he sexually abused my body. I did my best not to cry and focused totally on the television. My grandfather was gently affectionate once he had finished, and I would lie there wondering how I should feel about what just happened. This took an emotional toll that left me feeling ashamed and confused about my body.

In a twisted way, my grandfather's abuse wasn't nearly as hurtful as my parents' abuse. I remember one time when my parents dropped me off at my grandparents' house and I no longer wanted to endure what I knew was going to happen. I ran after the car as they drove away, screaming at them to take me with them. My dad slammed on the brakes and my mom jumped out, demanding to know what I was doing. Her anger made me afraid, so I simply said I wanted to come with them. She said that if I came with them, I would get my "ass beat," and she gave me the choice to go and get beaten or stay with my grandparents. I thought about the choice before me; on one side was the option of my grandfather pleasuring himself with my nine-year-old body, and on the other was my parents' violent anger inflicted on me. It was an impossible choice for a nine-year-old girl, but ultimately, I decided to stay with my grandfather. He raped me multiple times that weekend.

I had to recount my grandfather's horrific actions to several policemen, since they wanted to be sure I wasn't lying. I remember sitting alone in a blue room with a video camera in front of me, recounting in great detail what had happened. At the time, I felt the experience was as much a violation as the act itself, as I had to use words such as "vagina" and "anus" to describe what he had put where and how it felt. These moments still haunt me today, almost as much as the abuse itself. I was also subjected to a doctor's examination of my body, again to prove that I was not lying. I felt even more violated since I had to prove beyond a shadow of a doubt that abuse had occurred, while my grandfather was off the hook until my accusations were proven. In the doctor's office, I had to rely on my ability to remove my mind from my body, while the doctor poked and prodded me and talked with my mother about my "sexual activity." The doctor insisted that I'd been "having sex for some time," and my mother argued that I was "just a little girl." The doctor later informed us that I had various STDs, which was, to say the least, uncommon for a child my age. The shock to my mother came when she learned that my grandfather had the same diseases, but my grandmother did not. This ended the suspicion that I was lying to the police.

I opted to charge my grandfather with the least serious crime possible because I felt the emotional toll had already been too much for my family. My mom's brothers had accused her of lying and turned their backs on our family. My sister stopped talking to me and lay in her bed crying, night after night. My grandmother's health began to decline and there was talk that "this might kill her." My mom ended up in the hospital due to another emotional breakdown after being told I would never be able to have children because of the "extensive damage" done to my child body.

One time, at a powwow, not realizing that I was now an outcast, I attempted to talk with members of my extended family. They told me to leave and that I was not to associate with them as long as I kept up my lies. One aunt wondered why I couldn't just remain quiet, since my grandfather was a respected member of the community. At my grandfather's criminal trial, I thought I could help mitigate some of the hurts the situation had caused my family. My parents weren't too happy with me either, and all I could think was how much I wanted to die and not live through this anymore. Although school had been the one place where I could find solace, I suddenly found myself unable to focus, instead just going through the motions. My teachers worried about me, which only furthered my mother's anger.

Around this time, I began battling depression and entertaining thoughts of gaining my freedom by taking my own life. My grandfather had begun his six-month prison sentence, my grandmother had passed away, and my sister had announced that she hated me since she had lost the one person who cared about her—my grandmother. Eventually, my sister had a violent fight with my mother and was removed from our home. This left me to endure my parents' violent tempers on my own.

Growing up in an alcoholic and abusive home made it difficult to avoid, eventually normalizing the situation. Throughout my childhood I found great comfort in my Christian faith. I enjoyed attending church and reading biblical stories about people who could talk to God. I also enjoyed learning about how God took care of His children when they truly believed. Christian teachings state that God does not give you anything you cannot handle. When I first contemplated suicide, the hardest part was fearing that I would go to hell because I was not strong enough to deal with all that God had given me. I remember my mom telling me time and time again, "I don't have to worry about you because I know I can depend on you." These words became hurtful at a certain point, because I *did* want her to worry about me.

After I graduated from high school, my mom once again kicked me out, and my aunt and uncle opened their home to me. Their house was calm, peaceful, and stable. However, it was not my home and I couldn't shake the feeling that I didn't belong there. I hung out with my friends often, and sometimes stayed out late—particularly since I relied heavily on them without the support of my family—and eventually my mom told me that my aunt and uncle did not want me to live with them any longer. I was crushed and silently cried myself to sleep, but could not bring myself to ask my aunt and uncle if this was true. I didn't want to know the answer.

After that, I moved from place to place so much that I kept most of my belongings in the backseat of my car so I could easily access them when I slept in my car or stayed somewhere for only a few days. But it broke my heart. I didn't want to have to keep moving; I wanted to belong. I wanted a home—somewhere I could stay and feel safe. My life already seemed hopeless, and it showed no signs of getting better.

I was thinking about this one October afternoon as I drove to work. I was crying, the sound of my mother telling me I was nothing but a burden to her echoing in my ears. Lost in those memories, my car began to swerve. At first, I corrected the wheel, then something snapped. That day, I decided to let go of my hopes and dreams of a better life, let go of trying to please my mother, let go of trying to make my family different. The tears streamed down my face as I let the car swerve while keeping my foot on the gas. I was driving sixty miles per hour down a hill, and steered my car toward a cement culvert—then everything went blank.

I was knocked out for a bit, and when I regained consciousness I saw the shattered windshield covered in blood. I began to cry—I had tried to end my life and had failed. I heard another car approaching, and began waving my arms out the window. A Good Samaritan pulled over, then ran up to my car and knelt beside me. Soon, the lights of a fire truck surrounded me, the car was jerking as the Jaws of Life cut through the wreckage to free me. The Good Samaritan was still holding my hand to make sure I knew I was not alone. In the end my uncle who I had been living with was the first one on the scene, since he was the town's fire chief. The EMTs explained that my leg was broken at the ankle and they had to reset it before they moved me. They twisted my mangled leg back into place and stuffed it into a brace without administering any anesthesia. The excruciating pain caused me to lose consciousness; the last thing I recall hearing is the concerned voice of an EMT telling everyone I needed to be moved right away because I was fading. My next memory is of my family standing by my bed, tearfully offering words of encouragement—as well as good-byes in case I didn't make it through surgery. I was in a coma for a week, and when I awoke, my mother and some friends were sitting beside my bed. The doctors later told me I almost didn't make it. I had to have my face reconstructed because of the damage to my chin and my forehead, and was not able to walk for many months.

It took me a few years to admit that I had attempted suicide. I am a suicide survivor. Looking back on my life, I see that the wreck was a turning point for me. I came to the conclusion that suicide is not about being alone; it's about long-term suffering and isolation. I felt isolated because no one knew what I was going through. Even the people I told about my pain didn't truly understand the severity of this pain. I was expected to bounce back, to be resilient, and was told more than once that things would get better—but they never did. These platitudes didn't help, but instead, only further isolated me. I was suffering from internal pain that was never remedied. I could never catch my breath. I just went from one family crisis to the next, and was never able to relax and enjoy life. I cried by myself and then put on a fake smile, so I didn't burden others with my struggles.

I left Oklahoma when I was nineteen after a man that I was chatting with online bought me a plane ticket so I could fly to meet him. I left for the state of Washington and never looked back. I ended up living on a church campground with a family that belonged to a cultlike Christian group. I loved the family's structure and kindness, and the welcome I received from them and other members of the group. They made me feel

I might actually belong somewhere. I took a job at Target, where I met the man who would become my husband. I had been working there a few months when I started to notice one of my supervisors, who was an attractive guy with a good heart. His name was Christopher, and he helped change my life.

In a lot of ways, I was not in the best place to be in a relationship. I was working two jobs, living with a friend, and just then was learning to live on my own for the first time. I had dated guys before, but had never had a real relationship—everything was new to me. Christopher was only three years older than I, but at a completely different place in his life. He was goal-oriented, and owned his own condominium with a balcony view that overlooked the ocean. He was more than halfway through his college career and owned his own car. He was nerdy, like me, hardworking, and very confident. He came from a middle-class family and knew what he wanted out of life. He appeared to have everything going for him. Some other women dismissed him as shy and socially awkward. He wore big, thick glasses and enjoyed things like folk music, foreign films, and art. He wasn't attuned to popular culture and didn't see the point in things that other people his age found interesting. I saw him as genuinely kind, and didn't feel I was good enough for him.

Once Christopher and I started dating, we were inseparable. Less than a week after our first date, I moved in with him. He later told me that he was in love with me six days into dating, and knew he wanted to spend the rest of his life with me. He didn't tell me because he thought that I would be scared away. It took me longer to realize my feelings for him.

Our dating life was rocky, to say the least. I was uncomfortable living in his house because I had been kicked out by others so often. I lived with my things in suitcases and bags in case I needed to leave immediately. Whenever we argued, I would walk out, anticipating that this was the end of our relationship. He always came after me, assuring me that we could work things out and that arguing didn't mean separating. I remember walking out one day, sure our relationship was over. After walking about a mile into town, I looked behind me and there he was, following me. I stopped and yelled at him to leave me alone, but he just said no. I turned around and looked at him; his eyes welled up with tears as he told me he would continue to chase after me despite how much pain it caused him, because he loved me. When I saw how much he was willing to endure for me, I knew that I loved him as much as he loved me.

Love, however, didn't necessarily mean trust. I had low self-esteem and was very much insecure, and it was years before I could tell Christopher about my childhood. I told him pieces at a time, fearing he would think I had too much baggage, and introduced him to my family long after we were married. I didn't want to scare him off, but Christopher was gentle and understood everything I revealed to him about my past without ever judging me. Our relationship was strong and we were married six months after our first date.

By 2008, we had two daughters and were living in Kansas so we could raise our family near his parents. I gave birth to our first son in February that year, and everything was going pretty smoothly. It was a great time for our family—my husband had a high-paying job, my older daughter was starting school, and I had become accustomed to the stay-at-home-mom role. Things were exactly how I imagined life should be. I felt that all the suffering I had endured when I was young was worth it because it seemed I had achieved my happy ending. However, my husband lost his job that April and things changed quickly. When he was "let go," my crisis-response instincts immediately kicked in. We signed up for benefits for needy families, and I got a job at a local salon and looked into enrolling at a nearby tribal college, since I knew my tribe provided scholarships that would help support our family while I attended school. Although attending college was a huge decision for my family and me, I didn't really give it a second thought.

I started classes at Haskell Indian Nations University in August, and I knew from day one that things were going to be different for our family from there on out. It was hard at first, because we didn't have a vehicle, and I had a five-hour round-trip bus commute—it was tough to be on time for my first class at nine o'clock in the morning. Nevertheless, I loved being in school again, and was reminded of the feeling I had back in high school that school was an escape from the chaos at home.

On the morning of September 27, 2008—one month after my classes began—our lives were changed forever. I woke up to a scream from my husband, like nothing I had ever heard before. Sometime during the night our son had passed away. He just stopped breathing. My husband snatched our son's stiff, lifeless body out of the crib and held him in his arms. Christopher instinctively began performing CPR, trying his hardest to get our son to breathe again. I called 911, telling them in the calmest voice I could muster that my baby wasn't breathing. Then I called my father-in-law, who was a physician's assistant, and asked him to come quickly. I couldn't make myself go back into the bedroom—it broke my heart to hear my husband begging my son to wake up as he tried to breathe life back into him. Sitting on the couch for six minutes waiting for the EMTs to arrive felt like forever. I rocked back and forth, listening to my husband's pleas, feeling that I needed to prepare myself for what I did not want to hear. The EMTs rushed in, and I pointed toward the bedroom. They quickly returned with my son, and in one sweeping arm movement, pushed everything off the dining-room table so they could assess my baby under the lamp. They took one look at him, looked at each other, and just shook their heads. They turned to address my husband and me, and my in-laws, who had just arrived. As they shook their heads, I felt my whole body stiffen, and I began to shake my head in total resistance to hearing what they were about to tell me. "Ma'am, he's been gone a while." I still remember these words, which confirmed what I knew the moment I saw his body lying in the moonlight—my son died while sleeping. I screamed so loudly, feeling as if I had just been stabbed, then my legs gave way and I crumpled onto the floor. I lay there, crying and screaming, repeating over and over again, "This isn't real, it's just a dream." The paramedics and my mother-in-law attempted to comfort me, reminding me in kind voices that he was gone. I asked whether his outfit or blanket could have strangled or smothered him, and the paramedic answered my questions as gently as she could. She explained that this was a case of sudden infant death syndrome (SIDS), but no matter how much she explained it, I couldn't accept it. I felt like I was dying.

At the funeral service later that week, somewhere between the chair I was sitting in and the door leading back into the sanctuary, I lost control of my emotions. I lay there and cried, reaching out for my mother—I wanted something that I had never had before, the comfort of my mother's arms. We both cried, and she held me tight; my mother was actually taking care of me when I needed her most. It was a rare moment. Between my sobs, I heard my husband quietly singing "You Are My Sunshine." I had never seen my husband cry so hard as he cradled our son and fought through his tears to finish the song he had sung to our baby boy so many times before.

After my son's death, my husband and I separated for a while. He needed to feel closer to our children, while I needed to grieve by myself. My husband and children moved back to Washington State so he could be closer to his best friend and siblings. Meanwhile, I had nowhere to go. I could have returned to Oklahoma, but that was the home of all of my pain and suffering, so I decided to return to the place I now considered my home—Haskell Indian Nations University.

My first semester back was the roughest time for me. I was mourning the loss of my baby, trying to focus on what I was supposed to be learning, and processing the anger and sadness I carried with me every day.

Meanwhile, I was spending time with people who had no clue what I was going through. Many judged about how I was handling my grief, although only a few people had walked the path I was on; and the few who did knew better than to judge someone else's grief.

In a lot of ways, I truly was alone. I again felt emotionally unstable, and I didn't trust my own thoughts or feel safe in my own mind. My only way of coping was to rely on substances to separate my mind from the pain I was suffering—the only time in my life I have done so. People now saw a careless student who spent her time drinking away the nights and living the days in a haze of apathy. What they didn't see were the open wounds of my heart and a woman trying to figure out how to continue in a world that no longer included the son who had been born only a few months earlier. They didn't see the struggle I faced each morning to convince myself I had something to exist for and that I had the strength to keep fighting despite all my instincts telling me that I was weak. This was my life for the next few months. I wasn't concerned about my kids, as I knew that they were being well cared for, and I felt I was not a person I wanted my children to be around, not at that time.

After a few more months, it was clear that my husband and I were not ready to give up on our marriage. He came back, and our desperation to be together despite our pain was the only thing that gave us purpose. We knew we loved our girls, and that we had to find a way to heal from our tragedy together. I felt I could put my pain aside to do what was needed to ensure my family's continuity.

At that time, I heard about an internship that paid students a lot to do research over the summer. I saw this as an opportunity to help my family, since it would give us some income to pay for housing and the other things we needed at that moment. I spoke to the professor in charge of the internship and he immediately turned me down, since I was a freshman and the internship was for upper-level students. He suggested that I wait a few years and then apply again. I was crushed. It was the only plan I had, and I knew I couldn't take no for an answer. I told him I would check back with him closer to the start of the internship to make sure all the spots were filled. I wanted him to know I was serious about doing whatever the internship required me to do.

At the end of the semester, my family and I drove to Oklahoma to stay with my "aunt," who is a family friend who has always encouraged me to pursue my higher-education goals. She let us stay with her and encouraged me to find a job nearby so I could support my family. But I was stubborn. I wanted only the internship position, which I knew would pay much more than any local job I could find. I checked back with the professor a few days before the start of the internship, and once again he refused my application. Sure that I could convince him he was wrong about my capabilities, I asked if I could talk with him in person. He agreed, and the next day I drove the six hours from southern Oklahoma to Lawrence, Kansas, just to prove I was someone worth taking a chance on. My plan was successful. After speaking with the professor and assuring him I could keep up, and that I was prepared to do the hard work required by the internship, I secured my spot.

This internship paved my way to Dartmouth College. I ended up being invited to speak at conferences and other events about the research I was doing, which involved the impact climate change is having on tribal communities. This was something I could relate to, since I come from tribes that were forcibly relocated, and am all too familiar with the generational trauma caused by relocation. I took the feelings I had experienced throughout my life and turned them into a passion for advocating for Natives facing climate adversity. It worked, and people wanted to hear what I had to say.

Soon after, I was asked to serve on a planning committee for a conference involving other higher-education institutions. I took advantage of every opportunity presented to me because I didn't have the luxury of waiting until I was ready; my husband, daughters, and new infant son needed me to succeed. Some professors encouraged me to submit a transfer application to Dartmouth College, known for its Native American studies program, but I had little interest in transferring. I was struggling to do well at Haskell and considered it my home. However, the professor who had given me the internship assured me I would be able to succeed in a more rigorous academic environment. I trusted him, and submitted my late application to Dartmouth, after which the college's Native admissions officer flew me out for a campus visit—uncommon for a transfer applicant. I was accepted to Dartmouth and decided to attend. My husband and three children came to New Hampshire with me.

Being a nontraditional older student isn't much different from other students coming to an Ivy League university; they all face same question, "Is this where I belong?" But being an older student definitely had its challenges, and having a lot of life experience made for some memorable exchanges in class. I remember once sitting in a government class as we discussed Foucault's *History of Sexuality*, specifically his story about having sex with children. I listened as my classmates interpreted what he might have meant and offered their opinions about the morality of having sex with children. I had so many thoughts as I reflected on my experience of being sexually abused, but could not put them into words. There was no way the other students could understand what I was feeling, unless they too had been through it. I sat silent, feeling that what I had to say was too real for this conversation. As a survivor, I also had little interest in being questioned about my life experiences, unless I could speak with intention, purpose, and total honesty. I had many similar experiences while at Dartmouth since my life experience often informed what I was studying.

One of the biggest challenges in my education at Dartmouth was the overwhelming feelings I sometimes experienced while doing course readings. When I read something that referenced suicide and Native Americans, it stirred my emotions. Because of my personal experience, reading about trauma, political marginalization, or overworked and underpaid poor people provoked strong feelings in me. Once, I heard about a Native woman who committed suicide while attending Dartmouth Medical School, and although I did not know her personally, it affected me deeply because I could recall my own feelings of isolation and suffering that had driven me to attempt suicide. I believe that once someone attempts suicide they are always vulnerable to that "dark place," not because it's somewhere I want to be, but because I often get stuck there when something happens to unbalance me emotionally.

I once explained to my academic dean that my age and life experience gave me a sort of freedom. I did not have to be consumed with dating or finding a mate, which defined so much of the undergraduate social scene. I also had gained a lot of self-confidence over my lifetime, and wasn't as concerned with my appearance as my younger peers were. In a lot of ways, my sense of security gave me more time to focus on what I learned in class, but on the other hand, my free time was not something to be coveted. I was the mother of young children and had given birth to another son during my senior year. Instead of having the freedom to make social connections or join extracurricular activities, at the end of my school day, I spent time with my four kids, helping them with their homework, running errands, doing household chores, or working. I have had to maintain a job throughout my academic career just to meet our expenses. I was pursuing an education to provide a better life for the children and husband I was responsible for, and there were very tangible consequences if I failed.

As college graduation approached, I began to feel depressed again, and couldn't figure out why. This was supposed to be a time for celebration, since I had finally achieved the goal I had worked so hard for. I came to realize that I couldn't be as happy as my classmates because, as usual, I was not like them. It made me sad to hear classmates talk excitedly about their family members coming to cheer them on at graduation and how proud their family was of them. I heard one Native student say that more than thirteen people were driving across the country to see her graduate. It brought me to tears, since almost no one was coming to see me. My sister was the only one in my family who took time to celebrate my life accomplishments. No one else had the time or resources, or even understood what this meant to me.

In tribal communities, someone who feels sorry for themselves is looked down on; one need only look around to see that plenty of people are much worse off than you, and yet they still work hard for everything they have without complaint or expectation of glory. That's the way I was raised, which made me feel worse whenever I had moments of sadness. When I came to Dartmouth, I knew that my education was not free; it was paid for with the blood of my ancestors. I have learned the history of all the atrocities that my ancestors experienced so that we, their descendants, could thrive again. I have never forgotten this. I had not endured what my ancestors had and I measured my own endurance against theirs. My self-pity felt shallow because I wanted to make my ancestors proud. So I kept my feelings to myself and didn't tell anyone I felt cheated by not having a loving extended family.

My sadness would lift every day when I came home to smiling little faces that lit up when they saw me, and to a husband who never failed to tell me how proud he is of me, and how much they all appreciate my hard work. I knew that despite what I lacked, I had so much more to be thankful for. Recently, a friend of mine advised me to find one truth about myself and hang on to it. For me, that truth is that I am a survivor. I hold on to that truth every moment of every day, and remind myself in the midst of the chaos and stress of life that I have survived.

Nevertheless, in the days leading up to graduation, I couldn't shake my sadness. I wasn't sure I wanted to partake in the celebration, since I didn't feel the Dartmouth commencement traditions applied to me—there were no celebrations for nontraditional students. In reality, I just wanted to go somewhere and cry and cherish my son's memory, alone. Then I remembered a promise I made the last time I held my son at his funeral. At the time, I wished I did not have to live in a world without him. However, in my tribal culture, we are taught to let go when loved ones pass on and to wish them well on their journey, so I promised my son I would let him go, honor him, and one day make him proud. At the time I questioned whether I had the strength to continue, but I wanted him to know that he could go and I would be OK.

In June 2014 I graduated from Dartmouth College, fulfilling my promise to my son. It was a day of bittersweet feelings. Afterward, my children, husband, and I celebrated with our friends—the family we chose—and we celebrated each other. My success was their success. I was proud to walk across the stage with my diploma, but sad to be doing it without my first son, who was there at the beginning of my academic journey but not at the end. That broke my heart. To honor my son's memory I wore his tribal band patchwork sewn onto my gown. It is the design of the Wind Clan of the Miccosukee People, the strong ones, of the Seminole Nation of Oklahoma. I carried the memory of my son who couldn't be there in my heart, and my new infant son in my arms. My footsteps were heavy across the stage since it had required so much strength for me to get there. I completed the journey I promised I would complete, and my tears reflected my feelings of both joy and sadness.

Ma'Ko'Quah Abigail Jones, a citizen of the Prairie Band Potawatomi Nation, graduated with a master's degree in environmental law and policy from Vermont Law School in 2015. Previously, she graduated from Dartmouth College with a bachelor of arts degree in government and in Native American studies. She also holds an associate of arts degree from Haskell Indian Nations University. Currently, she works in the Environmental Protection Department at her tribe in Mayetta, Kansas, as the environmental/GIS technician. She plans to pursue a PhD/JD and a career advocating for underrepresented communities facing climate adversity.

6

My Journey to Healing   Kalina Newmark

A young Dené woman and her family arrive at K'álǫ Tué (Willow Lake).
They set up their canvas tents and eat with the other families who have
already arrived at the traditional gathering spot of the Dené people.
The young woman leaves the others behind and walks from the grassy
meadowlands to the muddy waters, where the boats have been tied
together and brought to shore.

As she looks down into the shallow water, the young woman sees a flash
of light strike across the rocks. A few moments later, the Water Woman
appears and points toward the edge of the beach. The young woman shivers
in nervousness and turns her head sideways. Suddenly a wolf appears in the
distance. The woman walks slowly, so that she does not bring attention
to her movements.

As soon as the woman reaches the wolf, the wolf whispers in her ear, "Come
follow me. I promise you will be safe, but make sure no one notices you are
gone." The woman peers over her shoulder, wraps her red-and-white striped
handkerchief over her long brown hair, and follows the wolf.

As they walk farther and farther into the night, the beach slowly changes into
a leafy green forest filled with tall trees and chirping birds. Gasping for air,
the woman stops and asks the wolf where he is taking her. The wolf says,
"I'm taking you to the new world, so you can see how all of our lives
(Dené and non-Dené) will begin to change in the coming years."

With a puzzled look on her face, the woman collapses onto the ground,
dirtying the white dress that her grandmother made for her. As she gets up
from the dirt, the wolf tells her, "Your children and grandchildren must
learn how to adapt and live in both worlds. If not, our Dené ways will be
lost." With tears slowly dripping down her brown cheeks, the young
woman tells the wolf that he is lying.

In Sahtúot'ı̨nę Yatı̨ she asks, "How can the Dené world be changed?" The
wolf looks at the young woman and slowly transforms into a young man.
The man explains to her that things in life are not always what they seem.
He leaves the young woman with the following lesson that she must pass

on to her people when she arrives back at K'álǫ Tué: the Dené must teach
their children to live in the new world—giving them both the necessary skills
to carry on Dené traditions and beliefs while learning how to adapt those
qualities to their environment.

Harriet Gladue, "Family Oral Tradition Passed Down
from Generation to Generation," oral history

With each passing year, I have come to a greater understanding of the
obligations I carry for my Dené people. I am a member of the Dené First
Nation, specifically from the Sahtu region. My band is the Tulita Dené
located in Tulita, formerly known as Fort Norman, in the Northwest Territories of Canada, where nearly all families are related. Although we call
our land *Denendeh*, meaning "the Land of the People," many of us, including myself, no longer live on or near our homelands. However, with
traditional stories like the above that are passed on from generation to
generation and by making frequent trips back and forth to the Sahtu,
I have managed to stay connected with my Native family. On each trip
home, I learn a little more of what it means to be Dené. This story is about
the difficulty of creating and reconciling an Indigenous identity in exile—
away from one's traditional homelands.

The Dené people are taught from a young age to care for others, and
often to place the needs of the group over those of the individual. As
a matrilineal society, the Dené people place great importance on the
women's role in the family. In her book on the Dené people, *Drum Songs:
Glimpses of Dene History*, Kerry Abel describes how Europeans viewed the
roles and responsibilities of Dené women: "Europeans were outraged that
women were expected to carry such heavy loads, but to the Dené it was
only natural, since women were believed to be the stronger of the sexes."[1]
Within Dené society, the division of work between men and woman was
clearly outlined. Men determined traveling routes, hunted large game,
and manufactured boats and hunting tools,[2] while women did everything
else—raising children, gathering food, preparing meals, chopping wood,
and sewing clothing items. The Dené system was balanced. Men and
women worked together for the purposes of their family and community's survival. However, because of the impact of colonization in Canada,
the Dené were discouraged from practicing their traditional belief systems and philosophies, and familial relations were slowly broken down by
forced governmental policies.

As a Dené woman, I still gain extraordinary strength from the women in
my family—my eldest sister, mother, grandmother, and great-grandmother,

and many others. When I was born, in May 1989, all the Native women in my family welcomed me, including my grandmother and great-grandmother, who were both visiting from the Northwest Territories. When my parents brought me home, my great-grandmother, whom we called Small Granny, sang and told me stories in *Sahtúot'įnę Yatį*. Small Granny would wrap me tightly in my blanket and hold me beneath the covers while we both fell asleep. Small Granny was a kind and respected woman who truly exemplified what it meant to be a Dené woman. She was born in the early twentieth century and became a midwife while still in her teens, delivering over one hundred babies. She would travel with her dog team for hundreds of kilometers in some of the toughest weather conditions to ensure Dené women would have a professional present to safely deliver their children. She was known for her bravery and courage. The Northwest Territories recognized her work and named the Tulita health clinic in her honor. She was married twice. Her first husband was Chief Albert Wright, who was several years older than Small Granny. When she was thirteen years old, Albert left Tulita to attend school in Montreal. He told Small Granny that they would marry when he returned home. He kept his promise. As a wedding gift, Albert gave Small Granny a sewing machine, cut-glass beads, and velvet material, the likes of which no one in the community had ever seen before.

When Albert returned from school, drastic changes were taking place in the community. The Canadian government was negotiating treaties with Native people in the area, and they brought their own translators to Tulita. As a result of my great-grandfather knowing both English and the Native language, he became an important figure in the community. None of the government negotiators knew that Albert understood English, so he would attend the meetings and take note of all that was said. He alone knew that the government negotiators were translating incorrectly.

After the meetings, Albert would meet with the community and tell them what he had heard. After a few days, the community wanted to make him their chief, but he did not accept right away. Small Granny told my mother that Albert was gone most of the day during the negotiations, returning home only to sleep and eat. On the last day of negotiations, Albert came home to talk with Small Granny about whether he should accept the community's offer to make him their chief. In his eyes, being chief would be not only his responsibility but that of his wife too—it was a partnership. Small Granny agreed with her husband, and Albert Wright became chief. Our community believes that our treaty was well negotiated because of Albert Wright's knowledge of the English language. Without Small Granny's support and guidance, Albert Wright would not have been the man he was.

Although Small Granny passed away when I was only few years old, she has had a profound impact on my life. She has given me strength by demonstrating that women play an important role in our culture. A few years after my birth, Small Granny gave me my Dené name, which is one of the most important gifts a Dené person can receive. My Dené name is *Góhtsiya*, which translates as Little Robin, because she knew that I would always live far away from home, but like a bird I would return to my nest when I needed to feed those who relied on me and, most important, when I needed to be fed. When you are given a Dené name, you are also given a responsibility to the community and to your family to carry yourself with honor and respect. Moreover, a Dené name gives you a place among our people—both those still alive and those who have passed on.

My family's transition from the small Arctic coastal community of Tuktoyaktuk, Northwest Territories, known simply as Tuk to its residents, to Penticton, British Columbia, was difficult. My father remained in Tuk to work and provide for our family, while my mother, who had never lived outside the Northwest Territories, cared for us. Although we frequently traveled back and forth between Tuk and Penticton, we had no family nearby to rely on for help. As a result, we treasured our visits to the Northwest Territories, where we were near our family and a network of friends who understood who we were as Dené people. Although the majority of my childhood was spent in Penticton, I still consider the Northwest Territories my home; it is a place where my ancestors spent thousands upon thousands of years building a nation, and where I feel most at peace. Conversely, I consider Penticton the place I grew up and where I was recognized for my academic and athletic achievements. I reflect on these years in Penticton with both pride and heartache. Although I was able to make strong relationships with people in Penticton, I was also physically far away from my father and my Dené community. This separation from immediate and extended family coupled with the lack of Dené culture did not help our living situation in Penticton.

My mother tried her best, but she suffered from a paralyzing addiction to alcohol that affected not only her life but her children's lives as well. In our culture, we believe that, without intending to, parents who do not take care of themselves pass on their negative emotions to their children. To stop the cycle, these emotions must be dealt with immediately, and I was dedicated to taking care of my emotions. I also soon realized that, although I could encourage and support my mother, at the end of the day she bore responsibility for her own recovery.

Until I was older, I didn't realize that my mother's issues in large part stemmed from her childhood experiences within the residential school system. Children are shaped by the environment they grow up in. In my case, life could have taken many paths, but I was fortunate to have the right people in my life at the right times. Ultimately, my *Ama*, my mother, has become one of the most influential women in my life, as she has taught me to laugh through the struggles and, most important, to live courageously. Until I was in grade eight, her struggles were a major part of her day-to-day life—and mine. I often arrived home from school to find my *Ama* in the carport sitting on the ratty blue chair, holding a burning cigarette in one hand and the phone in the other, sobbing uncontrollably. I would run to my room and lock the door, for I feared she would have one of her verbal or physical outbursts. Until I finally sought counseling in college, I did not fully realize the impact my mother's disease was having on my self-esteem and the way I viewed relationships with others. I believed relationships were inherently unstable and that problems could not be resolved effectively through calm and clear communication. That simply had not been my experience. Through counseling, however, I gained a better understanding of my mother's upbringing and could empathize with her struggles, although I did not and still do not excuse or condone her choices.

Throughout my family's history we have had tremendous successes, but we also have faced challenges such as depression, alcoholism, untimely death, and sexual assault. Being exposed to these issues early on, I learned to create barriers and to shelter myself emotionally from others. Instead of sharing your emotions, it was better to just go on with your daily activities as if nothing had happened. Thus I was forced to grow up quickly. I took on responsibilities that many of my friends did not have, which at the time seemed normal.

Even as a young child, I felt responsible for the welfare of my youngest sister. I wanted her to live without the struggles I had experienced, and to have a childhood free of stress and worry. I learned to channel my emotions through positive outlets such as school and sports. I would wake up every morning at eight so I could catch the thirty-minute Sports Center segment on TV. I found sports extremely calming, and while some children do their homework on the dining room table, I did mine on my bed while watching basketball games. I spent my free time practicing soccer footwork on the front lawn or shooting hoops at the local elementary school. Through sports, I achieved tangible results such as scoring a goal or dribbling the ball, which gave me joy. For once, I was allowed to freely express myself without fear of being ignored. Sports were my safe haven; they shielded me from the struggles I faced at home. Nothing else mattered when I played sports.

While I found solace in sports and academics, our family situation was not improving. As a result, my father took drastic measures to ensure that my sister and I had a healthy living environment. When I was in grade seven, my father flew from the Northwest Territories and drove me the four hours to Vancouver, British Columbia, where he signed me up to take a standardized test that would determine which elite high schools I was qualified to attend. Fortunately, my mother stopped drinking after that school year, and my younger sister and I were able to continue to live with her. I never found out why she stopped; I was just happy she was doing better. When I reflect on that pivotal time in my life, I feel the stars must have been aligned in my favor. I am not sure what else can explain my academic success.

I excelled in high school, and many of my teachers and advisers believed in my talent. Mr. Nackoney, my high-school counselor, understood my home situation, and although he never mentioned it, he was a great comfort to me. He would listen to me when I had issues in my classes and he coached me through the college-application process—he even helped me improve my basketball game. Simply put, he was there when I needed someone to talk to. Mr. Nackoney had been my brother's coach, and thus had known me since I was a little child watching my brother's games. Now that I was a promising high-school graduate, he had become an integral part of my success story. I owe much to his continued guidance and support.

Based on my academic merit and extracurricular activities, I was accepted by several premier colleges in Canada and the United States. On the last day in May, I chose to attend Dartmouth College. Before applying, I had never heard of Dartmouth, but a friend of my high-school principal who recruited on behalf of Dartmouth was particularly interested in First Nations students. My principal referred me to him, and he set me on my path. I first visited Dartmouth when I applied to the Native Fly-In Program, which provides talented high-school seniors the opportunity to visit Dartmouth's campus. During this trip, I was exposed to Dartmouth's strong Native American community, which was one of the main reasons why I chose Dartmouth over the other schools I was accepted to. Part of the decision to go to Dartmouth was based on both instinct and the hope that I could make a positive difference in my family's life. I had no doubt in my mind that I had made the right decision to attend Dartmouth and I was excited to start this new chapter in my life.

Nonetheless, as my father drove me from the Boston airport to Dartmouth College in Hanover, New Hampshire, I was nervous. This was the first time I would be living without family or friends close by. I suddenly realized that how I was feeling was probably similar to how my mother felt when she moved to southern Canada. When my father left me at the college, he kissed me on the cheek and told me that everything would be okay. Although I would face many challenges during my college years, Dartmouth College really was the best setting for me—a small liberal arts college that fosters undergraduate development in a safe learning environment. I truly believe we are drawn to places for a reason, and I would soon find out why I was drawn to Dartmouth.

The transition from Penticton, British Columbia, to Hanover, New Hampshire, was not easy. While I had excelled in most of my high-school classes, this was not the case at Dartmouth. I could no longer rely on my intelligence to get me through; I now needed to learn how to think critically about the texts we were reading and to formulate my opinions based on academic research. At Dartmouth I took challenging courses that forced me to think objectively—based on facts rather than purely on feelings. At times I felt uncomfortable and unsure of my opinions, but listening to others and engaging in the classroom dialogue helped better equip me for life after college. Instead of focusing on a subject area that would help me secure a job after graduation, I studied what I was interested in—Native American studies, anthropology, and linguistics.

Dartmouth has one of the nation's oldest and most prestigious Native American studies departments. It gave me a unique opportunity to learn about Indigenous issues—the environment, public policy, history, the arts, and law—from Native and non-Native professors. I often found myself harboring negative feelings toward students who did not understand why Native people faced racism or prejudices within society. I remember when, during a discussion in a Native American studies class, a student raised his hand and asked the professor why Native people could not get over their issues and conform to American standards: "Native people need to pull themselves up by their bootstraps and do what Jewish people did hundreds of years ago." I was sitting next to a Native friend who could see how upset I was getting. My hands were shaking as I tried to explain to this student why Native people are in the situations they are today. Instead of recognizing the harmful effects of colonization, this student chose to ignore those discussions we previously had in class. I thought educated people, especially at a place like Dartmouth, would have known better. In that moment, I wondered what it was like before Native American studies classes existed, particularly how Native students felt being on campus before the college instituted programs to recruit and retain Native students. If I thought it was difficult addressing this one student in class, I could only imagine what it would have been like decades before when the Native student population was significantly smaller.

Although Native people are marginalized within Canadian and US society, this was not generally the case at Dartmouth. While Natives were a small percentage of the campus population, we knew we were a part of an elite group being afforded advantages that those in our home communities could only dream of. This passion for understanding and learning inspired me to volunteer for many leadership roles within the Native American community, including helping to organize the annual Dartmouth Powwow and holding the copresidency of the Native Americans at Dartmouth (NAD) student group. I also attended many Native American events put on by NAD and the Native American Program. One of these was the Native American pre-orientation session, where I met Native people from places I had never heard of before. Through my interactions with other Native students, I started to understand more fully the broader issues Indigenous communities faced, such as educational achievement gaps, health disparities, and economic and political struggles. I had witnessed or experienced many of these disparities, but when I spoke with other Native students and professors, I finally felt that my feelings were validated.

Despite my initial reservations, I slowly started to welcome the realization that Dartmouth College was now my home. I built a strong community with Native and non-Native friends, and this made things easier, although I still struggled with my sense of being alone. I was comforted through these times by phone calls with my mother. I remember calling her one night and crying, telling her that I wanted to leave college and come home immediately. Instead of telling me what to do, my mother told me stories about her experience in boarding school, when she was taken from her family and flown hundreds of miles away from her home community. I appreciated her softness and her ability to relate to my situation. Although my mother did not understand what it felt like to be at Dartmouth, she was able to relate to my situation and encourage me to do my best. I acknowledged this change in my mother's behavior and I was proud of her.

I began to reflect on my mother's boarding-school experience in the papers I wrote, which helped me feel more empathetic and understanding toward her. Most important, I realized how the boarding-school system targeted Native ways of life in an effort to break down traditional family systems. The phrase "Kill the Indian, and save the child" was used to describe the assimilation of Native children into Canadian society. To accomplish this objective, the Canadian government worked with religious organizations to set up boarding-school systems throughout the country. Native children were then forcibly taken away from their families and placed in these unfamiliar environments. I could not envision what it was like to be living in an isolated community one day, and the next to be transported to a school without your parents, elders, or traditional foods, and where it was forbidden to speak any Native language. I now understood why my grandmother had disliked floatplanes—it was because they were used to spirit the Native children away to school.

Although my mother doesn't like to talk about her time in boarding school, her stories provide an important glimpse into her childhood and the kind of experiences many Native children went through during that era. My mother was taken from Tulita as a young girl, along with many of her brothers and sisters—part of an entire generation of Native children who were removed from their families and communities. Although she was sent away with her siblings, she was not housed with them, as the boys and girls were separated by gender and age.

She often told us about the time she was not allowed to see her older sister. Shortly after arriving at boarding school, my mother was walking through a hallway when she saw her sister playing volleyball in the gymnasium. She stopped, peered through the window, and began to cry. She wanted to open the gym doors and run to her sister, but was not permitted to do so. She was living so close to her siblings yet she felt so disconnected from them. Stories like these enable me to understand my mother's childhood and why she struggled to be a parent herself after being denied the opportunity to grow up in a traditional Dené family setting. I have learned through my own healing to accept my mother as she is without judgment. I have also tried to use my mother's stories as lessons in my own life.

When I got to college, I realized how much personal healing I had to do, including dealing with depression. As usual, I thought I could deal with my issues on my own, without the support of a counselor, but this soon changed. Once during my junior year I didn't leave my dorm room for nearly forty-eight hours, and I didn't eat or drink anything. Later, I understood that I was severely depressed, and knew that I needed help— I could no longer pretend that I was fine. In the past, I had feelings of isolation, but that night it was particular strong. I do not know what changed in me that night, but I called the campus police and asked for a ride to the health clinic. While so many other students seemed to be having the most freewheeling and exciting times in their lives, I felt alone; but at last I had made the decision to seek help.

The campus police drove me to the clinic, where I was admitted and shown to a bed. The attendant who admitted me was cold. He asked if I had eaten anything, and I told him, "No, I am not hungry." He shook his head and left. He returned with a cup of noodle soup, Gatorade, and a bagel. I drank the Gatorade and left the rest on the table. I remember lying in that bed and feeling like a failure, and wanted so much to escape. I didn't know where I'd go, but I wanted to get out of there. Then the nurse who tucked me into bed said gently, "I hope you feel better, I do not want you to hurt anymore." She made me feel better, and her kind words assured me that I had made the right decision to reach out for help.

I met my counselor the next morning. Through our sessions together, I learned some invaluable skills, such as how to process my emotions in a healthy way. Our sessions typically started with the therapist asking me, "What have you done to take care of yourself today?" There were no right or wrong answers in these sessions, but simply a process of reflection that helped me sort out what I was thinking and what was my truth. At first I thought "taking care of myself" had to be something extravagant, but I slowly learned this was not the case. I had also thought that "success" was defined by a clear achievement, like getting a good grade, but I soon learned that completing little tasks like doing my laundry was a kind of accomplishment and that things I was already doing—taking a long bath or drinking my favorite jasmine green tea—were also ways to take care of myself.

The first few sessions were the hardest. I remember feeling before each session that I did not want to go and I would try and find any excuse to reschedule my appointment, but each time I spoke with my counselor I felt better, and lighter, as if a weight had been lifted off my shoulders. I no longer had to pretend that everything was fine when it was not. I learned to be more open and, most important, I learned to be honest with myself. The shift to being so authentic was difficult at first, as I was used to my childhood coping mechanisms, to pretending everything was fine when it was not. However, I learned that being honest is one of the most powerful gifts you can give to yourself and to others. I gradually came to own all my feelings, which gave me a sense of accomplishment and enabled me to use the skills I was learning in my sessions in my daily life. I no longer felt imprisoned by depression; instead I felt free and able to express myself in a healthy way. Each day I did what I could to make my life better.

My counselor was a sweet woman who kept me on as a patient well after my days as a student. She taught me to be compassionate, and not to hold on to negative feelings. In an effort to end our sessions on a happy note, I often would tell a story about my younger brother, "Money Mike." Michael, who is my half brother, as we have different biological mothers, entered my life in a unique way. My dad came to Penticton for Christmas one year, with my two younger half brothers in tow. After Christmas, Michael asked to stay with us longer, and in fact he never left. My mother soon enrolled Michael in kindergarten, gave him his own bedroom, and he was acting as if he had lived there his whole life. At the time I was in eleventh grade. Despite him being my half brother, it never felt weird to have Michael around. It was only later that it occurred to me how uncommon it was to have a half brother living with his father's ex-wife. When I asked my mother some years later why she decided to take Michael in, she told me it was simply the right thing to do. After I prodded her a little, my mother admitted that she had talked with my grandmother about what she should do. My grandmother told my mom that if she decided to take Michael in she could never turn her back on him. In my grandmother's words, Michael was now my mother's son.

Bringing Michael into our family also brought healing. He fit in with our family right away, and it was as if we had been waiting for him our whole lives. My mother adored Michael. She laughed at his antics and sang to him at night when he was scared. He would often sneak out of his room at night and crawl in next to my mother in her king-size bed. She would wake to find Michael at the foot of her bed, curled up in the fetal position and snoring loudly.

There was also a period when Michael would wear his Spider-Man costume every day, refusing to take off the green mask and pajamas. He would run around the house pretending to be Spider-Man and climbing anything he could—doors, cabinets, and fences. My mother once bought him silly foam, which he sprayed all over the windows. Clearly upset, my mother told Michael not to do it again. Next thing you know, four-year-old Michael was outside with a bucket of water, a sponge, and a small stool cleaning up his mess. I came to realize how much joy Michael had brought into our lives, which is why I liked to end each counseling session by telling a story about him.

Once I learned to take care of myself through my counseling sessions, I became more spiritually attuned and began to pay more attention to my surroundings. I vividly remember walking across the main part of campus one day when I suddenly smelled Vicks VapoRub, wild grass, and blueberries. From a distance I saw my grandmother (Small Granny's daughter), who had passed away the year before I started at Dartmouth. She was sitting on a wooden bench, with her white hair, a blue-buttoned top, and black pants. As I got closer, the woman disappeared, but I knew that my grandmother, the woman I was named after, was there with me. I cried because in that moment I felt she was telling me I was in the right place and was still connected to my people, despite being so far away from my traditional homelands. I knew I was no longer alone.

My academic journey at Dartmouth College ended with my graduation. When I crossed the stage at commencement, my great-grandmother, Small Granny, came to my mind. By building on her legacy and those of my fellow family members, and with the guidance of my counselor at college, I have been able to do my best and accept my faults. Sometimes I wonder what my grandmother or great-grandmother would think of their granddaughter attending college so far away from home. As a young child, I always had big dreams, and though not everyone close to me believed in them, my father and mother always pushed me to do my best. While my father completed high school and attained a postsecondary degree, my mother never graduated from high school. For this reason, my mother even more so did her best to support my academic pursuits, even helping me the night before it was due to decorate my wooden car for my high-school physics class. Both of my parents knew education was the key to being independent and successful.

One of the philosophies my Dené family taught me was that every person has a gift, and I understood that my gift was the ability to bridge the gap between the Dené and non-Dené worlds through higher education. While it was difficult growing up and attending school so far away from my Dené homelands, I have learned that giving back to my community doesn't necessarily mean physically living in the Sahtu. Similarly to the lessons I learned in counseling about taking care of myself, I recognized that I was already giving back to my community by carrying on the Dené beliefs and traditions through my personal and professional work.

When I had the opportunity to attend a work function where David Johnston, the governor general of Canada (the queen's representative), would be addressing the Economic Club on "The Diplomacy of Knowledge: Innovation Exchange across Borders," I immediately took it.

Johnston was giving his speech at a downtown hotel, where nearly two hundred people were in attendance from several organizations. In his speech, the governor general mentioned First Nations as an group essential to Canada's success. He said, "First, Canadians believe deeply in the value of working together and learning from one another. We came to this belief early and out of necessity . . . our climate and geography can be challenging, to say the least. The first Europeans were wholly dependent on their willingness to work together and to learn from Aboriginal peoples."[3] When he finished, the moderator allowed for one question—mine. I asked the governor general what he saw as the biggest obstacles facing First Nations children in the education system. He answered honestly by saying that the most important domestic issue facing Canada today is the treatment of Aboriginal people, especially in regard to educational achievement gaps. Instead of sitting quietly, I decided to become an active participant in the conversation. While the question may seem unimportant to those in the room, I felt that I was using my "gift" to engage with an important leader in Canada on a topic that many First Nations (including myself) are passionate about. In that moment, I felt a sense of accomplishment. Although my family was not around when I asked the question, I knew they would be proud of me for not being afraid and for speaking my mind.

Leaving Canada to attend a small liberal arts college in the United States was not easy. At Dartmouth, I experienced some of the most difficult times in life. However, I learned how to deal with my depression and, most important, I learned to love myself again. Throughout my own healing process I have tried to inspire others to do the same. I want to offer my thanks to my older sister, mother, grandmother, and great-grandmother for their unconditional love and guidance. They have taught me what it means to be a Dené woman. *Mahsi cho* (Thank you).

Kalina Newmark is an enrolled member of the Tulita Dené First Nations in Tulita, Northwest Territories. She graduated from Dartmouth College in 2011 with a double major in Native American studies and anthropology modified with linguistics. While at Dartmouth, Newmark was the president of Native Americans at Dartmouth, chairperson of Dartmouth's Annual Powwow, a Stefansson fellow, and a member of Delta Delta Delta Fraternity and the Casque and Gauntlet senior society. In her senior year, she received the Dean's Plate Award and the Class of 1965 Achievement Award in Memory of Charles Eastman for her outstanding contributions to the social and cultural life of the Dartmouth Native American community.

After graduation, Newmark worked at Dartmouth for two years; first as a presidential fellow in the President's Office, and second as the coordinator of the Indian Health Service Partnership at the Dartmouth Center for Health Care Delivery Science. Afterward, Newmark secured a position as a marketing communications specialist at Cargill in Minneapolis.

Outside of work, Newmark has a passion for her Dené culture, travel, wellness, and fashion. She plans to pursue a master's degree in business, working to address the political, economic, and social needs of Indigenous people in Canada and the United States. She hopes that through her essay other Native students understand they are not alone in their academic pursuits, and that they too can bring healing to their families and communities through their education.

PART III

FULL CIRCLE

Returning and Remaking Home

7

Little Woman from Lame Deer   Cinnamon Spear

Growing up on the reservation means your first thought every day is "I can't wait to leave here and never come back." We see people on TV in nice houses with green lawns going on vacation. The only escapes we know are a week or two shacked up at our snag's place across the rez. We walk from town to town along rural Montana highways in the deathly heat of summer or the frigid winter cold. Cars pass us with duct-taped bumpers, others with no hoods. We laugh when we see those brave suckers in sunglasses driving a truck with no windshield.

There's nothing to do in the middle-of-nowhere town of Lame Deer. We're a hundred miles from anything and everyone is bored. Our parents drink and fight each other, or sometimes us, and we go to school comparing tragic stories from the night before without missing a beat. There's a belief that "getting off the reservation" is the thing to do but not many know how to leave, or where to go and what to do. Education is one way out. But white teachers lack energy and don't care enough to spark a fire in the hearts of impressionable Cheyenne youth. We hear stories of the ones who go off to school, but we never see them again. I always said I would go to college and never be that person who doesn't come back.

My parents both grew up on the reservation but their education led them to Missoula, Montana, where they connected. My dad's two-year stint at Lewis & Clark Law School meant moving their young family to Portland, Oregon. Drug use, failed coursework, and a miscarriage culminated in their premature return to Lame Deer. They knew how it felt to be far away, and in that distance, their appreciation for home grew. Every summer since I was five, my dad sat us down under the farthest tree at the limits of our big yard. For hours on end, we had to stare at the hills behind our house while they illegally drank eighteen-packs of Budweiser on a dry rez.

"Look at that!" he would say over and over, sometimes hollering, sometimes slobbering. "My grandpa used to own all of this before the BIA came. These hills, the hills behind them, from here all the way to over there," he'd say, waving a fully extended arm. "Isn't it beautiful?"

Despite his excitement, he had four, sometimes five, unhappy kids sitting like bumps on a log. It wasn't long before we were whining to Mom, asking to go inside because it was too hot or it was getting cold, the grass was itchy, we were scared of spiders and wood ticks, or because the mosquitoes were biting. From the hottest parts of the day until a million stars lit the black sky, Dad would sit consuming countless sunsets. "Come. Sit with me. Come look at this." But I complained, "It's the exact same as yesterday! The same field, the same creek, the same trees, the same hills, the same sky." But this view was his breath.

Later, it became mine.

At eighteen, I moved from the Great Plains to the granite hills of New Hampshire, where I was suffocated by towering, claustrophobic trees. Now when I go home, the simple size of the sky leaves me speechless. My eyes skim in vast circles trying to swallow all that is above. Every time I descend the big hill into the valley of the Northern Cheyenne, I get butterflies and my heart races—that's the feeling I long for. My spirit reconnects with the land. *I'm home.*

Those nights under the trees with Dad, sitting on a log or in the grass, he fantasized about birthday parties, barbeques, and stargazing on a wraparound deck. I would imagine this freshly stained, elegant hardwood sculpture attached to our dilapidated HUD house. I laugh now when I recall these images of grandeur I had in my head about that deck. We never had the money to build such a thing, so I took note and made it a personal life goal. *Build Dad a deck* was right up there with *Take Dad to a Denver Broncos game at Mile High Stadium.*

Working toward significant milestones like this drove me to do well in school. Luckily, school came easily for me. I constantly wondered how things worked. When I was four, I concluded that our station wagon's air conditioner was probably a huge ice cube under the hood that turned the air cold before it came inside the car. Around the age of six, my theory was shattered when I realized the ice would melt. I was sent straight back into the world of wonder, but I enjoy it there.

Fortunately, my parents were two college-educated individuals who understood that there was a bigger world out there, and in order to maneuver it, one must be educated. My mom would start mornings with "Wake up, you've got to go to school!" More than that, going to college was an expectation in my home. In seventh grade, I made my two best friends promise me we would go to college together to try to inspire them. It didn't work.

In order to want to learn, one must know what learning is worth. Nearly every home across Indian country is riddled with distractions and discouragement; mine was no different. I will never forget the times we had to improvise when we were out of toilet paper, using coffee filters or crumpled newspaper instead; the times we slept three to a bed and cuddled in the wintertime because the largest window in our house was actually only thick plastic sheeting; or the times we put mayonnaise on bread with cheese and called it *the Cheese Deluxe* because that's all we had to eat. I carry one clear memory of my older brother looking in the bare fridge then turning around to ask me, "Do you want a *Cheese Deluxe?*" with the biggest smile, like he was about to serve me super-special ice-cream cake with extra sprinkles on my birthday. Matching his excitement, I gleamed yes.

We never had a lot but we always had each other. We definitely strug-gled, but we survived *together*. I made sure of that. When my parents didn't make it home from their drunk-weekend escapades, I stood on a chair to cook dinner for us and crawled on top of the drier to reach the washer's dial so we'd have clean clothes for school. When they brought the party home, I bathed the babies and put them to bed in the room farthest from the drinking. I sang them to sleep over sounds of fighting. In the morn-ing, I'd wake them and press on knowing one thing: I never wanted my children to someday go through what we were going through.

I joined every extracurricular activity possible so I didn't have to go home at night—student council, Indian Club, Math Club, volleyball, bas-ketball, cheerleading, cross-country, track—the list goes on. These sanc-tuaries were also résumé builders that I was unknowingly racking up. My parents never attended parent-teacher conferences because, they said, "we already know you're doing good. We don't need to listen to seven teachers all tell us the same thing." A few high-school mentors claimed I could go to any college I wanted, while other teachers suggested I be more "realis-tic" and enlist in the military instead. I even argued with an army recruiter once. He aggressively questioned how I thought I was going to pay for school and shoved the GI Bill down my throat. Honestly, I didn't quite know how I would but I knew I'd find a way.

* * *

School was my escape from the Little Mama responsibilities I had at home, but even school had its own set of dysfunctions. My junior-high English teacher moved to the high school when we did. We were in a different building with a brand-new classroom, yet she was teaching the exact same lessons.

"A noun is a person, place, or thing."

"Ugh, but we learned this last year."

Equally irritated, "We can't move on until everyone understands the basics," she said.

This meant *I* couldn't move on until everyone absent or misbehaving had learned the lessons from last year and the year before. Math class was similar. Ms. Williams would write equations on the board. "Now solve for *x* and give me an answer," she'd turn around to face the class. "Anyone but Cinnamon." On a good day, I'd sit and silently suppress my frustration. On a bad day I'd spout, "Well, what's the point of even *being here?*"

Ms. Williams knew she would lose me if she didn't keep my interest. Algebra material typically taught in one year anywhere else was broken into two years at my school. I began in Algebra IA, but she quickly bumped me up to Algebra IB with the sophomores. The following year, I started with Algebra II before Ms. Williams transferred me into Advanced Math and doubled that with Geometry. My brother wasn't happy when his sister from two grades below was all of a sudden in his class.

Ms. Williams believed in me when I didn't believe in myself, because I didn't believe in myself. Native youth are constantly hit over the head with statistics stating we aren't going to do much in life except make babies, go to prison, get sick, or die young. I never wanted to be one of those statistics, but I didn't always believe I could defy them either. Ms. Williams knew, and her acute attentiveness to my capabilities and partnership in challenging the norm was critical in propelling my academic growth.

Similarly, my literature teacher found ways to push me ahead. Mr. Nelson suggested that in addition to my junior English class I simultaneously take his Advanced Literature course, which was reserved for seniors. He routinely pulled me aside and gave me talks, "I want you to take this book home. When you get to college, they're going to expect you to have read the classics. *Catcher in the Rye* is on that list." So while the class was trudging through *Crime and Punishment*, I was expected to discuss Dostoyevsky, with Salinger on the side (not knowing years later I would share library space with J. D. himself). Mr. Nelson's bright blue eyes held hope for me. My heart understood the seriousness of their expectations. *You can do this. You're going to do this. Not just for you, for everybody.*

These teachers walked me to the unsupportive guidance counselor's office and spoke fervently on my behalf, vouching for why it was imperative I be allowed to take their advanced courses. They went to bat for me against the oppositional counselor. They stand out because they cared enough to carve a path for me; everyone else just schlepped along and expected me to do the same. It was always a fight against a failing system.

There's the story of this girl, Monique. She earned a full-ride basketball scholarship to Minot State University. Every Indian kid dreams of playing professional ball, and those who have a head on their shoulders aspire to play college ball. Just prior to her fall arrival, the university informed her she was one lab science short. She was told if she attended a community college for a semester to earn the credit, her scholarship would be held and they'd keep her spot on the team. Unfortunately, the immediacy of life on the rez has the power to force one's aspirations for tomorrow out of sight as they are blinded by the short-lived thrill of today. As it turned out, Mo soon got pregnant. The fans at Minot State were never captivated by our amazingly talented number 23. Just like that, the potential life-changing college opportunity she had earned slipped away. From the heights of excitement we had for her, we all watched this star fall. We fell with her.

I swore I would never let this happen to me. I studied the state graduation requirements as a freshman and kept a personal, unofficial transcript. During my junior year, the school switched operating software and in the transfer, my grades had not been entered correctly. The next consultation I had with the counselor included her pressuring me into a class I had already taken. She had no record so she ignored my word and enrolled me in a course I had already aced. I fled her office and returned with my little blue spiral-bound notebook whose opening pages listed each class I had taken, quarter by quarter, complete with grades as stated on report cards. She then began to update her digital records based off my handwritten notebook. I won.

But Indian students in underfunded, rural public schools don't always win. Basic administrative incompetence killed Monique's dream—and we all mourned because it was our dream, too. She was one of our brightest stars, a smooth ball handler with a killer three and the greatest laugh. She is still a living legend all her own, and her smile still shines, but she never got her chance to take classes at Minot, step foot on that court to play under those lights, or snap the net to make those fans go wild. *How many Moniques exist?*

The lives of our children are being determined by bitter indifference. I can count on one hand how many individuals truly believed I had a future. Betty, the Montana GEAR UP coordinator, was in the ranks with Nelson and Williams. When I was a freshman in high school, she encouraged me to attend the Montana Apprenticeship Program (MAP) at Montana State University in Bozeman. It was a six-week long laboratory research program that provided more than $1,000 in stipends. I refused to fill out the forms because I didn't think I'd get in, I wasn't technically old enough. The application only had boxes to mark if you were a sophomore, junior, or senior. Betty said, "So draw a box and check it." After eighteen years of existence, MAP accepted its first freshman.

Despite these academic successes, I was full of doubt. I had my sober parents prepping me for the "real world" and my drunk parents telling me I wasn't going to do anything with my life. In school, select mentors encouraged, "You can do it! Shoot for the moon!" But it was all a cliché. I read those words on stickers and posters for years. It meant nothing. I only thought I stood out because I did my work; that was it. I didn't believe I was smart.

The day I received my ACT test results opened my eyes. Standing there holding the paper in two hands, I learned that I scored above both the Montana state and national averages. That very moment took me out of Lame Deer High School and placed me in context with every other US high-school student. That day, I believed.

Later, I received a recruitment flyer in the mail for the Native American Fly-In Program at Dartmouth College. I was scared to visit the East Coast because I imagined that everything everywhere looked like Times Square. *What did I know?* That October, I was flown to campus, hosted by a Native student, and attended scheduled presentations regarding admissions, financial aid, and student life. I found "the College on the Hill" nestled cozily in the woods. Strangers smiled as I walked across the Green, and it made me feel welcome. I saw the Native students tease each other hard and laugh, then I thought: I could go to Dartmouth.

My college decisions narrowed down to (1) accepting a full ride at MSU–Bozeman, which I was already familiar with thanks to MAP; or (2) potentially taking loans at an Ivy League school that I knew nothing about, which was located clear across the country. Betty warned, "You're accustomed to chaos and you might gravitate toward it in life." She went on, "If you're only four hours away and something goes wrong or your mom calls you crying, you're going to do everything in your power to come home and help your siblings or save your mom. What if that's every weekend?" It was true; my heart is too big. So I intentionally made it nearly impossible for me to return home at the drop of a hat. I put more than two thousand miles between my family and me. That was the hardest short-term but most beneficial long-term thing I've ever done for myself.

My freshman floor mates were busy exploring the world as fresh-out-of-the-house eighteen-year-olds, but I was constantly calling home to check on my brothers and sisters. "Do you have clothes for tomorrow? Do you guys need bread?" I often asked teachers and friends to drop off a gallon of milk or spare roll of toilet paper. I played puppet master from thousands of miles away while "schmobs" incessantly toured frat basements, chugging Keystone Light. I couldn't stand the scene because it reeked of the same stale beer smell that plagued my childhood. More so, that "fun" didn't appeal to me because I was suffering from a reverse sort of empty-nest syndrome. Immense guilt shrouded me because Dartmouth provided a roof over my head, an open-till-2-a.m. food court, and endless water and electricity. Simple things most people don't think about. Meanwhile, I just abandoned my siblings back home and they sometimes went without.

I had real, faraway things to worry about, more important than Earth Science or Linguistics. Oftentimes while studying, I found myself staring at a light fixture that I knew cost more than my entire house. It was hard not to hate the light fixture. It was hard not to hate everything. I felt like Dartmouth carelessly threw money around and I knew so many people who could use it. I was infuriated that people were paid to bag leaves all day when the next time the wind blew, *more would fall*. Ungrateful students would brush past the quiet, gray-haired men who cleaned dorm bathrooms every week as if they weren't somebody's grandpa. They never said *excuse me* or *thank you*. I immediately saw two classes of people: those who clean toilets and those who attend Dartmouth, and the latter arrogantly deemed themselves more important. Everything that was prim and proper about my college caused me pain.

I was raised looking *up* at the federal poverty line, so I experienced a unique struggle in the Ivy League. While my classmates went on skiing trips and ventured up to Montreal, I had to work anywhere from one to three jobs to sustain myself (and my family, who often called asking for large sums of money). This meant I could never start studying until after dark. When I walked through the library on my way from class to work, I absolutely despised every student who could do their homework midday and socialize at night. But really, I was just jealous.

More than socioeconomic status though, the largest degree of difference I held was in my Indigenous worldview. In an ethics workshop, each member of the team was provided a false identity including age, race, and skill set. The team's goal was to determine which individuals should be tossed over the edge of a sinking boat in order to save the lives of others. Identities included an older Chinese scientist, a middle-aged African American surgeon, an autistic Caucasian child prodigy pianist, a two-month-old baby girl, and so forth.

The white kids in the workshop immediately assessed which individuals had the most to offer society once saved, valuing and devaluing people based on age or occupation—dare I say race unspoken. The one black student in the group was left repeatedly saying, "*Women and children?* What ever happened to *women and children?* No one runs into a burning building and starts asking what talents and education people have!" All the while, I sat in complete silence not wanting to expose the fact that this decision was easy for me: toss the baby overboard.

I was taught that we are not human beings on a spiritual journey; we are spiritual beings on a human journey. I believe that we come from the Spirit World and that our physical bodies, this flesh, is what the Creator gives us to live this life here. The spirits of the children and babies would be so new to this world that it would be easier for them to return to where they came from, as they weren't given a chance to fully learn how to live here yet. Sending the children back to their unborn state made sense to me. But saying that in the boisterous environment that was the timed ethics activity would have only served to depict me as a demented child killer, echoing the age-old Euro-American stereotype of "the Savage Indian."

My concept of life and spirit and my sense of self clashed violently with that of my peers. These fundamental differences were the hardest aspects of diversity to endure because I had few options: I could openly express my beliefs at the risk of being judged and ridiculed; I could give an anthro-history lesson every chance I got; or I could say nothing at all and remain misunderstood. At the end of the day, I just wanted to return to live among the like-minds and like-hearts in the lands where I grew up.

These moments make you miss your family, your culture, and your people. It's not the simple challenges of academia itself that makes us want to quit school and move home. It's our obligation to tolerate and educate our ignorant peers *and professors* that weighs heavily on us. I've watched Native students withdraw from Dartmouth, and I respected their courage. At the same time, I hated them for leaving us behind.

During my freshman fall, I took Writing 5 and was quick to find the course filled with nicely dressed, full-pocketed city dwellers. Almost all the other Native students had been placed into the lower Writing 2–3.

I was alone at this level. I was alone in the class. We read Sandra Cisneros's *The House on Mango Street*, and I was excited to discuss the similarities I found between the underprivileged protagonist, Esperanza, and myself. With every page, Cisneros handed me encouragement in the form of a Latino version of my own home. Her story of hope, using education as a ladder out of an extremely impoverished community, resonated deeply with me. To this day, my heart sings the same song as the last few lines. *They will not know I have gone away to come back. For the ones I have left behind. For the ones who cannot out.*

Professor Thum opened class for discussion, and before I could raise my hand, he called on the blonde Victoria from New York City. Bursting out of her wealthy mouth came a disgust-coated sentence that stopped me in my tracks, "First of all, I just have to say, I can't believe there are people in America that still *live* like this!" My intent to share deflated slowly and painfully. I retreated into silence as the others commented on the dire conditions of the poverty-stricken neighborhood, disadvantaged school, indigent family, and the violence and abuse present in the book. Their privileged lens of perception obstructed their view of the story. They couldn't see beyond the surface of destitution to appreciate the uniqueness of culture, the beauty of Esperanza's struggle, or the amazing triumph she achieved in the end. My triumph.

They couldn't see *me*.

Only those who come from where I'm from, or a place truly like it, can feel what I feel. Like Esperanza, I come from a special place with a unique history. Our tight-knit communities were traditionally governed by warrior societies before the Indian Reorganization Act of 1934. Now, each enrolled member is a citizen of the Northern Cheyenne Nation. Our grandmothers and grandfathers give us stories and songs, and we draw empowerment from that. They make us strong. There is a very particular love and pride that lives at home. It doesn't exist anywhere else. When you leave it, your heart aches for it. There is no money there but that doesn't mean we are poor. In fact, we are rich—rich in land, culture, and family. We are the blood of great leaders, resisters, and protectors. Expressing our inherent sovereignty and freedom was once deemed "hostile." That's us.

I will never forget the words of Professor Thum. He inquired about my lack of participation the day we covered *The House on Mango Street*. I told him I was reluctant to admit I lived in poverty like Esperanza, but I knew my home was beautiful regardless. I was the only one who held the perspective that I did. There were no other Natives in class to have my back. He responded, "Cinnamon, if you *had* shared in class, imagine what insight you would have given your classmates. The professor's assignments can only make up half of the college education. The other half must come from *you*."

From that point forward, I did my best to speak up in class despite the sense of inadequacy that floated around me. Professors lectured with words I had to take note of and look up in a dictionary later. When other students spoke, they always sounded so important. Often, I couldn't respond in discussions because I didn't understand certain words people used.

I quickly learned: if I had a question, I must ask, and if I had a statement, I must share. What mattered was *what* I said, not *how* I said it. My words might not have been extravagant but they held power. As time went on, my classroom presence grew stronger. After years of being in this intense academic environment, I began to inhale the words of those around me. "Random," "sketchy," and "booted" were a few of the first. Later came words like "Foucauldian," "dehumanization," and "Indigeneity." I was always surprised at the taste of these words when they came out of my mouth.

I've come pretty far. When I visited on the fly-in program, one of the Native students on a panel discussed the same issue. She said, "It feels like everyone here is articulate and speaks so eloquently." I focused on the word *eloquently* as it did slow-motion flips in my head, similar to a scene from *Sesame Street*. I think it was the first time I heard the word in context, which only contradicted her point: she was being articulate and eloquent while trying to explain being uncomfortable with everyone else being articulate and eloquent. Years later, I hosted a prospective student from home who was visiting campus through her fly-in program. I knew she was a shy girl but she seemed extra quiet throughout the program. When alone, she confided in me, "Errrret, I feel like I talk just purely *rezzed* out!" *A girl after my own heart.*

Lame Deer is the center of the reservation and home to the Chief Littlewolf Capitol Building. There is one high school, one post office, one grocery store, and one gas station. The only stoplight, a blinking four-way flasher, directs traffic where Montana Highway 39 meets US Highway 212. Beautiful hills colored with red shale and evergreen trees cradle my hometown, which is often splashed with vibrant sunsets and crowned with bright starry skies. In January, if we're lucky, the northern lights will share their subtle rhythms and movement. In July, we hold our largest powwow celebration and return the favor by singing and dancing into the night.

A passerby may only be able to see the trash that is constantly blown in from the unkempt local dump. There are often plastic bags stuck in tree branches and barbed wire fences. Graffiti splashes everything: churches, stop signs, houses, buildings, cars, and even sometimes mangy, starving dogs who wander unclaimed. Yards are not fenced and there are hardly sidewalks to speak of. Every lawn has a broken-down car or two, or ten.

The bottom concrete porch step to my house has disintegrated; the front door doesn't fit the frame; and our toilet bowl—rigged with a toothbrush—leaks through the rotting floor into the basement. Like many, we have holes in our walls and mice problems in the wintertime. It gets so cold that pipes freeze unless you keep water dripping all through the night. We have our share of substance-abusing homeless people; the difference is they're our family. That was my grandpa asleep by the side of the Chicken Coop cuddling Black Velvet in a paper bag. Despite everything, I *love* my beautiful home because that is where my people exist.

Home is shy Native girls approaching their prime with unbridled beauty eating sunflower seeds or pickles or sucking lemons while walking uptown. Home is little Indian boys riding horses bareback down the way to Grandma's house while their rez dogs run alongside them. Home is a tin hall full of pros, double-fisting bingo daubers with six cards in front of them, just waiting for the announcer to call out B-6. Home is a high-school gym full of screaming Indians watching a basketball game as if it meant life or death for *everyone*. Home is the spring flowing fresh and sacred surrounded by prayer flags tied to tree branches honoring that *water is life*. Home is the heartbeat of the drum alive in the same place it's always been—from back when we had everything on into when we had nothing—still strong, even now. Home is in my heart because I couldn't live without it.

I assumed the other Natives at Dartmouth were all going to be rez kids like me. I was quick to learn otherwise. At Native student events, we would begin with introductions. While standing in a circle, one by one, each person would share their name, tribe, hometown, and major. *Hello! My name is Cinnamon Spear. I'm Northern Cheyenne from Lame Deer, Montana, and I'm a Native American studies major.* But then you'd get these kids who would say, "I am so-and-so and I'm *part* Cherokee" or "I am *part* Choctaw." Part this or part that, and that confused me. I thought either you *were* or you weren't. Parts didn't make sense to me. I am from a community that is 99 percent Native and there is no other identity. It was simple: the border towns were full of whites and the rez was all Native.

Sure, you'd have those two kids in school who were black or white, but even *they* were Cheyenne.

Then you'd get, "I'm so-and-so and I'm this tribe and this tribe and this tribe and this tribe and this tribe and . . ." until the list was ten nations long. I never understood that either. I wondered to myself, "So which *one* are you? Whose *traditions* did you grow up with? Who are the *people* you come from? Where do you call *home*?" But a lot of these students do not know their traditional lands as home and their people have never made up their community. Sometimes these kids have never even *visited* their homelands or even *met* other Natives. I didn't understand them and they didn't understand me.

One time another student asked me, "What are you?" I responded, "Northern Cheyenne." Evidently, this wasn't enough. "Well, Northern Cheyenne and what?" My answer remained, "Just Cheyenne." Then, while scoffing, he saw fit to comment on my complexion, "Well obviously you're like white, so Cheyenne and *what*?" Unfazed but irritated, "*Just Cheyenne.*" I know what I look like, but my appearance leaves only others confused. I know who I am.

My identity is solidly rooted in the hills of the homeland I come from. My blood flows fierce and everlasting like the fresh water from Crazy Heads. My feet can walk among ivy walls, brick, and concrete only because they first ran red-shale roads, played in the dirt at Ice Wells, and stood on Morning Star Peak. My fingers can dance across this keyboard only because they first picked buffalo berries and plums with my grandma, hooked worms to catch fish at Green Leaf or Tongue River with Dad, and even made a million of my sister's favorite mud pies.

I know what I come from, and that drove me to do well. My success is everyone's success. When I felt like giving up on this foreign academic world, my motivation was the many smiling faces and open arms that welcome me home when I return; the little girls that run across the gym plowing into me, excited to see me and give me a hug; the aunties and cousins who love to hear my stories of travel and adventure; the young ballers and recent graduates who now know college is a possibility for them because they've watched me do it; the cars that pull over crazily on the street to say hi and show me their babies because they never know how long I'll be home.

It is them. They are me.

This community-as-self identity is the source of both my strength *and* my loneliness. College retention rates for Native students are lower than most and it has absolutely nothing to do with our academic capability, interest, or passion. In addition to the systemic racism and institutional-ized inequality, it's the simple distance and heartache of being removed from the people, homelands, and love that we were born into that makes higher education difficult for us.

The ruthless individualism and singular success of the "American Dream" directly clashes with the Cheyenne values I was raised to respect. Giveaways are embedded in our social structure to ensure that when one person does well, they share their success with other members of the tribe. Our society functions communally, everyone celebrates and struggles to-gether. There is a profound sense of isolation associated with being more than two thousand miles away, in the Abenaki people's original homeland, surrounded by a variety of personalities from all parts of the globe. But if you're not connected to a people or tribal community, you don't fully understand the impact of this separation.

Indian country revolves around basketball games, babies being born, funerals, ceremonies, rodeos, and powwows. My first year away, I called a friend who laid the phone by her stereo so I could listen to my little brother play his senior-year basketball tournament over the radio, over the phone. I wanted to welcome my firstborn niece into this world but I missed her Cheyenne naming ceremony by ten days that term. My fam-ily has mourned the passing of one uncle, two grandmas, and three grand-pas without me there. My education kept me from the Fourth of July Chief's Powwow when Northern Cree was our host drum and the Indian National Finals Rodeo where my little cousin was titled the bull-riding champion of the world! Each of these instances causes a degree of social separation. You can't retell those stories if you don't have the memories to share. Missing the highs and lows from home broke my heart, but no matter how bad I wanted to leave Dartmouth, I wasn't going to drop out. That would mean failing everyone.

I had to learn to bloom where I was now planted. I grew to find value and be thankful for the extensive diversity among the students that actu-ally came from other tribal communities. My first friend at Dartmouth was Quinault from the state of Washington. Her grandpa was a generous man, their family's totem was the whale, and she had a beautiful traditional cape in her room decorated with abalone buttons. My Great Plains sisters and I kept each other close because we were *home* for one another. We helped each other bless our dorm rooms at move in and smudge off during stressed out finals. My lacrosse player friend invited me up to Akwesasne Mohawk Territory in New York for a game, and his family showed us around their beautiful river waters on a pontoon. My Navajo friend from

Tuba City, Arizona, used Mountain Smoke to pray and taught me the importance of their four sacred mountains. My bear clan, Anishinaabe friend kept birch bark in her room, told me Nanaboozhoo stories, and cooked manoomin for me often. My Iñupiaq friends from the North Slope of Alaska told stories of seal hunting and whaling; they even had me eating tuttu and uunaalik. My friend from the Pueblo of Acoma in New Mexico invited me to his Pueblo's feast day, where I watched him participate in traditional dances atop their three-hundred-foot-tall mesa and was teased for having to eat from the "kids pot" because the chili was too hot for me.

Those of us who come from the depths of Indian country have an instant respect for one another based on the shared struggle of everyday life. We understand the intense longing for the beauty that exists back home. We also know how it feels to hear our classmate presume, "Wait, doesn't *everyone's* parents have a 401(k)?" Yet you're not even sure what a 401(k) *is* and your family still lives hand to mouth. Shooting a quick glance in class and locking eyes with another rez kid provides an unspoken comfort in a moment like this. We hold an undying support for one another because our hearts are made heavy, often, with good and bad news from home. The stories we catch over the phone range from the most beautiful doctoring ceremony, full of song and prayer, that healed a three-year-old boy and rid him of cancer to two teenage relatives who partied together, but one woke up bloody in a jail cell not remembering he stabbed his little brother to death while blackout drunk the night before. Everything echoes in our ear and rattles us from afar. But we stay on the grind and push ourselves to thrive in the environment that is Dartmouth—even if only to prove wrong every single person who ever told us, or silently thought to themselves, that we would never become anything more than a teen-pregnancy, prison, or suicide statistic.

When you bring Native students directly from tribal communities together, we provide each other with a unique support system that no institutional office can re-create. Administrative officers hardly understand its depth. You can offer "Speed Reading" classes and tutoring, but no sponsored activity will ensure our success. We need each other. We grow from the cultural exchanges that take place, often around food. We learn of each other's jokes, arts, languages, taboos, traditions, tribal politics, governance structures, environmental issues, and more. There is a real beauty in creating this Native network and it makes each of us stronger.

Families in Indian country encourage their relatives to go to Dartmouth because it has the largest Native student population out of any of the Ivies. Unfortunately, students who came from tribal communities were few and far between. For every rez kid there were nearly twenty box-checkers who merely "identified" as Native American on their college application. There's an injustice done when nearly two hundred of Dartmouth's four thousand students are listed on the books as Native American but maybe only fifty make up the on-campus community on a good day, while the other three hundred and fifty float around not even understanding the depth of the box they checked.

Being Native American is more than claiming an ethnicity because your great-grandmother was this or that type Indian. It is more than carrying a piece of government-issued paper with a number on it. It's more than teasing about living in tipis or loving commodity cheese. Being Native American is more than throwing on a jingle dress and dancing at every powwow, or using social media to take a stand on trending hot issues, because you can and you think it looks cool.

Being Indigenous means knowing you're alive because your ancestors fought and died for you. It means understanding you're the inherent recipient of blood memory, and the carrier of your people's past *and* future. Being Indian means you belong to a tribe. It means loving the living collective of which you are a part, not just knowing its name. It means voting for your tribal president and investing in contemporary local issues.

When I was growing up, my dad would always say, "We are a nation within a nation!" Then I got to Dartmouth and heard Professor Dale Turner echo, "Identifying as an American Indian college student is an intrinsically political act." So I learned early on and had reaffirmed that it's not about "race" or "ethnicity." It's about legal rights and sovereignty, and there's a responsibility in that.

Not everyone even realizes this. Furthermore, not every Native student at Dartmouth has basic familiarity with commonplace cultural and social standards. I knew students who weren't comfortable around the Native community until their senior year. They explained their distance was due to "not feeling Native enough." A girl once told me, "When I first met you, I was intimidated by you. My freshman fall, I heard you speak. You were *so* Native, and I was so *not*." I didn't get what she meant when she said it then. Now, I do.

Dartmouth is in the business of manufacturing Natives. These kids come to dinners and learn to make frybread and wojape. They learn how to smudge and pray, and they feel so sacred doing it. They listen to stories of rez life and learn that Indian jokes are really the funniest on earth—even though they don't get them at first. *Ayyyye.* Their friends teach them to bead and how to feel about Indian mascots. They take Native American studies courses on history and culture to arm themselves with an identity fed to them from books. They read *The State of Native Nations* to find out what Indian country looks like and lives like. They hug the older, wise, and intellectual Tuscarora professor at the end of class, and that makes them feel more human because through her and the love she emanates they feel connected to something real.

It's one thing to know who your people are but it's an entirely different thing when your people know who *you* are. During our Mother's Day Powwow, I sat on the Green in the sunlight at my vendor booth full of beadwork. I had my hustle going. This Choctaw boy excitedly dragged this girl by the arm and stood her in front of me. "Cinnamon, this is so-and-so. She's Northern Cheyenne!" *Oh?* I've never seen her before. "Where did you grow up?" I ask. "California." Per usual, "Who's your family?" She offered a name I didn't recognize. Curiously I question, "Have you ever gone home?" She said no, but added that her father was attending a college reunion somewhere in the state of Montana that summer, as if that was somehow relevant. "You should really try to visit home sometime," I encouraged, for I don't know what it means to be Northern Cheyenne and to never have stepped foot on our homelands. I don't know if she knows either but I didn't feel it was my place to teach her.

The other kids made me uncomfortable by asking questions and wanting to hear my stories while offering nothing in return. I shared, but grew protective of the knowledge I have after I watched one girl steal another girl's story about her grandmother. I was there when the first girl told her story and I was in the same room a time later when the second girl regurgitated it nearly verbatim to unknowing underclassmen acting as if it were her own, but *she* never knew her grandma! I couldn't believe it. I sat in conflicted silence putting walls up toward the culture vultures who took a little of this and a little of that to create their own pan-Indian identity. Exposure to this crazy amalgamation of nations perhaps made them feel more connected, but I was always left thinking they were just still so clueless.

Others read tales of government boarding schools while I've spent my whole life catching my mother's tears as she recounted her traumas, knowing full well that her mother was a survivor of the same destruction. Assigned readings on congressional policy and federal Indian law made me angry and sad because I saw how the government did it all, in writing. It wasn't Amnesty International's report "Maze of Injustice" that taught me that one in three Native women will be raped or sexually abused in their lifetime—my mother has three daughters. Students who come straight from Indian country have lived among the truth that these skewed statistics are reflecting only *reported* cases. This is our reality. Our Dartmouth education only supplements lived experience. So when we read our homework, we are not learning so much as we are reliving, and that takes a deep emotional toll on us.

No one can take college courses or spend a few years around other adolescent Natives and graduate knowing what it's like to *truly* be part of a tribal community. Our homes are made up of elders and babies, dancers and veterans, artists and philosophers, medicine men and drunks. There is a certain way you carry yourself around each member of your community. Culture is composed of social roles and unspoken cues. Living on the land and having a connection to earth, sky, water, and stars is important. Being raised within this structure is what helps fully shape a Native person and with over 565 different federally recognized tribes today, there isn't one set of rules. There is no one Native experience; even *this* is only *one* Native's experience.

Admittedly, it's like I'm writing on eggshells. Reflecting on my ignorant (albeit very visceral and real) reactions to many aspects of Dartmouth is not an easy thing for me to do. It took me years to dispel discomfort, set aside judgment, and actually listen to and learn from the different and difficult experiences of my peers. I eventually felt compassion for them—many of them are the living result of the forced assimilation policies of Indian removal, boarding schools, relocation, or their parents just moving away to give their children more opportunities, a better life. At the end of the day, it's not their fault.

So while we strive to find balance along the vast spectrum of Indigenous identity that exists in the world, Dartmouth should make sincere efforts to recruit, admit, and support not just "Native American" college applicants who likely come from urban prep schools and are sure to do well and make great numbers, but those students in rural tribal communities who are empowered by their cultural connection and draw from that strength to challenge their failed education system for a fair chance. There are standout, drug-and-alcohol-free young leaders who are currently enduring ridiculously unfair circumstances but continue to make good choices, therefore inspiring the younger generations who look up to them. They are fighting, right now, to create a better life for themselves and their siblings or unborn children. They are brilliant individuals, their families cherish them, their communities love them, and they are remarkable ambassadors for their tribal nations.

Dartmouth, as a historically wealthy institution, has both a great obligation and an amazing opportunity in its founding for the purpose of Native education. We are depicted in the college seal as naked savages, complete with feathers in our hair, being guided out of the wilderness toward civilization under the rays of "the Good Book." To this day, the weather-vane scene of founder Eleazer Wheelock towering above an unidentified "Indian" sitting cross-legged on the ground eerily overshadows our entire Dartmouth existence. For four years, we live under images of colonization that sit atop beloved Baker Tower. A feeling of inferiority can reverberate deeply within us because of this, but students from tribal communities come from and have access to arts, medicines, languages, songs, philosophies, entire *worlds* of knowledge that others do not. We have the power to reverse the roles and sit the colonizer and his descendants on the ground to teach above them. *I think I'm doing that right now.*

Dartmouth took me from my people in order to educate me about many different things. After a while, I decided, "You know what, Dartmouth? Let me take *you* home and teach you something." I spent seven months during graduate school on the rez and used my master's thesis project to produce a documentary. I took the beauty from home and put it on-screen for others to see, hear, and feel. My film, *Pride & Basketball*, explores the theory that, in the postcolonial era, the basketball court has transformed into a modern day battlefield where historic tribal rivalries are relived and non-Native race relations are played out. Since our young warriors are no longer riding up and down across the open plains stealing horses, earning war honors, or protecting our homelands, the court is one of the few places where our young people are acknowledged for their bouts of bravery and leadership. A sense of individual, familial, and communal pride is derived from what a person can do with a basketball in their hands.

While filmmaking, I was welcomed into the lives of the youth, their families, the school, and the community. My people honored me by opening their homes and hearts to me, sharing their words and giving me their tears. An outsider wouldn't have been able to create the product I did. I was fluidly in the classroom, locker room, and on the bus with these kids. I stood in prayer with my young relations, and sang the Cheyenne Flag Song with the drum at the start of every game. The coach asked the players to circle up and listen to me share stories of college and travel. I encouraged the youth to want more for themselves—not to *leave* the reservation but just to be a better person, and be the best at whatever it is they love to do. Formal education isn't for everybody;

and as much as we need people to leave and learn, we also need people to stay and learn.

In the history of Lame Deer High School, which opened its doors in 1992 and maintains a 50 percent graduation rate, I am so far the only student to have gone to a four-year institution and graduate in four years, the only person to attend the Ivy League, and by far the only one to receive a master's degree. I know what I represent and I recognize my responsibility in this. For the first time ever, the word "master's" is floating around my reservation. I've heard young men say, "You're making a film about basketball for your master's? Man, I want to get a master's!"

Just the other day, I got a message from a young girl back home. "Ever since I can remember, you've been my role model, graduating from Lame Deer and going to an Ivy League college. I want to be just like you, successful. You're beautiful in every way. There are like rays of sunshine that spring out of you every time I see you. You're spectacular. I love you." My heart soars. Words from the youth are the purest affirmation that I've done it the right way: I left the rez, but I've never left the rez; I am still there, and they are still with me.

We're taught to be humble about things so it always makes me a bit uncomfortable to speak this way, especially awkward having to write it. When I shared my uneasiness with an older lady friend of mine, she responded, "I know it never feels right tooting your own horn, but you, my girl, need to blow it loud for your relations!" People ask me, "How did you do it?" and it's always hard for me to answer that question. One step at a time, I guess. Creator has and continues to bless me as I journey in this life. I have been gifted with voice and the ability to craft words to create images. It's time for us to tell our own stories, and I will tell them for all those who share my experiences but cannot write them down this way.

Writing is my sanctuary, my freedom, but also my duty. As I fly back and forth between poverty and privilege, both states existing on and off the reservation, I realize I am a super-exposed, bicultured hybrid. With that, it is my responsibility to teach the world about the Northern Cheyenne people, and, likewise, it is my responsibility to teach my people about the world.

Mókéé'e náhesevéhe. Natsistahe.

"You have a strong name," my aunt told me. "*Little Woman*. That was your grandmother's name. You should always let the people know who you are, in Cheyenne, when you speak."

I am of the Morning Star people; I dance with and for the Thunder Valley tiospaye. Though I come from the sky, my heart beats from deep within the hills. At the core of my identity is the land—it is who I am, and I am where I come from.

Cinnamon Spear was raised in a large family on the reservation in Lame Deer, Montana. She earned a bachelor's degree in Native American studies from Dartmouth College in 2009. Cinnamon then moved to Pine Ridge, South Dakota, where she worked at Red Cloud Indian School. Her time there allowed her to strengthen her spirituality with her Oglala Lakota relatives, historic allies of the TsiTsisTas and Suhtaio. Returning again to her alma mater, she received a master of arts in liberal studies degree with a creative writing focus in 2013. She is currently serving as a public affairs specialist at the Indian Health Service headquarters in Washington, DC, and continues to share her story outside of work.

8

Village Girl   AlexAnna Salmon

We lost my father on February 27, 2008. I was five thousand miles away at school when I got the life-changing phone call from my family in Igiugig, Alaska: "We think Dad has been in a plane crash." At that moment, my world stopped turning. I fell to my knees in sheer desperation, praying my heart out for three hours, when he was confirmed dead. In shock, I packed my bag and embarked on the longest journey home. I did not stay home long to deal with the aftermath: I knew my dad wanted more than anything for me to graduate from Dartmouth College, so I returned to school for my final semester. School was my escape from the shock, but it was rough and I ran into every problem imaginable. I was in a time crunch to complete my thesis, my laptop crashed, the funeral set me behind in all my classes, and I didn't feel the drive to accomplish anything.

One day I hit rock bottom and retreated to my dorm room to cry myself to sleep. I was so alone, and the only person I needed was my dad. I knew that if he were alive, I would just call him, and he'd jump to help me and take care of my problem with lightning speed. I would express my gratitude and say that he never ceases to amaze me. "Daddy did it again!" would be his response, and deep down he'd find great satisfaction in being able to help. I had taken it for granted that I had a father who'd do anything for me. This thought made me cry even harder, and I sobbed into my pillow that my life was over!

The vivid dreams that followed his death haunted me, until they forced me to see the silver lining:

My dad and I were flying together in some type of floatplane through the mountains at Battle Lake. The day was beautiful and sunny, the view one of our favorites. We were so content. Suddenly, my dad sat back, pushed his seat from the controls, and folded his arms. I thought he was joking and smiled . . . I thought he would take the controls as the plane swerved through the mountain pass, but no, he just waited for me to respond. I couldn't believe it; I had flown with my dad hundreds of times but never learned to fly myself—why bother if you have someone to do it for you? I hollered for him to fly, but he refused. After a playful minute, the mood turned serious, and I panicked as I realized he expected me to land the floatplane on the lake. I was so angry I could feel my blood boil! My heart was practically jumping out of my chest, but after a long standoff I grabbed the controls and safely landed the plane. I slammed out of the airplane screaming at him that it was not funny and he should never do that again! My dad just laughed at me! I screamed the obvious: "I DON'T EVEN KNOW HOW TO FLY AN AIRPLANE!!!" He simply said, "I knew you could do it," and walked off without a worry in the world. He knew that I had never flown, but his bet was on me. That was so typical of Dan Salmon— to have complete confidence that I could handle anything I put my mind to. He just knew I could do it.

The silver lining, which it took me some time to realize, was that my dad could no longer solve my problems for me. It became clear to me that I could continue to lie in a dark room not wanting to face another day of life, or I could step out and draw on my twenty-two years of Dan Salmon "boot camp" and figure out how to help myself. In the months following my father's death, I focused completely on myself—particularly how to finish college. I put thoughts of the internships I had been pursuing aside for the time, because I could not silence the underlying obligation I felt to return home to Igiugig.

I was born in the winter near my home village of Igiugig. I chose a stormy night to arrive. A medevac plane landed in the snowstorm, and my parents and the health aide were evacuated to the nearest hospital as the aide coached my mother not to deliver in the airplane. It was a close call, but we made it. No matter what my gender I was to be named Alex in honor of my great-grandfather, Alexi Gregory, my mother's dearest relation. Annie Wilson, the health aide who was soon to be my godmother, suggested that AlexAnna would be a beautiful name for me. So I carry the names of two people, my *Amau* (great-grandfather) and my *Kelussnaq* (godmother), as well as the Native name *Apapigainaq*—meaning "genuine grandfather," in following the Yup'ik tradition of naming a newborn after someone who has recently passed. He was described to me as "a funny old man who liked to tell jokes and pull pranks."

I was the second daughter of Daniel and Julia Salmon. My character was shaped by my upbringing and by this place called Igiugig to such an extent that most people will truly understand me only if they visit my village, for although I can recount story after story, no one from the Lower 48 can even begin to understand my home. My experiences are such that I cannot fully capture them in words. Igiugig is one of those places you must see to believe—or even imagine.

Igiugig (ig-ee-ah-gig) is located where Lake Iliamna—the largest lake in Alaska—flows into the Kvichak River (kwee-jack), home of the greatest sockeye salmon run in the world. I was born in the era before sewer systems, satellite television, and wireless Internet, and before the population of our village reached fifty. Igiugig's "main road" is in fact a little stretch of dirt road bordered by a bunch of homes and outbuildings clustered together between the river and the airport. We lived next door to my grandmother, across from the Russian Orthodox church, and a stone's throw from "downtown," where we had a general store, a health clinic, a recreation hall, a "washeteria," and a post office. A five-minute walk beyond town lies the school—the heart and soul of the village.

The village activities in Igiugig change with the season, and when I am away I sometimes miss the scenery and the activities even more than I miss my family. Every season brings scenery so spectacular that I find myself proclaiming in each, "This is the most beautiful time of year." In the spring, the main attraction is unquestionably the fracturing of the ice on our ocean-sized lake. The icebergs clink and chime as if toasting the renewal of the world; we all are lured to the river to watch it. Then the birds begin to return and it is time to hunt for bird eggs on the river islands. The defrosting tundra trails and rain showers create pond-size puddles to splash through on four-wheelers. Millions of salmon run up the river—first silver and then bright red as the season comes to a close. Bordering the rivers are the guest lodges, where visitors from all over the world compete for the best fishing and the finest trophy rainbow trout.

The locals keep themselves too busy to be bothered by the influx of tourists. There is always a lot of work to do: driftwood to be gathered for steam baths; salmon to smoke, can, and freeze; and berries to pick—first salmonberries, then blackberries and blueberries, and last cranberries. Beach gatherings, picnics, and riding four-wheelers are popular summer activities for those not headed to Bristol Bay for commercial fishing. These activities are all "extracurriculars" for people who work full-time in the community. They often leave work early on a nice day to participate in subsistence activities or simply to enjoy the outdoors.

My father, a white man from Penfield, New York, met my mother during the winter of 1984, when he was trapping along the Kvichak River while working for the Alaska Department of Fish and Game. Daniel R. Salmon measured six feet, five inches tall and wore size 13 boots. He attended the University of Alaska in Fairbanks, where he earned a degree in fisheries biology. When he met Julia Olympic, a village Native, they immediately were attracted to each other—perhaps he saw her as an inroad to life in Igiugig, and she saw him as a ticket to the great wide-world. Our family of seven was the largest in town and we lived in the center—the ideal location for "grand-central station," which our house resembled, with its constant flow of people coming to visit or borrow something. Our phone rang off the hook because my dad was tribal administrator of the Igiugig Village Council and also ran several businesses. He made no separation between home and work.

Once he became a father, my dad had a vested interest in the village and dedicated the rest of his life to making Igiugig a place where his children would want to stay forever. He said that he took me everywhere he went, carrying me on his back where I had an eagle-eye view of all that he did. He always treated me like an equal and valued my thoughts and opinions as he would those of an adult. Because we were born in an era before fresh groceries or running water were available, he acquired a pilot's license. Once my dad had wings we were truly spoiled in comparison to other village children, as he could fly to our regional hub and buy fresh fruits and fresh—NOT powdered—milk. My mom would cut up all the fresh goods and keep them on the table for all the village children to exclaim over. Because of that our house always had visitors and we gave away a lot of food. In our small village—a tiny dot on a great expanse of tundra, lakes, and ponds—we use airplanes like cars, only they are ten times more expensive. My dad slowly assumed more leadership and management titles, such as land use program officer of Igiugig Native Corporation, operations manager for Iliamna Lake Contractors, assemblyman of the Lake and Peninsula Borough, and Igiugig Airport manager; he also owned Igiugig Transport and Igiugig Boarding House.

As my father's schedule grew more demanding and mentally, physically, and emotionally taxing, so did that of his children. The Salmon kids grew up understanding four meanings of work: school, community service, chores, and employment, which were instilled in us so young that I can't remember not knowing. The first three were understood as "what was owed" and the last was "what was earned." Our family operated on the punishment/reward system, and hard work in all four areas was generously rewarded. Refusing or failing to accomplish "what was owed" resulted in various punishments, as my father had worked in a juvenile delinquent correctional facility before having his own children and he ran a tight ship. His authority was unquestionable, and he had endless ways to correct our wrong behaviors and attitudes. In fact, our New York relatives disciplined their unruly children with the threat of sending them to Uncle Danny's "boot camp." These four understandings of "work" were instilled at an age before I can even remember.

My mother provided a good balance to my father's parenting style. She was raised in Igiugig and was a lot more lenient than my father. She was the one we cried to if our feelings were hurt or we didn't feel well, and we would always ask her first if we wanted something. She didn't work outside our home, and she always planned fun activities for us: creating a garden, beading bracelets, baking cookies . . . She worked from home doing the bookkeeping and secretarial work for the village Native Corporation and managing the local store. She could sit at the kitchen table and process a pile of paperwork despite her many children running around the house. I couldn't wait for the day I would have my own pile of paperwork to handle and write checks. I would also browse through the grocery catalog and make suggestions about what I thought the store should sell, and I often helped my mother stock and dust the shelves. The bond I share with my mother is more about enjoying similar hobbies, our family history, and work in the Igiugig Native Corporation than spending quality time together, the way I did with my father.

I enjoyed a blissful childhood along with my siblings (Christina, Tanya, Jonathan, and Jeremy), our only first cousin, and whatever other kids were in town. We made friends with anyone, despite age differences. Our companions included kids who were visiting their relatives in Igiugig, and the teachers' kids, who lived in the village for only a few years. We spent the warmer days stomping through puddles and making mud pies, getting atrociously dirty. We loved to drive four-wheelers through the deep puddles— the faster we drove, the bigger the splash. We just could not keep away from the water and often spent our days at fish camp helping Gram, Mom, and our aunties pull in the fishnet, count the number of salmon, and transfer the fish to a large bin. The women would sharpen their *uluaq* (traditional Yup'ik knife) on large flat stones, and we kids jumped at the opportunity to lift a fish out of the bin and place it on the splitting table for them. We made miniature drying racks and tin smokehouses out of pop cans, feeding the fire with dried grass. Our attention soon shifted, and we would start to untangle our homemade fishing sticks—a piece of driftwood with fishing line wrapped around it. We would bait the large hook with fish eggs, stand on the stick, and swing the line out to the river, and then wait impatiently for a nibble. Once I caught a fish that fought so hard I almost had to give up and release my stick. We usually caught grayling—not a prized fish—and proudly offered then to Gram. She would split them along with the salmon and put them in the smokehouse too. Fish camp was like an amusement park of activity. Besides fishing we could swim, explore, spy on fishermen, and watch the fishing boats cruise by on their way to "the bay."

The Salmon kids were extraspoiled in terms of water activity because my dad worked the night shift for Fish and Game. Sometimes we would camp out with him, and that meant getting in a boat, traveling downriver, and spending the night in the "smolt tent." The tent was full of sonar equipment used to count the salmon smolt as they swam upstream. His job was to pull a net and get smolt samples to ship out. We would eat peanut butter sandwiches or canned chili for dinner, lay our sleeping bags on the floor, and get treated to one of my dad's famous ghost stories. Then he would say, "Stay here while I go check the net," and hop into the boat to go check the fish trap. Of course we would lie there scared out of our wits and wishing he would hurry back because of the "wolf" we heard howling in the distance! We would also help my dad with the smolt samples. His job was to take the scales and place them on a slide, and ours was to tally them on his clipboard. Throughout elementary school I thought I would grow up and work for the Alaska Department of Fish and Game. As it turns out, science and math are my worst subjects, and I am lucky if I can tell an arctic char from a grayling.

The long daylight hours made the summer season feel especially long, but in the far north fall approaches quickly. It seems the tundra turns to flame-colored golds, oranges, reds, and yellows overnight. It makes me envy the skill of a painter, especially as flocks of geese, ducks, and sandhill cranes form giant Vs overhead. Once the leaves change color, they fall with the first harsh autumn winds. Then it is moose-hunting season and the hunters go out every day, their anxiety escalating until they catch "their" moose. A moose will feed a family for a long time, much longer than a caribou, but I prefer the taste of caribou. My favorite food is caribou *patuq*—boiled leg bone, which serves up rich marrow and soft meat. For special occasions—my birthday, a "welcome home" or "going away" meal—my family will make a patuq bone just for me.

Fall was also when my family made our annual excursion to the big city of Anchorage. We flew out on a small bush airplane and stayed at a hotel. When we were very young the most exciting part of the trip was the hotel bathroom. We were obsessed with running water and bathtubs that were easily converted into swimming pools. The only thing more exciting was the Alaska State Fair. Our aunties and parents would team up to take my siblings and me to the fair to be filled with cotton candy and candied apples, which got us pretty hyped up as we raced through our ride tickets. We also did all of our school shopping in the city: four new sets of clothes each, two pairs of shoes (indoors/outdoors), new winter gear, and all the academic accessories.

My parents' favorite holiday arrived next: Back to School. We kids also could not wait to meet the new teachers, who would stay for an average of three years, or welcome back the old. Every morning we walked or biked to school early enough to play in the gym or on the computer before classes started. Most days we would hustle home, do our homework while eating a snack, and then run outdoors to enjoy the last of our freedom before dinnertime. After dinner it was time for chores, relaxing and reading, taking a steam bath, and then bed. I spent all day every day with my siblings. In hindsight, it was this togetherness that created our special bond and was why we enjoyed living in the village. But at the time there was a lot of fighting and competition among us, and we longed for our idea of "real friends."

Igiugig's Post Office Hill bears the remains of the old post office, which is nothing more than an overgrown shack. But when we were young it was the greatest place for sledding and thus a hubbub of activity. If we did not have sleds we rode downhill on plastic garbage bags or tarps. One Christmas we woke up to two sleds each from Santa Claus—a runner sled and plastic tow-sled—which made for the best sledding season ever. We impatiently (and sometimes daringly) awaited the "go-ahead" to cross the frozen ponds and lakes that surround Igiugig to find the best skating, ice fishing, and towing grounds. After we reached the age of seven and proved our driving ability on four-wheelers and snow machines, we were allowed to tow each other along the trails within walking distance of home, in case we got stuck in a snowdrift or ran out of gas. I miss the love of winter I had as a kid.

When I was five years old I was the only one that age in the village, so I started school when my older friends started taking classes. Igiugig is a village that supports its youth: I have worked in the general store since I was eleven and I was hired by the council when I was fifteen. The village constantly supported me and encouraged me to dream big, but because of the size I was the only person to graduate in my high-school class. When I first attended Igiugig School it was a two-story building with one classroom upstairs and a shoe-box-sized gym downstairs. The large K–12 room was divided by a fold-out wall. Halfway through my primary education the school was expanded, which added two classrooms downstairs and quadrupled the size of the gym. The curriculum was standard K–12 materials and Saxon math books. However, throughout much of my education my teachers specialized in writing or language arts, so I did not receive adequate education in math or science.

By my tenth-grade year, the district fortunately transitioned to a standards-based system. Students were required to take classes in all subject areas, and if you proved proficient in a subject area you could advance. There were several required targets to qualify for graduation, but once you met them you could take college courses while still in high school. The new system was tailored to the learning needs of each student and allowed a student to excel and exceed the typical grades.

In my senior year of high school I had my favorite teacher, Kristin Hathhorn. She helped me with my college applications, wrote recommendation letters for scholarship programs, and encouraged me to look beyond Alaska colleges. I loved her enthusiasm in the classroom, and she treated students like we were her own children. I would see her again during my college commencement, when Dartmouth president Jim Wright recognized her for her excellent teaching in "Uh-goo-a-gig." She has remained a good friend and confidante.

I was the first in the family on my mother's side to leave the state for postsecondary education, and now the first to earn a degree. I did not even know Dartmouth College existed until I received an application for the Native American Fly-In Program. I immediately filled it out, jumping at the opportunity to travel, even if it was only to New Hampshire. I was in awe when I arrived on the Dartmouth campus: the architecture, the Green, the "live free or die" attitude—it is the closest thing to love at first sight I have ever experienced. Nevertheless, I waited until the deadline to make up my mind about Dartmouth because I had negotiated my own financial-aid package and was intimidated by the cost. When I received the acceptance letter, my dad ran down the hallway waving his arms in the air and yelling, "We are going to Dartmouth!"

When I left for college, I thought I was going to another world. My mom cried so hard she made me cry, and I left Igiugig with mixed feelings. She told me during Christmas break that she had thought she would never see me again. That's when it really hit home that New Hampshire to her seemed like the other side of the world. Our people just don't go *that* far away.

I began my Dartmouth experience with an Outing Club hike in the New Hampshire woods, which was the beginning of my freshman-year heaven. I missed the Native American orientation because of the hike, so my first friends were my fellow woodsmen. When I returned from the hike it was time to move into the fourth-floor of French, an all-freshman dorm near the Connecticut River. The moving in gave me second thoughts about my decision. The weather was really hot for me, and I had to lug my boxes from the post office all the way to the river, and then up four flights of stairs. I watched enviously (and with a little disgust) as other parents helped their college-bound kids move into the dorms. But I had a three-room double, which meant a room all to myself! My undergraduate adviser was the nicest, most energetic and helpful person I ever met. She arranged a number of fun "get-to-know-each-other" events so that our floor bonded quickly into "4th Floorgy." I called home often to report about all the wonderful activities the campus held for freshmen, such as the '08 Birthday Party in Collis Common Ground. There were so many exciting things to do and I always had a packed agenda. My first classes were English 5, Native American Studies (NAS) 34, and a theater class. Outside of my NAS class I did not associate with other Natives at Dartmouth (NAD) very much, nor did I participate much in the frat scene or partying of any sort.

I found it an easy transition to Hanover from Igiugig. The remoteness of the dorm was similar to my home, and the seclusion made me feel secure. Just as we did in isolated Igiugig, the campus community created its own entertainment with parties, day trips, and bringing the outside world to campus. The students' strong pride in being part of the Dartmouth community reflected the spirit of my hometown. Both communities were very aware of the need to contribute, to recognize our role in the world, and to build a strong network of friends that would be an asset in the future because we will all be connected for life. One advantage of being at Dartmouth was that I developed a network of peers that will be with me no matter where in the world I go.

Late fall semester of my freshman year a Native American student was posting fliers for a large gathering at the Native American House. He convinced me to go, and soon I found myself attending weekly council meetings, joining the NAD intramural basketball team, and enjoying NAD meals and parties. I discovered that NAD are a big family that reminded me of home, and the upperclassmen really supported the younger NADs. Yes, there was more gossip than people in the community, but we looked out for each other, helped each other through thick and thin, and whenever we gathered laughter reverberated throughout the house. I learned more from my peers about life on the reservations or tribal politics than I did in the classroom. The friends I made in the NAD community have remained my closest since I graduated from Dartmouth.

I moved into the Native American House in my sophomore year and stayed there for four terms. I worried that I was missing out on learning about our history, traditions, and other cultural knowledge that I would be gaining if I had stayed in my village. I did not want to pursue postsecondary education at the expense of my cultural knowledge, so I found a way to combine the two. I pursued a double major in Native American studies and anthropology, and found that these two disciplines enabled me to maintain a strong connection to home and to keep up with current affairs by applying events in my hometown to concepts in the classroom. The school's extensive resources enabled me to pursue my passion. At one point I opened a book in the NAS library and looked directly at a photo of my great-great-grandfather, who was over one hundred years old at the time. I didn't even know he had been interviewed.

In the fall of junior year I took courses at the University of Alaska in Fairbanks, and that winter I went to New Zealand as part of Dartmouth's anthropology program. It was the experience of a lifetime. After the program ended, my boyfriend Terek and I traveled for another month, exploring New Zealand, Australia, and Fiji, including the Indigenous peoples and their relationship with their states.

Returning to campus senior year, I underwent a series of life-changing events. Socially, I became part of a senior society and met a whole new group of friends who introduced me to a side of campus that I didn't know existed. We had meetings and supported one another—a lot of us are still really good friends. I also broke up with my boyfriend. Terek was from another village on Lake Iliamna, and having a long-distance relationship was getting old. I also was enjoying all the changes in my life and was not sure where my future was headed.

I drew on all my resources to complete the year academically. Some students used campus counseling to get them through tough times; I called Gram. During freshman year I called her with the day and time of my daunting final exams so that she could pray that I passed. She's practically a saint, so I knew God would answer her prayers. It worked so well that I may have abused the system in senior year.

Needless to say, getting to June 8, 2008, my graduation day, and earning high honors took devoted teamwork from the East Coast to the far North. My academic success was boosted by my wonderful study aids— a combination of sugar, caffeine, and carbohydrates to get me through all-nighters and nonstop reading and writing. Occasionally I would clear my head on the weekends by hanging out with friends on frat row to gear up for another hectic week. I do not recommend this lifestyle, as it resulted in my gaining twenty-five pounds and having countless cavities.

That said, Dartmouth has prepared me to do whatever I want to do in my future. I often called my father when I was drowning in paper deadlines and/or upset over the fact that I was cramming in information simply to pass a test. I would say, "I am never going to use this information, so why am I trying so hard?" He would tell me that it was like intellectual boot camp, that it was not necessarily the information but the training that I would apply in the real world. He was absolutely right.

My mother, of course, was simply proud that I was in school. Even if I had dropped out halfway through, she would have been proud that I tried. She always supported any decision my siblings and I made, and did not try to steer us in one direction or another. It was reassuring for me to have one slightly overbearing parent and one who would be proud regardless of what I did. Growing up in Igiugig and then attending Dartmouth College have unquestionably given me the tools to do whatever I set my mind to.

I am deeply grateful for my NAS major, as it brought the relationship I enjoyed with my father to a whole new level and provided a degree of intellectualism about tribal sovereignty that I otherwise might never have had the opportunity to discover. My thesis was the crowning achievement of my Dartmouth career. It earned me high honors in anthropology and a Pendleton writing prize. Titled "'Igyararmiunguunga': Qallemciq Nunaka Maani Kuicaraami-llu ("'I Belong to Igiugig': The Story of My Home on the Kvichak River"), my thesis allowed me to explore the social, economic, and political forces that shaped the settlement of Igiugig Village, as well as the challenges and opportunities of living in a Native Village in rural Alaska. Copies of my thesis are now being sold at the Igiugig Gift Shop!

On graduation day, my New York and Alaskan family members crowded around me as we traversed the booming metropolis of Hanover, New Hampshire. My family's enthusiasm for the shops on Main Street and for Dartmouth attire reignited my enjoyment of the town, which had grown a bit stale after four years. I had mixed emotions at graduation. Perhaps it was the 90-plus temperature, the fact my best friends and I would be dispersing forever, or the sadness I felt that my dad could not give me a few words of encouragement that would make the day extra special. When it was time to pack and say last good-byes, I wandered into my dorm room on the edge of depression.

I returned home after graduation and began working for Igiugig's tribal council almost immediately. I had once planned on easing back into "reality" by joining Teach For America or doing an internship that would allow me to travel. I knew that Igiugig was the place where I would "settle" with a husband and raise children, but I intended first to attend law or graduate school, travel, and experience what the world has to offer. But after my father died, I knew that I would have to return home and try to fill his size 13 shoes. I was not merely returning home to help my family; I wanted see my father's visions fulfilled and his dreams for our community become a reality. I knew how much it meant to him, and I did not want his work to be in vain. I also knew that if I did not go home immediately, I might not ever be able to.

Returning home was difficult because we all were mourning the loss of my dad, but my sisters and I helped each other through. We had a common mission—to make our father proud—and we set to it without thinking twice. Since coming home, I have taken a path that is very different from most twenty-three-year-olds on the planet. You could say that I am indeed filling those size 13 boots. For nearly two years I have provided a home for two local foster children, written grants to create a community greenhouse and establish a recycling center, and was elected president of the Igiugig Tribal Village Council. The largest projects I am currently working on include building six homes and solving the village's "fuel crisis." Most of my time is spent researching and writing grant proposals. I work in the Igiugig Native Corporation office because I am also the organization's bookkeeper. I volunteer at the school, where I am teaching a five-year-old how to read. At noon I open the post office, sort the mail the plane brings in, and then return to the tribal council office to finish up the workday. After that I walk over to *Sayak Lavguq*, Salmon's Store, the general store I have owned since 2005. I make it home in time to cook dinner, do house chores, review the girls' homework, and get them through the bedtime routine. I am exhausted by the end of the day. This routine is broken by an occasional trip to the city to attend workshops and meetings, or to get supplies for my store.

The summer season brings an additional list of duties, including managing our seasonal family businesses—a rental cabin and boats, and a barge transportation operation. The summer also brings an influx of tourists and a flurry of activities. Fortunately, the long summer days make it possible to get a lot of work finished in one day. I have followed my passion for Igiugig down several different avenues: the village council, the Native Corporation, my family businesses, school activities. It is exhausting and sometimes alienating, in that I walk a fine line between business, family, and governing fairly, and conflicts of interest lurk around every corner. That is also what makes the work so special and challenging.

What I love most about my life right now is that there is no separation of work, life, and love. They are all rolled into one, and it is fulfilling beyond words. I love easily and unconditionally, yet also fear to trust. I am no longer afraid to show emotion, or my vulnerability—life is too short to get caught up in the small stuff. Sometimes I wonder if my practical idealism is too optimistic for the state of my village, regional, national, and even global affairs, but the two girls I have adopted have helped renew my optimism. They have not had the opportunities I had at their age, yet they are just as happy as I was. Despite losing their mother to an early death, their father to alcoholism, and being separated from their closest family members and their older sister, they arise each day with smiles on their faces. I am experiencing the stresses of parenthood, which has helped me understand my own upbringing more fully, including the stress I caused my parents.

Most people do not know that I went to Dartmouth College with the intention of returning to Igiugig. During my four years at college and in my travels, people who learned that I come from a village in rural Alaska with a population of only thirty would often ask, "Do you see yourself returning to Igiugig? Would you ever go back?" The expressions on their faces suggested that they thought they knew the answer: What for and why? But most people do not know that I went to Dartmouth College with the intention of returning. I would tell them yes, although I could not articulate the reasons why, other than that it is my home. My dad made Igiugig a place I want to raise my own family, and I have an overpowering drive to honor him by keeping Igiugig sovereign and proud, and to make it a model community for our future generations. But I think one must experience village life in order to fully understand. It is my memories of being raised by an extended family with strong cultural values and a connection to a place that makes me proud to say *Igyararmiunguunga*— I belong to the Village of Igiugig.

AlexAnna is currently raising a family of four in Igiugig, Alaska, with Terek, her longtime partner. Their family includes three daughters—two teenage girls by adoption and one girl in preschool—as well as a three-month-old son.

Professionally, AlexAnna has enlisted the help of three other Dartmouth graduates to aid in the tasks of her tribal government. In 2012 she participated in the First Nations

Futures Program, hosted at Stanford University. Through her ongoing work as a leader in rural Alaska, AlexAnna takes part in several forums to address community concerns. Most recently, she participated in the Salmon Project, an initiative designed to address the sustainability of salmon in the state. She is looking forward to working with the First Alaskan Institute in Fairbanks, Alaska. Along with other Igiugig leaders, she also fundraised for a community-wide visit to New Zealand in late 2015.

Balancing family life and community engagement, AlexAnna still reflects on her Dartmouth experience daily and hopes her children will one day embark on their own Dartmouth experiences.

9

Future Ancestor   Hilary Abe

Look around you, feel the wind, the sun, the energy from the great-branched trees. Something very different is going on. We are so vital, so alive. And we are all here one final time, in order to celebrate the fact that you have acquired knowledge. With this knowledge you have the makings of mino bimaadiziwin, in Ojibwe, the good life. Knowledge with Courage. Knowledge with Fortitude. Knowledge with Generosity and Kindness. . . . It says knowledge without compassion is dead knowledge. Beware of knowledge without love.

Louise Erdrich '76 (Ojibwe), an excerpt from the class of 2009
commencement speech at Dartmouth College

My name is Hilary. I am Hiraacá, Nueta, and Sahnish—a citizen of the Mandan, Hidatsa and Arikara Nation. I am Mexican-American. I am Japanese-American. I am a living confluence, the point where many rivers of history culminate in my flesh.

My first name is often a curiosity to people. When I was a young child, my mom asked if I would prefer to go by my middle name instead of the name Hilary, since I was born a male. I must have been about six years old and I likely came home from school with tears on my face. My mom, in her gentle and open way, made it clear that it was my decision to make, and I sensed that it would be a significant decision for me. I considered it seriously for a moment—I can't tell you how many times my peers and adults teased me relentlessly, always calling me Hillary Clinton! Nonetheless, I chose not go by another name. Even then, I could feel that my name expressed a dimension of who I was and who I hoped to become.

When my mother was pregnant with me, my parents made a wager. They were sure I would be a daughter, so they felt confident when they made a bet with my Grandma Virginia, that she would name me if I were indeed a boy. So, to my parents' surprise, when I entered this life my grandma offered my new name, Hilary. My parents thought she was confused about the bet—I was a boy not a girl. My Grandma Virginia explained to my parents that she was naming me after her own grandfather, *Mashuga Ti-eesh*, Old Dog. Grandfather Old Dog was a Hiraacá chief and warrior who was born in Like-A-Fishhook Village, in our homelands— what is currently called North Dakota. Although he was seldom known to go by his baptized name Hilary (I do not think he was a devout Catholic— missionaries or a priest likely saw to his naming), I draw power from the connection my grandma drew from him to me in my name.

Old Dog was born around 1850. Anyone born in my community during that time was a survivor of utter devastation and transformation. Smallpox and other diseases brought to us by European colonizers worked through our homelands in swift and repeated waves. In their wake, an estimated 95 percent or more of our people perished. My grandmother's grandfather was born in this wake of unfathomable hardship, in our last earth-lodge village of the time. Old Dog was a formidable person—it's rumored he reached seven feet tall and his deeds in life were just as large. As a young leader, he readily put the protection of our people first, before his own well-being. From the stories I gather, this ability to be selfless even in the face of hardship was not at all an uncommon trait among our women and men of that time. Compassion was certainly a fundamental trait expected of our leaders. The people in my community continue to embody and strive toward this ideal—to let go and give freely of the things you most value, to be generous and kind. It defined my grandmother's generation, who survived the Garrison Dam and the Indian Relocation Act of 1956. It continues to this day.

My name has given me fortitude by reminding me of my connection to the family who came before me and safeguarded my future well before I was conceived. In all things I do, I must pay homage to my rope of life— to the women and men who have come before me, bound to me by lineage and blood, or simply through stories, thoughts, and ideas. As much as I want to live up to their example, I don't wish to glorify my ancestors either. My ancestors were human beings and I don't expect perfection of them; I am certainly not perfect—far from it. I am simply a new iteration and combination of them. My intelligence, my gifts, my features are all in great measure inherited directly from my forebears. I try to remember that one day, my own legacy, for bad or good, will be felt and lived by others—eventually beyond any memory of who I was. I try to remember that I am a future ancestor. We all are.

I remain in great awe of the physical and mental strength it took for my relatives to endure much in life, but I take greatest pride in their ingenuity and propensity for developing compassion. I am deeply fortunate to experience the compassion of my Hiraacá and Nueta ancestors through our ceremonial ways. From what little I understand, I believe compassion is one of the central teachings; it is a key component of our ongoing survival and a basis for peace in times of abundance. The compassion practiced by my ancestors was expansive, not solely limited to one's family or even to human beings. They recognized that a form of compassion that fails to acknowledge our responsibility to the land and our relation to the countless living beings around us is far from complete. In fact, in this current society we can see the inverse—a narrow view of compassion has proved deeply self-destructive to ourselves and our planet.

I have come to realize that the land is perhaps the greatest source of compassion, our greatest teacher. We owe it to ourselves and to all our living relatives to deepen our understanding of its mysteries. Repairing our relationship with the earth and with each other must form the basis of our long-term survival beyond the twenty-first century. Today's generations will have to contend with the legacies of violence that have shaped the modern world if we are to spare our descendants from profound and incalculable suffering. Any education that purports to be moral and relevant today must explicitly cultivate and reinforce the marriage of compassion to deeply critical knowledge. This is why, as a student, I so often wondered: Can an elite and wealthy college, founded in an era of genocide, built on stolen Abenaki lands and chartered with the express purpose of assimilating Native peoples, achieve this marriage of knowledge and compassion? Can it do so without openly and meaningfully confronting its past?

My ultimate goal in education has always been to use the knowledge I acquire for the good of other people. As a young person, I may not have had these words but I certainly sought to pursue a college education with the exploration of these themes in mind. I feel that many Native students I've encountered at Dartmouth and elsewhere feel such a strong commitment in their hearts to their communities and the land—the reason why they are able to follow impossibly arduous paths to acquire an education. In order to get there myself, I had to navigate my own obstacles, and every step of the way, I felt it was unlikely that I would be successful.

I still remember the moment quite clearly when I walked outside on a clear, sunny day to check the mail. It must have been the weekend—all was relatively quiet and peaceful outside and I was at home alone. A typically beautiful spring day on the rural outskirts of Flagstaff, Arizona. At that moment, I wasn't full of anticipation—in fact I was distinctly calm. Maybe I just tricked myself into being momentarily cool when I was really brimming with anticipation. When I reached the mailbox, I opened it, and my eyes landed on a large envelope addressed from Dartmouth College. I opened the package. I had been admitted to one of my top-choice colleges. Excitement flooded in. A huge weight was partially lifted from my shoulders that I wasn't completely aware had been there. Being accepted to a college like Dartmouth meant that I was at very least guaranteed to have a paying job, assuming I was able to graduate. I couldn't remember a time when money wasn't a constant source of stress in my life. To me, attending Dartmouth was a ticket for my future and that of my family. It was also something to regard warily; I had to consider the possibility that my ego could be weak and that I could become detached or distance myself from where I came from. I was deeply afraid of that. But I was hopeful too. Though I was sure the path would not be easy, this seemed like a step toward greater stability in my life. My need-based scholarship was very significant—a financial-aid package that covered nearly all my tuition as well as room and board. I went inside and sat alone at the kitchen table chewing on this new information and excitedly awaited the moment when I could deliver the news to my mom.

On the evening of my departure to college, the sky was ablaze with fiery colors and the clouds arranged themselves in strange columns and figures that reached high into the sky. Driving beneath this tapestry, I studied the shapes for meaning. The ride to the airport was blanketed in silence as my mother, father, and uncle accompanied me on the long drive from Flagstaff to the Phoenix airport on I-17, coasting down a surreal stretch of winding desert interstate. My dad and mom displayed a quiet, thoughtful countenance—they might have been pondering what I would encounter there since they had not attended college themselves. I had some clue, as I actually visited Dartmouth the previous fall as part of the Native Student Fly-In Program, but the experience was largely ominous for me. Ultimately, I chose Dartmouth first and foremost because of the Native American Studies Program and the Native student community. I would also be lying if I didn't say I chose it for its reputation as well. I wanted to believe that I could have an amazing experience there but my heart told me to be cautious. For the thousandth time, I tried to imagine what my life at college would be like—I had no idea. I felt a mixture of excitement and nervous anticipation.

The drive and subsequent good-byes came and went, dreamlike. My father said a prayer for me at the airport and wept. My mom stood on her toes and kissed me on my cheek and my forehead. My uncle George gave me a thoughtful hug. I was so grateful for their send-off; it was bittersweet. We exchanged some final words. I navigated my way through security—then suddenly, I was on a red-eye flight to Manchester, New Hampshire. As I slipped in and out of an apprehensive sleep, one thought seemed to linger more than any other: Who had I fooled to get into this school?

After I had completed nearly three thousand miles of travel, my bus from Manchester, New Hampshire, pulled into Hanover around eleven in the morning, after fourteen hours spent in transit. I was weary but excited. I arrived with two sixty-pound bags containing all my clothes and a guitar. I recall that I was wearing my usual baggy black cargo pants, a fitted plain white T-shirt, and worn combat boots—my black hair was short and spiked. Folks stared at my pierced labret, and I must have looked bedraggled from the trip. It was hot and humid. I could tell from the strange glances I got that my look was out of place and my appearance somewhat an anomaly. Immediately, I felt a stinging self-consciousness. Even though my entire wardrobe came from secondhand stores back home—before, I had always felt cool enough. Here, on this first day, I suddenly felt vastly out of place. These feelings would gradually subside over the next four years, but they never truly disappeared. As I looked around, pastel colors and polo shirts were a recurring theme. Dozens of white kids running in all directions, sporting short track shorts and athletic tank tops seemed to populate campus. Parents and students in the occasional BMW or Land Rover were a common sight. There were signs of class hierarchy everywhere. At this moment, it became clear to me that my normal way of dressing and acting would likely be scrutinized in this place. Was this really the right environment for me? Each moment fueled my concern but I resolutely decided to keep an open mind. All the brochures and images of diversity couldn't be completely false.

I dragged my bulging bags to check-in near Robinson Hall and then proceeded to lug them in the opposite direction to my dorm, a good half mile away. After a few blocks, I could only carry my bags about fifty yards or so before having to drop them at the edge of the sidewalk as I wiped my face. I watched as the ends of my hair gathered beads of sweat. I was about 145 pounds then and certainly healthy, but it was still a struggle to carry nearly my weight in possessions with me. It seemed like a tremendous walk to my dorm and I felt utterly foolish for having no one to help me carry my belongings. What made those earliest moments worse was that no one along the path looked me in the eye or seemed to notice me.

It was a busy day on East Wheelock Street and I must have passed at least fifty people—no one asked if I needed help and most people avoided any interaction even as I smiled or nodded at them when I passed by. Was it silly of me to expect anything else? In my hometown, most people at least smiled or acknowledged you to some degree as you passed. I didn't necessarily expect help, but by the end of the walk, I felt utterly invisible. I finally found my dorm and carried the bags up three flights of stairs, pausing at each landing and dodging people on the stairs until at last I approached my door.

Andres Hall, my dorm, was far nicer than any building I had ever lived in up to that point. As soon as I opened the door, I caught view of someone's luggage. I immediately knew it belonged to my new suite mate. I noted his bags were new and clean—they looked costly and accompanied a large ski bag. By contrast, one of my bags was an old army rucksack that had been purchased at an army-surplus store, and the other bag I carried had its zipper broken. My new roommate was a tall and muscular redhead—he sported an Italian crew team shirt and a clean-cut hairdo. I found out that he was a heavyweight crew recruit. I had no clue what that meant. I suddenly felt like a poor-student cliché. My new roommate's parents drove him to school, purchased furniture for him, and made sure he was settled in before they left. I suddenly felt the absence of my own parents. Meeting his felt awkward and confusing for everyone; it was clear they did not fully know what to make of me, and in turn I was hesitant. I was disappointed and somewhat hurt by their cool and distant attitude as I unpacked my belongings and settled in. I glimpsed the framed portraits of Ronald Reagan that my suite mate had placed prominently on his desk. I had the distinct impression that I must have landed in an episode of *The Twilight Zone*.

My first year was a jarring mix of social and academic adjustment. Classes started, and I didn't have the money to buy books right away. I didn't even know where I was supposed to go to buy books. Small details hurt my confidence right off the bat, as I couldn't do my first homework assignments in that first week. In every space, I felt self-conscious. Everything was new. Everyone else seemed to know where to go. My roommates and I were friendly, but I tried my best to pretend everything was just fine.

I took Japanese 1, 2, and 3 in my first year and it was incredibly time-consuming and demanding—drill every morning at 7:45 a.m., 8:45 a.m. classes, and weekly quizzes and tests. We were not allowed to speak English at all from the get-go and were expected to write assignments solely in Japanese *hiragana* and *katakana* characters after our first week. Course work went so fast for me—it was absolutely anxiety producing. All-nighters became a fixture. I had no one at all to commiserate with— I couldn't really call or ask anyone for advice. I refrained from calling my mom or sister, and when we did speak, I pretended like things were just fine. I didn't want to worry them. After the first few weeks, I learned that about half of my class had already taken Japanese in high school, several years' worth in some cases. I barely clung on. While I studied with students from my class for thirty-plus hours a week, I still felt so distant from them. Japanese was probably among the hardest courses I took in college, but I stuck it out. My other courses were also difficult—at times perplexing—but I managed.

While my academic transition was difficult, it was actually the social transition that proved to be the hardest part for me. In high school, I had no trouble making deep and lasting friendships with a variety of people. Here, people were strangely distant or competitive, unsure of each other perhaps, and finding common ground was often confusing and difficult. For a while I was friendly with a female student from my Dartmouth Outing Club trip. Then I found out that her grandfather had been a prominent Nazi Party member and her part of the family had fled to Argentina—something she readily admitted to without even feigned shame. That was an eye-opening lesson. In my time at Dartmouth, I became acquainted with the son of a well-known Hollywood director and writer, the daughter of the CEO of Condé Nast, a daughter of a Dartmouth trustee, and the son of owners of Chick-fil-A. It became normal to see and hear about wealth everywhere—not only that but many middle- or upper-middle-class students who seemed wealthy to me were pretending to be more affluent than they were. Nothing made me feel more like I had grown up in alien circumstances than spending time around these students.

In my first year, I also started working for Dartmouth Dining Services. When I started, I was in complete awe. It was the most incredible job. I got paid ten dollars an hour for mild duty work and it was so flexible too. But then I realized that it was yet another thing that made many of my privileged peers feel uncomfortable around me—to see me in the dining hall in my green DDS shirt and hat, serving food or cleaning. One of my most powerful learning experiences in college was working for dining services during my four years at Dartmouth—seeing who among my peers, people I knew well enough, would flat out ignore me when I was working in the dining hall.

The only place on campus that offered significant relief for me in my first year was the Native American House and the Native American Program office. It was one of the only places on campus where I felt like I shared any common ground with people. This community helped me feel sane and human again, even if the feeling was momentary, in between classes or extracurricular obligations. Without the Native community I have no clue what I would have done. It was truly a relief to be around students who were facing similar adjustments even if we weren't always comfortable enough to talk about them.

When freshman year ended I wanted to get the hell out of Hanover. I considered transferring. My professors, however, were strong, and academically I was doing well enough. But my self-esteem and overall view of the college had taken a toll. Everything remained strange to me—the elitist behavior and lack of compassion I saw in many of my classmates, the contrived hollowness of campus traditions, the overwhelming male whiteness of campus social practices, and the way alumni imbued these occasions with almost comical reverence. I was not able to shake the feeling that I was an outsider.

Dartmouth is a deeply conflicted place when it comes to Native people. There is no better example of hollow tradition than the retired Indian mascot, a symbol that alumni old and new claim is part of their deep and meaningful experience at the college. It was always disgusting and disappointing to see so many people deeply devoted to that racist imagery— seeing the Indian head around on frat jackets and in *The Dartmouth Review* or on the graduation canes of alumni. During my freshman year, a vivid T-shirt was made depicting an Indian receiving head from the College of the Holy Cross mascot. There was a themed party hosted by sports teams on campus called "Cowboys, Barnyard Animals, and Indians." In response to Native students' critique of these images, *The Dartmouth Review* published a torrent of abhorrent and racist content depicting Indians scalping white settlers and claimed that NAD students were "on the warpath." These frequent encounters were a constant source of aggression for my peers and me.

But it wasn't just students and alumni that condoned these attitudes. Although the college had retired the Indian mascot decades ago, I regularly met the Dartmouth Indian in the library—the silhouette of an Indian with two feathers sitting at the feet of a white settler who is reading the Bible to him, an image that is genocidal in its roots, stamped on the inside cover of most books in the library. Whenever I gazed toward Baker Tower, I was reminded that the same image also sits at the highest point of the Dartmouth campus, immortalized atop the weather vane. The Hovey Murals, located in the basement of the dining hall, and which depict caricatures of naked and fetishized Native women, drinking alcohol and fawning over Eleazar Wheelock, Dartmouth's founder, were usually boarded up—but these offensive murals were purportedly uncovered at the request of alumni for certain reunions and functions. And don't forget the official seal of the college, two naked Indians under a gleaming Bible in the sky, in front of Dartmouth Hall! These images stand in bold contrast to the recommitment of the college to its charter. And there is very little that recognizes Samson Occom, the Mohegan man who helped found Dartmouth by raising the funds necessary to start the college. These images quietly curate and condone racist mentalities as a part of a living tradition. Every day when I saw them I would feel a burning and mounting disgust.

I realized early on that being a Native student at a predominantly white elite college in the United States meant constantly encountering and resisting these ideas. And you were often doing it alone—inside and outside of the classroom, over e-mail LISTSERVs, educating peers and professors alike, attempting to dispel myths about Native people, day in and day out. It was emotionally and intellectually exhausting to engage in that unrecognized work. There was a lot of pressure too. For many non-Native students, this may be the only time in their life that they would be around a real group of Native people. The pressure to dispel myths was felt deeply precisely because many of your peers go on to occupy positions of power. If I didn't try to educate them in some way, I felt like I was failing Native folks everywhere. And as a result, I can say my grades slipped. Many of my peers and I helped coordinate a campus-wide response called the "Solidarity Against Hatred" rally during my junior year in response to various racist incidents that popped up on campus at the time. That work stole a lot of time away from my classes, on top of the other commitments I maintained. Ultimately, I learned that these unprompted hostilities, mostly directed toward communities of color on campus, frequently resulted in little to no accountability for those who committed the racist behaviors.

The Native American Studies (NAS) faculty and curriculum were a godsend to me as well and were perhaps the greatest antidote for the anxiety and alienation I felt being a Native student at Dartmouth. The program allowed me to intellectually engage with concepts and ideas that were directly relevant to me and my family's experience—I am a proud NAS major. At the same time, NAS classes were often emotionally crushing. Non-Native students often had difficulty understanding how small Indian country could be and just how directly affected by historical policy our families were. My blood would boil every time I sat in my NAS history courses while the front row was occupied by students who regularly surfed the Internet for sports scores in plain view of all those behind them, and while our professor lectured and recounted the horrible and grim process of genocide and highlighted how resilient Native people had to be in order to survive. These students failed to understand that my family and the families of other Native students who were personally present in the classroom experienced this violence, even after we would speak up about it. I was struck and frightened by this absence of empathy. It was an education in itself. Truthfully, all these experiences made me into an angrier person. But my family did not raise me this way.

My father, Eugene, was a tough but gentle man with a sparkling sense of humor. He was born in Elbowoods, North Dakota—a small village-town that was a hub for Fort Berthold, our reservation. My mother, Sofia, is a petite but wiry-strong woman with a sharp intelligence and jet-black hair. She was born in her home of Mexico in the state of Puebla—she grew up poor on her family's farm, *en el campo*, and immigrated to the United States in her twenties. My parents met in Chicago and married. I grew up in a variety of homes throughout my childhood in different states—Montana, Utah, Michigan, and finally Arizona. I spent many of my summers in North Dakota visiting family and supporting ceremonies at home. Together, my parents had my two older siblings fourteen and nine years apart from me. My parents had me in their forties.

My mother and my father decided to separate when I was three years old. I have only vague memories of a time when my father lived with us, but I recall that there were tensions present in my home and spells of unhappiness. Before I understood what was happening, I was living with my mother and sister in a small apartment in Battle Creek, Michigan, and I attended day care while my mother worked long shifts. My older sister was in middle school and was charged with watching me a lot. My older brother had just begun attending college in Montana, and my father had moved to Arizona to live and work. I was very sensitive to the fragmentation of my family at this time.

When I was five years old we moved to Arizona and lived for a brief while with both my parents while my dad worked at a Bureau of Indian Affairs boarding school in Tuba City on the Navajo Nation reservation as the manager of a school cafeteria. After a few months, my sister, mother, and I moved into a pink single-wide trailer on the outskirts of Flagstaff, where I would attend school from kindergarten until my graduation from high school. We moved fairly often in those first years, and I ended up living in a number of homes on the outskirts of Flagstaff before we settled in one home about a thirty-minute drive east of town when I was in fourth grade.

Flagstaff is located at the edge of a reservation community, and just one hour's drive to the north lies the Navajo Nation. Many of my friends and residents of the Flagstaff community are Navajo and Hopi, and this helped shape my perspective on Native people outside of my own community. My first cousins are also Navajo and grew up in Tuba City—I really enjoyed spending time playing with them on the reservation during my vacations. At times I felt connected to my Diné and Hopi friends; at other times, it was hard to explain who I was—I was still learning myself and sometimes it felt like our two Native communities occupied similar but ultimately disparate worlds. Rightfully so, I was merely a guest in their homelands.

I liked elementary school and made friends easily. When I was in first grade, I became best friends with a couple kids who liked getting into a little trouble. Almost all of my friends' parents were divorced, some had parents who may have been alcoholics or abusive. I spent 90 percent of my time after school playing outside. I smoked and had my first taste of alcohol before I hit fourth grade. We'd pretend to get into fights on the side of roads and would flee when people would suddenly stop their cars. Two of us would zoom around the neighborhood on a mini bike. My earliest friends and I engaged in some graffiti, we shoplifted occasionally from the gas station nearby, played with fire and firecrackers, and we even broke into a couple of neighborhood homes when it was clear the owners were away. We took small trinkets—lighters and neon plastic cups for our forts. I knew it was wrong, but it was easy to be influenced by older kids—one of whom was already in sixth grade and exerted some control over us. In truth, I was very ignorant of what any of these choices really meant. Even so, I felt sheltered compared to some of my friends. Although I had a lot of freedom as a kid, my mom saw to it that I was always fed, clothed, and cared for.

In fourth grade, we moved to a new house on the other side of town and that put an end to that. My new neighborhood was mostly white, low income, and conservative. There were few opportunities to make similar friends in my new area of town, and I turned my boredom to books. Our new home sat on a large stretch of dusty brown land flecked with juniper scrub and overshadowed by the sacred San Francisco Peaks. While it was an endlessly beautiful landscape, the neighborhood we settled into was also very isolating for me. I often felt powerless there. But I was also very fortunate to call it home—I would explore the woods on my own and I believe I grew intellectually from the time alone.

My mother was an exemplary single mother and is the toughest person I know. As a certified nursing assistant and home health caregiver, she kept us fed and clothed on an extremely tight budget. Somehow, with utter determination, she would consistently make ends meet and accrue some savings as well even though we were a very low-income household. I have endless respect and adoration for my mother. She lived through our successes and triumphs with little care for her personal comfort. She is the most selfless person I've ever known. It was hard to see her so tired all the time. That was her gift to us and it was the steadiest demonstration of love I've ever seen—I've been able to build my life on the foundation my mother so carefully laid for me, and so I learn from her example greatly.

I also credit my mother for sowing the seeds of my education by developing my reading habits from an early age. She would take me to the public library and we would check out huge stacks of children's books—then we would go through them all together. As a result, I developed a healthy appetite for reading, which was strengthened by my brother's and sister's reading habits, as I grew older. Equally, I will always be grateful to my mom for giving me freedom as a child but also keeping a watchful eye. It gave me the space to figure things out for myself and helped me cultivate a strong sense of independence early in life.

It was during my early years that my older brother, John, sought out tribal ceremonies. My brother was fourteen years older than me and had started pursuing his spiritual path when I was very young. Beginning at age eight or nine, I spent many summers driving with him back to our reservation in North Dakota. On those summer road trips, in the quiet of the car, the rushing landscapes served as a backdrop for our many conversations. He treated me like an adult and would explain a lot to me—illuminating certain concepts and helping me understand a broader context for our family situation and our position today as Native people. I credit these early conversations with priming me to understand a broader context for settler colonialism. I learned a lot about this country by driving through border towns and stopping in areas where we were stared at for our brown skin and especially for my brother's long hair.

When we arrived in North Dakota every year, I noted a land largely populated by the descendants of white settlers. Stolen land. The erasure of our history and the whitewashed narrative of US history was so tangible in peoples' attitudes and ignorance toward us. But I could always sense an abundance of subconscious guilt too. Indians always serve as uncomfortable reminders that this land was taken violently and unjustly. This guilt is everywhere in the United States—Dartmouth was no exception. However, nothing can suppress the boundless emotions I experienced when coming home to North Dakota. I can't begin to describe the feeling I got when I entered our lands and when I was among family. Even though not all my ancestors are from that land, I felt no other ties that could compete with it since my dad's side of the family was closest growing up. And being away from it for the better part of each year helped me appreciate it in a way that might be hard for those who live there all the time. I loved spending time there and experiencing everything—the people, the hills and buttes, the water, each place with its own stories and mysteries attached. This is the geographical center of North America—a beautiful, endless, and captivating place; it has sheltered and nourished the ancestors of my father and grandma's family for generations. That connection has always been real and tangible to me. It remains my favorite place on earth. These experiences were among my most formative and they continued into my teenage years.

I always felt guided and loved unconditionally by my brother, and I deeply admired my father, too. My dad was a compassionate person, like my grandmother, and his life was riddled with hardship from an early age. As a young person growing up between North Dakota and Chicago, he had enlisted in the marines at the age of seventeen and ended up signing up for duty as the Vietnam War was just escalating, not conscious it was in fact impending. My father spent part of his childhood in the notorious Cabrini-Green housing project in Chicago. As the second of seven siblings, he decided to leave my grandparents' overcrowded residence to begin a new life in the military. After being sent to Vietnam and having nearly finished his first tour of duty, he was witness to a friendly-fire incident in which a close friend accidentally shot another close friend in the head. As a result, he was required to stay well beyond his allotted time and was finally permitted to leave after a year or so by petitioning his congressional representative. His time in Vietnam coincided with heavy Agent Orange campaigns, and my father would often relay stories to me of his time ingesting stagnant, gray-colored water that had been purified with halazone tablets. After the war, my father was diagnosed with type 2 diabetes. When I was fifteen and a few years later, after an excessively thorough evaluation process, he would receive a rarely administered 100 percent disability rating for a pension from the Veterans Administration for kidney failure, hearing loss, and post-traumatic stress disorder. By this time I was a sophomore in college.

My father was conflicted by many things in his life, I think—including the guilt he felt about leaving my mother. As a child, I was largely unaware that my father and mother had permanently separated. My mother has always worn her wedding ring and, when I was young, always told me that my father simply had to work elsewhere. She wasn't in denial, and my siblings knew, but she was protecting me as best she could. My father visited every few weekends when I was a kid. I never visited my father where he lived and I never even thought to question the unorthodox living situation between my parents. My brother and sister never told me anything different if they knew, and I was too busy living the life of a kid to think about it too much.

When I was thirteen, my father and I had a conversation that shook me to my roots. We were in the car when he asked me if my mother had told me why he didn't live at home with us, to which I nodded yes. But she hadn't—I thought he was talking about his job. He then proceeded to explain the reason was because he had an entire other family and that I had three younger half siblings whom I had never met. I had no clue. In a moment, I became an older brother. However, I pretended like I knew because I could sense his shame. I learned that my youngest sister was already four years old. My eldest half sibling was closer to my age. My father had recoupled with a Navajo woman and had been living with her and raising my three new siblings since I was three or four. Eventually they married. Though I often wondered over the years what the lives of my father and unknown siblings were like, I did not get to meet them until I was twenty-two, having just graduated from college in 2008.

My father suffered from many health complications while I was in high school and college. He had received a kidney transplant when I was fifteen, but it was rejected when I was a junior in college. It was heartbreaking when he had to go back on dialysis. When I was a sophomore in college, he was diagnosed with life-threatening heart disease and stage 4 throat cancer—he was told by his doctor that he had less than a year to live. On top of my social and financial struggles in college, this made it very hard for me to concentrate. Toward the end of his life, my father surprised us by becoming a born-again Christian, but his fundamental nature did not change. However, he became wary of medical procedures and reluctantly accepted medical help. It was always a special anxiety for my sister and me when my father would go months without taking his antirejection medication for his kidney despite our frequent protests. I worried about him endlessly; my whole family did. Miraculously, my father's faith seemed to keep him going despite his ailments. He passed away when I was twenty-three, when I was working at my first job after college.

Aside from the quiet moments I spent with my father, I came to know him through my brother. My brother was fourteen years older than me and had grown up with my father at home. It was hard on him when my father and mother split apart, but he was also a young adult and was able to understand their relationship in a different way. My brother had great respect for my father and together they had belonged to the Native American Church. When I was growing up, my father used to tie a water drum and sing church songs for our family in overnight ceremonies. I watched carefully at the way he would sit and tremble while his hands stretched the soft deerskin over a cast-iron kettle. He delicately wrapped stones along the edges of the kettle, holding them in place under the leather with a white rope. He wove and wound them into an intricate pattern. Then he tuned the drum, and the rich sound of the water within it reverberated throughout our living room. In these moments, I watched as he sang songs, drew deep breaths, and cried in prayer. As he prayed aloud for our family, I was overcome by my own sadness. In those moments I learned the strength of vulnerability, that the strongest men and women can cry. I learned that those tears can embody generations' worth of suffering and simultaneously encapsulate the hopes and prayers my father had for us. I learned a lot from my father.

My brother and sister were the first of my family to graduate from college, each facing a difficult path to higher education. I grew up under my brother and sister and looked to them for guidance. My brother taught me to put my education at the service of my family and, after securing a job, he made sure that my mom had enough money to cut back on hours from work. My sister Marisa taught me self-sufficiency and how to be thick-skinned. Certainly, my ability to persist and graduate from Dartmouth was at least partially due to my brother and sister paving a path in higher education that I benefited and learned from.

Nothing mattered more to my brother than ensuring our safety, our happiness, and well-being. My brother, seeing our family's need for healing and reconciliation, became immersed in ceremonies in our community. Over time, he sought out mentors and began the steps necessary to pursue his spiritual development. He fasted and gained rights to carry a pipe. I remember bits and pieces of his time praying and fasting on the high buttes on our reservation. I was still a young kid running around and camping out in the tall green summer prairie grasses during the four days that he went without food and water. I did most of my maturing while watching my brother sacrifice time and again for the well-being of our family and community in his way. Eventually, he made the commitment to participate in a Sun Dance—a commitment spanning four years. My brother always treated me as an adult when I accompanied him each year and as he scraped together the cash to make the annual pilgrimage home to Grandma Sadie's grounds on Fort Berthold. I stood in the shade of the arbor watching him as he sacrificed for my family over seven years, three years longer than his four-year commitment. Life-defining moments.

I was fifteen when I found out that my brother died. He was living in Oregon at the time. On a cold and foggy November morning, he died in a head-on collision near his home in Corvallis. He had just bought plane tickets to spend the Thanksgiving holiday with us at home. I was in Alabama at the time, visiting an arts high school with representatives from my own school. I didn't find out until I arrived home two days later. As I pulled up that evening, relatives from both sides of my family were at my house. I was confused. As soon as I walked in the door, my mom and dad rushed to me and grabbed my arms on both sides. They were crying. They took me to my mom's bedroom and I immediately saw the cedar box my brother kept his sacred pipe in on my mom's bed—as soon as I saw it I knew. When they told me that he had been in an accident and did not make it, I crumbled. I was utterly broken.

A part of me had been amputated. My family was devastated and the nightmare persisted. My mother grieved for at least ten years, keeping a candle burning for him nonstop during all that time. These were among the darkest times of our lives, and I look back amazed at how we each were able to make it through. At school I acted as strong as I could, like nothing had happened, and I spoke little with my friends about his passing, though they all attended his funeral with me and sensed how deeply I was hurting. What could I say? I was grateful to have my friends there for me when I needed them most and they helped pull me back into life.

I continue to feel my brother's presence in my life. He remains one of my biggest sources of inspiration—a person that strived to embody the compassion of my ancestors and developed it through action. I knew I had to follow his example and obtain an education if I were ever to be able to help heal my family as my brother had done. My family and I traveled to North Dakota the following summer to scatter his ashes on our family's old place, on a hill overlooking the Missouri River and my grandma's home growing up, the place where my uncle was born. When my father passed away, he requested for his ashes to be placed there too. By then, my grandmother had joined my brother on the hill too.

I had not been a dedicated student until I started to turn it around in the year leading up to my brother's death. Many of the students I attended middle and high school with saw school as a graduated form of day care, an obstacle to what they really wanted to do. I concurred. What was the point exactly? Arizona schools were consistently ranked among the last in the nation and I think we felt it. School was a routine that could be fun, could be distracting, but mostly it seemed like we were just floating in a sea of requirements with no clear purpose. So it was exhilarating when that rare teacher came along who was open, engaged, energetic, and successful in generating excitement among the students about their subject. My theater and freshman English teacher was known to get angry and hurl chairs across the room at students for not living up to their potential. He cared in an eccentric and irregular way. That was one of the first times I had ever been treated like a young adult in school. It was also the first time in my life that I had ever been outright challenged, even antagonized by a teacher, and I enjoyed it a lot.

I had never been so engaged in ideas as I was in his class. I was becoming an adult and beginning to explore and further understand myself as a person but needed some nudging to look deeper. One day, he confronted me outside of our portable classroom and told me in his typically point-blank way, "You know, Hilary, it's not cool to suck at school. So stop sucking."

That summer, I read for the first time *The Autobiography of Malcolm X*, *1984*, *The Catcher in the Rye*, and *Slaughterhouse Five*. I remember with emotion the moments in Malcolm X's autobiography as if they were extensions of my own experience—I was so thunderstruck by the book I read it twice, and when high school started back up, I was carrying it in my backpack regularly. This book in particular drove me to think about taking charge of my education.

By the time I graduated from middle school, I was convinced that I had already let myself down and would not be able to go to a college on scholarship. At the beginning of high school I had a mix of grades. I didn't understand that grades in elementary school and middle school had no effect on college choices and I just assumed that I had already limited my options. It wasn't until high school that I learned perhaps it was not too late to build a strong academic record. But doing so would not be easy for me.

I was lucky to attend a small arts charter school—made up of eight portable classrooms and a handful of young teachers. When I began high school, if I could do well enough by participating in class, I would do that and no more—especially if it was a class I didn't particularly feel engaged by. And if any of my classes required the completion of homework, that's where my grades invariably slipped. No one sat down with me to explain how I should structure my time. No one in school fully explained why it was important. My mom couldn't help me, and my brother and sister assisted when they could, but no one was going to lecture to me about the ins and outs of time management. I had never been punished or disciplined seriously in my life, so grades were usually not a point of contention between my mom and me. I did well enough—I rarely received failing grades. My mother was always very encouraging and wanted above all for me to be happy—but obtaining good grades wasn't something that was rigorously enforced, nor would I have liked it if they were. My father was not able to finish high school, and my mother was working her family's farmland by the time she was a young child. They tried their best to guide me toward college even though it had not been possible for them when they were my age.

At one point I had managed to convince my parents to let me drop out of school so I could homeschool myself. *Unschool* was the term. However, before I could implement that plan I came to the realization that I probably wouldn't have the requisite self-discipline, mentors, or resources to carry it off. So, in keeping with my teacher's admonition not to suck at school, I decided I would return to my classes and transform myself into a straight-A student. It was easier said than done, because after years of having little to no study habits, I had no clue how to motivate and set specific goals for myself. What made matters worse were the low expectations that others had of me. Many of my teachers expected very little from me. I was never much of a disturbance in the classroom, though I could be a clown—but I wasn't always an active participant either. In the classes I deemed more pointless, I deliberately sat in an area of the room where I could string three chairs together and lie horizontal across them with my hoodie over my face to nap. As a result, my math instructor would walk right past me when it was time to check for homework—sometimes he would justifiably scoff at me. It was easy to live up to their negative expectations and it represented a vicious cycle that bred apathy in me.

I did the only thing I thought could truly help me. My high-school girlfriend was an excellent student, having developed the habits to follow through with her assignments from an early age, and I was sure that if I worked with her and followed her lead, she would be able to help me the most. I asked her for her mentorship in order to become a better student and she agreed. Going forward, she had me sit down with her, where

I proceeded to hammer out every piece of homework no matter how painful. It took all of my fourteen-year-old willpower to complete each assignment and learn better time-management skills. With her help, I quickly improved. It took my teachers a moment to catch on, but when they finally did, it was impossible to stumble because their expectations for me had shifted. Halfway through the year, they started regarding me as one of the most responsible students in any of my classes. It was hard to believe and it had the dual effect of giving me more motivation. I didn't want to revert to my old habits, and it helped a lot when I knew that my teachers had newfound belief in my abilities. The higher their expectations for me, the higher my expectations were for myself too. It was so important to know that others believed in me in order for me to believe in myself. I graduated with straight As from that point on.

Yet in spite of my growing self-esteem and confidence as a student, I still felt frustration about having so little control over the immediate situations in my life. I decided I would have to imagine a different existence for myself—despite not fully believing it was possible. I determined that high school could be a jumping-off point to get to something better. I wanted to have *options*. At first, I never consciously decided that I would try to attend an elite or competitive college. Initially, my best-case scenario was going to school at the University of Arizona in Tucson on scholarship, but more likely to attend one of my local college options. I had no notion that a school like Dartmouth would be even remotely possible for me to attend or afford. I actually owe my entire college experience to one program called College Horizons. College Horizons is an organization and summer workshop for Native American, Alaska Native, and Native Hawaiian students, providing an extensive weeklong workshop on the college admission and financial-aid process. As soon as I heard about it, I applied. This program alone opened my eyes and made me realize the possibilities that I had been working toward already were within reach. I don't know if I would have graduated from college without the much-needed guidance I received from this program.

I entered Dartmouth ready for a new educational experience—one that would not be confined to classes. I did everything in my power to experience all that Dartmouth had to offer. Despite its challenges for Native and first-generation students like me, I believe I did. By my sophomore year I had joined an all-inclusive coed fraternity called The Tabard; early in my junior year I found myself running for and becoming president of the house. This was a second home for me outside of NAD, something I never imagined I would be participating in and completely different from most frats and sororities on campus. By senior year, I was tapped for two senior societies on campus. I was a member of a forum for the various under-represented communities on campus called Inter-Community Council, I was involved in the student assembly as a representative for the Native students on campus, and I was social chair for NAD. I joined numerous other groups on campus, applied for and received fellowships for indepen-dent research, and took PE classes in skiing, kayaking, and martial arts. I was able to make a short film, went on several spring-break service trips funded by the college, and through various groups and projects got to visit India, Poland, and Ukraine. I even exhausted the number of courses I could take—graduating with three four-course terms. The whole time, I remained aware of how extraordinary these opportunities were.

Although I tried to make the most of my undergraduate experience, I also wondered if Dartmouth was helping me to become a better human being. Being a Native student at an elite institution was a day-to-day struggle. I suffered from anxiety and depression during all four years of college, and in my junior year I finally began seeing a therapist who helped me process the sources of my anxiety, to untangle many of the issues that I had been trying to process alone. I later learned she had helped many other Native students do the same. Yet mental-health issues were not at all uncommon among many of my classmates, Native and non-Native alike; the mental-health staff at the college was so taxed that it took me weeks to get an appointment even when I found myself in a very dark place. I managed to function, but there were times that I felt completely hope-less. I wish I could have taken some time off, but I was afraid that if I stepped away, I might never come back. It was an unhealthy time for me. My family had endured a long and tumultuous road to position me at college, and I felt I had no choice but to proceed. In the end, things became more bearable as I finally acclimated to the environment over my four years, but in my time as a student, I was rarely able to fully enjoy the experience. Truthfully, there were a great many things worth loving at Dartmouth—from amazing students and professors to the immense beauty of the land surrounding campus. But in my heart and my mind, the warmth of those memories is often obscured and dimmed by the anxiety of being in a place where I rarely felt accepted as my full self. I want to remember it differently, but I can't. Still, I experienced so much compassion there too. I would not have made it through without countless individuals' support—I wish I could name them all here. And I certainly didn't have it hardest—I knew classmates who had overcome unbelievable hardship and were still treated as pariahs on campus. It has to be said that as a cisgender male with experience navigating diverse social settings, I certainly had more privilege and an easier time on campus than some. I cannot imagine what this college experience might have been for some of my more marginalized peers—students who came directly from their reservation or who live at the intersection of being queer and a person of color. I've heard many stories—I am immensely grateful to the alumni who carved out a space for us at the institution and endured their education in worse times.

My name is Hilary and I graduated from Dartmouth in 2008. I am grateful for all my experiences, including my college education. It has truly been life changing. However, my greatest hope is that my children and theirs can experience a more compassionate education, one whose rigor is focused on teaching what it means to be an intelligent and kind human being in equal measure. Dartmouth is not without its areas of excellence, but too often the experience yielded knowledge that lacked humility and love. It is through the teachings of my family and our stories of struggle, resistance, compassion, and courage that I have learned the value of living knowledge—an education that readily lends itself to healing and perpetuating life. I remain hopeful that Dartmouth and this broader society can grow to meet the mounting challenges of our time by making this key component of education more deliberate and integral.

Since graduating from Dartmouth, Hilary has worked in education—first as a teaching fellow then as an admission counselor at Phillips Academy in Andover, Massachusetts. He now works for College Horizons, the same program he attended as a youth. As a Native-led nonprofit organization, College Horizons is a small team dedicated to providing national college access and success programs for Native American, Alaska Native, and Native Hawaiian youth. Hilary believes in the power of their workshops because they openly address many of the concerns and issues that Native and first-generation students encounter in college and graduate school. He has also been active in the Native American Alumni Association of Dartmouth, an organization that does its best to connect with and advocate for current Native students on campus. He lives happily with his best friend and partner.

10

An Unpredictable Journey   John Around Him

One night our job was to guard a factory. White concrete walls with guard towers surrounded the building, which manufactured parts for Iraqi military vehicles. The factory, a tall, steel-frame metal structure, stood partially demolished, with its walls blackened from air bombings early in the Iraq War. The rest of the compound was littered with vehicle parts. Our mission was to provide security and prevent looting. Whatever civil order existed in Iraq before the invasion had now vanished. Locals, looking to sell just about anything to feed their families, commonly took to looting. Two sixty-five-ton, sand-colored steel tanks, call signs Bravo-33 and Bravo-34, provided us with both protection and shelter. During the war, tanks doubled as killing machines and living quarters—eating, bathing, and sleeping were done on the tank. Each consisted of a four-man crew: a loader, a driver, a gunner, and a tank commander.

Since this particular factory was notorious for being attacked, we were always on high alert. A highway lay between the factory and a large village, with a dense community of houses that allowed the insurgents to fire quickly and blend into their surroundings. This was the nature of urban warfare. Ambush, sniper fire, mortar fire—we prepared for the worst. Fear was constant. A gate on the south end of the factory provided the only way in or out. To prevent an onslaught, we positioned a tank in the gate. One soldier stood guard near the tank and another one in a tower along the wall approximately fifty yards away to provide support. Everyone took up shifts throughout the night, rotating through the two guard positions.

I remember it was dawn as my shift came to a close, and the sky was coated a rose-pink hue. The air was crisp. The rest of the crew was sleeping in a small guard building near the gate, most likely a previous security checkpoint for the factory. This was home during the guard missions. I proceeded to wake Specialist Russo for his shift. A medium-built white man from Chicago, Russo was honest and hard working. I had a lot of respect for him, and we were good friends both in war and on the home front. That morning, we talked for a little bit, mostly about four-wheeling, American food, and family. Later, my body fatigued, I staggered toward my cot to lie down. I untied my bootlaces, which were tightly bound, and the relief to my feet was instantly gratifying. Aside from boots and Kevlar helmets, which were optional, we slept in full gear: socks, undershirt, DCU (desert camouflage uniform), and armor vest. Most of us wore our helmets to bed because, in this environment, chances of surviving a hit were slim.

I always did a quick weapons check before sleeping. It was routine, like brushing your teeth. My dirt-covered rifle, locked and loaded, stood upright against my cot. I felt for my pistol, attached to a holster on my thigh. For me, there was something strange and bone-chilling about the routine weapons check. It added to the constant fear of attack, but it was also a reminder of the possibility of death. My life depended on how fast I could reach my weapon. Weapons check done, I closed my eyes for what seemed like a few minutes. Then suddenly, Boom!!! An orange light pierced my translucent eyelids. My immediate thought was "What the hell was that!" Simultaneously with the explosion, I heard Specialist Russo shriek, a cry horrifying and unnatural. His cry made me cringe, like nails on a chalkboard.

My ears were ringing. The inside of our sleeping quarters was shrouded in dust as I tumbled out of my cot. An object, lodged in the wall of the building, was burning red and sparking, orange embers falling to the floor. The object illuminated the dust in the room, encompassing everything in an eerie red glow. For a minute I thought I was dead. It all happened so fast; still deafened by the explosion, we all jumped to our feet, grabbed our weapons, and shot out the door of the guard building. We instantly began surveying the perimeter in front of the factory. Breathless and angry, I scanned the perimeter too. We were ready to kill anything with a weapon. Nothing! Some of the other guys attended to Specialist Russo. He was hit with shrapnel, but his injuries did not appear to be life-threatening. This was good news. Assessing the damage, we found the explosion was from an RPG (rocket-propelled grenade). Russo had been standing on the right side of the tank when the RPG hit the left side of the tank, exploding on the commander's hatch. The stem of the RPG, the propulsion piece, was catapulted into the wall of our sleeping quarters. By all accounts, Specialist

Russo was very lucky. If he had been standing a few feet closer to the front of the tank, he would have absorbed most of the explosion.

On returning to the safety of our base camp later that day, the tank crew sighed with relief, some joking to ease the trauma of the RPG incident. "That was fucking close!" someone said. "Specialist Grady, if you die, can I have your snack food?" pleaded another. Guys would facetiously joke about laying claim to a soldier's possessions if he or she were to die. After the wisecracks died down, everyone retreated to their bunks either to write letters home or rummage through care packages.

Standing alone near the tank I began to feel nauseous and had difficulty breathing. My legs felt weak. That was a close call, maybe too close. I was shocked to my very core. It is difficult to describe the feeling, but my existence was suddenly put into perspective, and I felt myself *change* in that moment. It was my first real experience with combat. It was dark out and as soon as I was alone, I kneeled next to the tank and could feel the tears trickling down my cheeks. I tried to act tough and "John Wayne" it, but it was no use. I could not hold back. A sense of submission began to overtake my body. I thought it was only a matter of time before my own death. I was amazed and sad at how easily life could be taken away. Crying near the tank, memories of family, friends, and home began to flood my mind. My dreams of going to college and making my dad proud—all of it seemed to be slipping away. I did not want the guys to see that I was so emotional. I did not want to discourage anyone. I nevertheless knew what I was fighting for at that point. I was fighting to go home.

It is remarkable how the chaos and violence of war brought into focus my deep affection for home, a feeling that from then on impelled me to stay alive during the war. Rooted in every Lakota family is this profound affection for home. Home is bigger than me or you, bigger than money or power. Home is not just a domicile, but an expression that is reflected on regularly, almost like a prayer, and it would go something like this: always put your home and everything in it—family and Lakota culture—before yourself.

Growing up in my home on the reservation was a time of great happiness and emotional contentment. I lived with my parents, John and Linda Around Him; my two sisters, Amaris and Clovia; two brothers, Milton and Samuel; and various relatives from broken homes whom we often cared for. Our home is located in the backcountry near Kyle, South Dakota, a small rural community on the Pine Ridge Indian Reservation. Our little, light-blue government house is nestled in a small canyon, a kind of oasis among the bare hills and rolling prairie, and accessible only by dirt road.

A stream runs nearby, and pine trees line the tops of the canyon cliffs; I fondly remember hearing the sweeping sounds of a cool breeze brushing over the treetops, the relaxing murmur of the streams, the hum of the grasshoppers in the meadow, and the sweet smell of ash trees. My dad and I often went on hikes near the stream to open beaver dams. I spent many summers sitting on the porch of that light-blue house, watching the dust from the dirt road do a little pirouette. The land is rich in chokecherry, wild plum, and crabapple trees. The family often picked chokecherries for my mother, who used them to make *wojapi*, a type of pudding and one of the traditional foods of the Lakota people—my people.

My mother was a slender woman with dark-brown skin and long black hair. She was very pretty, and when I was growing up we had a loving relationship. She read bedtime stories to me—my favorites were the *Care Bears* books. Although she only reached the eighth grade, my mother was quite literate. She was a fantastic cook as well—the intoxicating smell of her sweet oven bread often filled the house, which was always stocked with food and coffee in case any guests were to stop by. To be a Lakota meant sharing your home with others, a principle my mother personified.

My father, too, enjoyed making people happy, especially his children. When we did a good job, whether in school or doing the chores, my father would praise us. He believed in education and made that known to his children. He also took on a lot of responsibility in the community—helping Native American inmates find a spiritual path, fighting to revive the Lakota language, and conducting Lakota prayer services for families. I admired his optimism, selflessness, and devotion toward seeing improvement in the lives of others in the community. We occasionally made trips together to Martin, South Dakota—a small farm community located off the reservation—to buy house and lawn supplies. During our trips to town we would listen to old Lakota ceremonial songs on the stereo, and my father would tell me about the old ways.

My father was a singer and song keeper. He sang for many traditional Lakota medicine men from the Pine Ridge reservation who have since passed away. He often regaled us with the songs he sang during ceremonies held by Dawson Has No Horse and Joe Eagle Elk, medicine men not known to the outside world but highly revered on the reservation for their connection to an ancient past, a connection that the US government tried to deny the Lakota people by outlawing many traditional customs for most of the twentieth century.

In the 1980s, my family and I often attended Lakota *yuwipi* ceremonies, a type of prayer service conducted by local medicine men. Yuwipi ceremonies were often held in a basement and conducted in the dark. I especially enjoyed the time right before the ceremony started, when all the people would gather in the basement and sit on blankets that lined the cold floor. Shaking hands with the elders was important, my father said. Originally a social custom of the West, shaking hands on the reservation has come to symbolize one of the four sacred values of Lakota culture—respect. So before the ceremony started, my family and I walked around the room as if in some kind of procession, greeting and shaking hands with everyone. Then I would sit with my mother and watch as others greeted each other. The smell of prairie sage, bitterroot, and flat cedar filled the basement, creating a very sanctified environment. The medicine man would address the people and instruct the singers on what songs to sing. The drums cracked like thunder and the floor of the basement seemed to shift beneath us. This powerful experience often moved me. Most important, ceremony connected us all.

Those days of quiet rituals of family and community life were forever altered just eight days before my eleventh birthday. I was home with my mother, up late watching TV while she was doing some chores around the house. I can distinctly recall the house smelling like ashes and kerosene, which came from the woodstove. I remember walking down the hallway and, for a split second, seeing my mother in her bedroom. I bid her good night and was off to bed. She was preparing to take a bath after a hard day's work of cooking and washing clothes. Exhausted, I fell asleep fast, but the time between falling asleep and the ensuing chaos seemed short.

"Jon Jon, wake up, there is something wrong with Mom!" urged my sister Clovia. Needless to say, I was startled and quickly sat up in bed. My room was dark, but I could see a light coming from the hallway and set out to investigate. At once, I heard a commotion. I walked into the hallway and into my parents' bedroom. Blinded from the bright lights in the room, my eyes took time to adjust. As the room came into focus I saw the family circling the bed where my mother lay motionless.

Apparently my mother was in the bathtub when they found her. I saw my father kneeling next to the bed, nudging my mother and calling her name. "Linda!" he pressed. His austere expression characterized his approach to any challenging situation. Meanwhile, my brothers, sisters, and I stood behind him, our aunts surrounding us, watching, as my father tried repeatedly to wake my mother. The fear in the room was palpable.

While waiting for the ambulance, I too began to panic. My body, my emotions, and all my thoughts were suspended. I will never forget the moment when they called me over to the bed where my mother lay. I did not understand why I was summoned to stand next to her, everything was happening so fast. My aunts encouraged me to try and wake my mother. I walked over to the bed, my body trembling. "Call mom's name," Clovia urged. My aunts, brothers, and sisters said the same, "Call her name!" The pressure was unimaginable. I stood next to my mother's motionless body, calling her name. "Mom." No answer. The room was silent. I tried again, this time with more force, "Mom, wake up!" My voice shaking, I was frustrated and angry. "Mom, wake up!!" It was no use. She would not wake up, and soon after the ambulance arrived.

I remember feeling relieved when the ambulance came. Two tall men, reservation paramedics, put my mother on a stretcher and carried her out of the bedroom, down the narrow hall, and out the front door. A cold chill moved through the house as they carried her from our home. I remember the sky was clear that night, and the stars were out. The air was cold and crisp. They put my mother in the old white ambulance, its red lights flashing, as they drove her to a nearby hospital off the reservation. My father and a few others followed the ambulance. I stayed home telling myself that the hospital will fix her and I did not need to worry. Besides, I had school the next day. I remember feeling anxious but expecting to see my mother in the morning. Hours passed before my sister woke me again.

"Jon Jon get up," she said in a subdued voice. Finally, the anticipation was over; I was going to see my mother. I climbed out from under my sheets to my parents' bedroom. The house still felt cold and damp. My father sat whimpering on the bed where my mother had been lying just hours before, his elbows on his knees and his face in his hands. Everyone was quiet. My father could not control himself, and his cries became louder until they filled the house. I put one arm around my father's neck and I, too, began to sob. None of us slept that night. We just sat there in my parents' bedroom—confused.

It was not until later in life that I began to understand the impact that my mother's death had on my family. Growing up, we were loved, protected, appreciated, and had stability. I could not ask for a better upbringing. After my mother's death, our home life changed dramatically. The family now lacked stability in an environment that was already prone to family dysfunction, and we were forced to take care of ourselves. We had to cook our own meals, wash our own clothes, and clean our own rooms, things my mother did for us. I often cooked for my little brother, nephews, nieces, and my father. I constantly took on house chores like sweeping, mopping, and washing the dishes. My father would often say, "Jon Jon, you can't depend on anyone. You have to take care of yourself." My father's lesson on independence, I think, was born from his watching, like a powerless spectator, this dysfunction move into our once stable home.

Black mold spread through our house. The light-blue carpet that came standard with the home was chock-full of dirt and discolored. Clouds of dust would engulf the hallway in the wake of children running through the house, likely the cause of several cases of pneumonia. Eventually the decision was made to remove the carpet and we walked on untiled floors for some time before my father could afford to fix them. I also remember that a male relative, his wife, and their children were living in a tent on the lawn outside our home. There was a wobbly table outside the tent, on which they had placed an electric pan used for cooking. There were also a few canned goods and bowls that sat on the wobbly table. I could not imagine the hurt and shame they felt after being reduced to living in a camping tent. Like some families on the reservation, we lived under these conditions for some time.

When my mother was alive, we faced hardships, but managed to keep our home in balance. Her death left us in a haze. We were absent any instructions to understand or take action against the unfavorable changes that were happening in our home. On occasion I would ask myself: Are Lakota people supposed to live in disrepair? History books, news outlets, and research articles are always highlighting the latest calamities of Lakota people—high rates of violence, dilapidated homes, poor health, etc. After centuries of resilience in the face of challenges, it is easy to see how one additional tragedy in the lives of so many Lakota families could be enough to drive them to surrender to the low expectations imposed on our reservation. It is a virulent cycle of marginalization and disempowerment. Having the power to control one's destiny, for some Lakota families, seems like a fairy tale entirely removed from the realities they experience every day.

Growing up, I held on to the belief that the power to defeat dysfunction and poverty, which plagued the reservation, resided in education. Education as power was difficult to believe in when the very schools that were tasked with providing that education were crippled by dysfunction too. The truth is I was far from academically prepared for any opportunities after graduation. In fact, a majority of students in our area perform below grade level when it comes to reading, writing, and math. Most reservation schools have not been able to reach a level of function that will allow for greater academic outcomes and opportunities for students. When I graduated, I walked across the stage with approximately seventy students, and roughly five entered college directly after high school. That is less than 8 percent!

With a lack of proper preparation, students progress through school with low expectations, and it is hard to believe you are destined for the best schools or the best jobs. Why? First, there is a pervasive notion among students that it is OK to settle for less—community college or dead-end jobs. Many Lakota students in this context do not even entertain the idea of applying to or attending a quality college. Second, faced with limited job options, so many students become dependent on assistance from the US government. Last, it is most depressing to see students slip into a life of violence, drugs, alcohol, and poverty. Like me, students from my reservation oftentimes do not take the direct route to college that is so common for many non-Native students in this country. I understood that, without a quality education, it is significantly more difficult to find one's way through life. With all my hope for a better future, I still could not help but feel "lost" to the cycle of dysfunction and poverty.

This sense of being "lost" was difficult because it had a strong effect on my sense of identity. I was proud to grow up on the reservation. I identified myself with one thing and one thing only—Lakota. I lived and breathed the Lakota culture and way of life. I was given a Lakota name—*Ozuye Cikala* (Little Warrior), went to ceremonies, and sang with my father at various Sun Dances throughout the reservation. I attended an all-Indian, tribally run school. These, I thought, solidified my identity as Lakota. So, as a young man, to have my identity questioned was difficult.

I felt that the foundation on which my identity rested could give way at any moment. Students would insinuate that rather than being Lakota, I was of more Hispanic or Middle Eastern ancestry—no doubt because of my thick black eyebrows and dark wavy hair. These were heavy blows to my sense of who I was, so I had to be tough to counteract the insults. Like so many other kids on the reservation who feel uncertain about who they are, I began to carry a lot of anger as a defense mechanism. I started to wear angry facial expressions like a mask, so that my anger was apparent to everyone around me. The mask let the other kids know, before they had a chance to make fun of me or hurt me, that there would be consequences. Unfortunately, a side effect of maintaining this outward appearance would come in the form of anxiety. I became anxious in just about any setting—in the classroom, hanging out with friends, and sometimes around my own family. With a dysfunctional home life, the challenging social and academic maze of high school, and my increasingly repressed feelings, exhaustion began to set in. The idea of furthering my education was losing its strength. I was beginning to entertain the idea of settling for the low expectations set for people from the reservation—a low-paying job, little education, and dependence on the government.

Identity, I feel, is something that not all families talk about on my reservation. There are many positives—culture, community, and love. Fears and insecurities, however, get brushed under the rug. The reality is that teasing and indirect comments about identity are common, but positive and direct discussions about forming a strong self-identity often do not occur, perhaps because of a lack of education on the subject. Not only did I live with this sense of not having a direction in life, but I also felt that I somehow did not belong. Is it not clear how some students from the reservation are sent adrift in this sea of dysfunction? In this tempest of uncertainty, I was reaching a breaking point. Then, at a critical moment in my life, I was given a much-needed push to keep the idea of furthering my education alive.

My high-school English teacher, Giles Morris, was a young, energetic, jovial white man from Boston, Massachusetts. Reservation schools often rely on outsiders, usually young white people from the East who will stay two or three years, tops, or the cast-offs from the surrounding school systems, which can make the quality of education inconsistent at times. Giles, however, was able to bring into focus my fondness for reading. He was the first teacher that I can remember to require his students to read an entire novel. In fact, it was the first time I read Shakespeare and *The Great Gatsby*, literature considered critical in most schools. One day, Giles introduced the class to *The Catcher in the Rye* by J. D. Salinger. I will never forget this book as I immediately related to the main character, Holden Caulfield. I could not put the book down and read it every chance I got. Despite all our apparent dissimilarities, I, like Holden's character, was displeased with my school and the way my life was unfolding. Like me, Holden was dealing with the loss of someone very dear to his heart, a loss that disturbed the normal function of his family, life, and identity. Holden affirmed for me not only that life is full of hardship, but that holding on to those hardships can make life's journey much more difficult. I needed to somehow *let go* of all the pain I was carrying and further my education. I did not want dysfunction and poverty to be my fate, so I went with my conscience and decided to enlist in the army, face the perils of combat, and later solve the puzzle that is applying to college.

I made the trip to MEPS (Military Entrance Processing Station) in Sioux Falls, South Dakota, during my senior year in high school and signed up to join the army. I did my eighteen-week basic training at Fort

Knox, Kentucky. A year later I was deployed during the initial invasion of the war in Iraq. We spent a week or so near the Kuwait/Iraq border. There were a few fights during the invasion, but it was not until we got to Baghdad that the level of combat increased. In addition to providing security for key locations such as municipal buildings and factories, we also conducted routine security checkpoints throughout the city. War, at times, seemed like an impassable hurdle in my journey to attain an education, but there were familiar hurdles that I continued to negotiate.

To a certain extent, a soldier expects to find himself imperiled by enemy fire, but facing bombardment on my identity is quite a different thing. It happened during our convoy, thousands of military vehicles inching toward the capital city of Baghdad. The sky was a clear blue, and the day was dusty and hot. Our convoy drew to a halt near a small Iraqi town, so we decided to dismount our tanks, get some fresh air, and stretch our legs. It was common for some Iraqi locals, mostly men dressed in traditional Iraqi robes, to approach our tank. We were wary at times because you never knew where the enemy was coming from, but these encounters were mostly cordial. One of the Iraqi men looked to me and casually said, "Are you Kuwaiti?" My tank crew had a good chuckle. My tank commander caught his breath and said, "No, he's Indian! Red Indian? You know, feathers?" While I recognized his attempt to remedy the confusion, and forgive his stereotypical depiction of Native people, the question was yet another glancing blow to how I identified myself. Why couldn't I just be a Lakota warrior or an American warrior? Serving during wartime was seen as a huge honor in Lakota country, an honor connected to the history and traditions born from the countless deeds carried out by Lakota warriors of the olden days. Yet how am I supposed to live up to this honor when my identity as a Lakota warrior was put into question? What I began to realize was that issues with identity do not fade over time and, instead, they become heavy burdens to carry unless you choose to deal with it.

I had no intention of staying in the military after my enlistment was up, so five months following my tour in Iraq I was honorably discharged. I became a counselor's aide at a drug- and alcohol-treatment center back on my reservation. Providing a service to my community through working with troubled youths was rewarding. It was during this time that my own life started to take a turn for the better. I had the good fortune to meet my future wife, Deana Wagner, a member of the Cherokee Nation of Oklahoma. She graduated from Brown University and joined Teach For America as a member of the inaugural South Dakota corps. She was placed as a high school science teacher at my former school. When I first met Deana I was afraid to reveal my world to her, a world that had been so full of dysfunction, but she was completely understanding and nonjudgmental. She also has a passion for helping Native people. Most important, she accepted me for who I am and where I come from. She is everything I could ask for in a friend and companion. It was the start of a strong and beautiful relationship.

Overall, the two years I spent on the reservation after my military service were positive, because I was thankful to be home and surrounded by family and friends once again. My relationship with my father evolved and seemed renewed. While I was growing up, we never spoke of anything too deep or personal, but now, as veterans of war, we had something in common. We often talked about war. We would talk about the psychology of the mind during wartime and how fellow soldiers often would resort to brutal tactics. He confessed to me the few times he came close to death. My father was, in fact, wounded during Vietnam and awarded the Purple Heart. We also talked about his time growing up and his struggle with alcoholism. He talked about a time when he would receive his paycheck, leave some money with our mom and my brother Milton (who was an only child at the time), then proceed to the nearest bar and spend the rest of it on booze. It was a dark chapter in his life, but he eventually stopped drinking for the sake of his family. He wanted to provide a better life for his children and did so by turning to a life of Lakota culture. Singing was my father's calling, and it helped set him on a positive path. We found room in our relationship to talk about our feelings, which was long overdue. It was healing to see this side of my father because it showed that he, too, felt lost in terms of his place in the world. We began to talk about the difficulties we experienced around the time of my mother's death, an ordeal that prevented us from having an ideal father-son relationship. I cherish the conversations we had and the time we spent together after my discharge from the military. I think the conversations with my father gave me the courage to continue examining my own identity, this at a time when a secret about who I was suddenly emerged.

One afternoon when I was twenty-four years old and working on some client files at the treatment center, I received a phone call from a woman I did not know:

"Hello son," she said.
"Who is this?" I asked.
"This is your mom," she replied.

I was not sure why, but at that moment I was quickly boiling with anger inside. My anxiety kicked in and my heart began to race. There was nothing left to do but react.

"You're not my mother!!" I said, and I slammed the phone down.

I was furious! Who does this woman think she is? I knew my mother was Linda Around Him. I sat in the office of the treatment center for a few hours, trying to gather my thoughts and composure. I was shocked by the mysterious woman's statement as well as my very emotional reaction. Why was I so emotional? The truth is there had been nagging incidents in the past that had unsettled me.

I remember a hearing at the tribal offices in Pine Ridge where a man motioned his hand toward me and said, "OK, so the child's name is John Little Hawk?" My father quickly responded, "Little Hawk? No! His name is John Around Him." I turned to my sister feeling confused and anxious. She shook her head in disagreement and reassured me that I am an Around Him. On another occasion a relative walked up to me and said, "My mom says Linda is not your real mom." I remember these incidents vividly, and in each case my siblings were quick to reassure me that we shared the same parents. Growing up I was never treated differently from my brothers and sisters, and so I never doubted who my biological parents were. Nevertheless, the strange incidents piled up over time and the doubt gradually increased. After the call from the anonymous woman claiming to be my mother, I finally decided to confront my father and family about it.

One evening soon after the unsettling call, I beckoned my family into the house for a meeting. My father often brought us together whenever there were any issues in the family, but never would we meet at the request of any of us kids. My father, my sister Clovia, and my little brother Samuel sat around our dining-room table in our small, light-blue house. I was very nervous and could feel my palms getting sweaty. I sat next to my father and told him that a woman had called claiming to be my mother. My father appeared uneasy and shifted a few times in his chair. I finally mustered enough courage to ask: "Dad, was I adopted?" His head dropped immediately and he began rubbing the back of his neck, concentrating on what he wanted to say. His lips gathered and contracted. Then he said, "Well, son . . . yes . . . you were adopted." His voice was a bit shaky. He paused for a moment. I noticed I was shaking too and couldn't swallow. My father pressed on: "When you were a baby, you were abandoned at the hospital. Your biological mother was having a hard time with alcohol and drugs. The nurse at the hospital knew who I was, she knew I was related to your biological mother, so she called and told me what happened. So Linda and I went to the hospital. Linda picked you up. She said in Lakota, 'Let's take him home.' That night we brought you home with us."

The words "Let's take him home" resonated with me on a deep and profound level. My deep affection for "home" was cultivated from the dawn of my existence. It was an emotional moment for everyone in the room. Inside, I felt a sense of relief at hearing the truth. The revelation of my adoption began to shed more light on who I was, and I felt like I could begin to bring some closure to this gray area in my life. I tried gathering my thoughts, and spoke through tear-filled eyes: "Well, Dad, thank-you for telling me. I don't want you guys to worry. I am not mad. This does not change anything. You will always be my dad. Linda will always be my mother. Milton, Amaris, Clovia, and Samuel will always be my brothers and sisters. You raised me and brought me into your home, and I thank you for that."

I hugged my dad, turned, and embraced my brother and sister as well. I have since come to find out that many of my relatives and family members knew about my adoption and that they collectively tried to keep it a secret. My aunt says they feared I might rebel if I knew about the adoption, which is understandable. Would I have rebelled or run away like some adolescents dealing with adoption or divorce do? I do not know. What I have learned, however, is that life is not only a journey of discovering your identity, but also one of confronting the difficult question: Are you willing to accept your identity, imperfections and all? Wrestling with this question is a step toward reaching some semblance of peace with who you are.

A friend who was a counselor at the alcohol- and drug-treatment center helped me put things into perspective. The counselor said, "John, these things are difficult. Just know that your dad (John Around Him) probably saved your life." These were powerful words at the time. Indeed, who knows where I would be had John and Linda not walked into the hospital that day. This part of me, the adoption, would no longer be a source of insecurity but a reminder of how lucky I was. From what I am told, my biological mother still struggles to this day with some of the challenges that led to her choice of giving me up for adoption. I discovered that I have several other biological sisters and brothers who have been raised by other relatives. Some of these siblings I have met and others I have not. I have also discovered that we share Mexican ancestry through my biological mother, confirming early suspicions of my having mixed ancestry, the truth of which was comforting. My father, John, always told me that a part of being Lakota is having the ability to forgive. I decided that I would no

longer hold on to to my feelings of anger and resentment, which came
from my troubles with identity. Instead, I would forgive myself by accepting my adoption and my mixed heritage. I also think that I am willing to
take steps toward forgiving my biological mother. Talking about it here
has been an act of forgiveness in itself and a step toward achieving peace.

After two years of working on the reservation, a fire inside of me was
stoked and I was driven more than ever to pursue higher education. Deana
was accepted to the Harvard School of Public Health to pursue a master of
science degree. Around this time my father, whom I had come to respect
and love with all my heart, and who also believed in education, lost his life
in a battle with cancer. I followed Deana to Massachusetts and enrolled in
Boston's Bunker Hill Community College (BHCC) in hopes of finding
better opportunities. My experience living in Boston, which included
working in a pastry shop and attending community college, opened my
eyes to the challenges of inner-city life. Many of my classmates were minorities. Several were from countries in Africa and Asia, and all lived in
low-income neighborhoods with inadequate public education. Growing
up, it was easy to think that life was less troubled for those off the reservation. As my horizons have expanded, I have come to realize that poor
education does not discriminate. Even though these students often held
multiple jobs, had families to care for, and made long commutes, they still
came to school.

At BHCC I met Wick Sloane, an adjunct English professor who taught
expository writing and was to become my mentor and friend. I came to
learn that Professor Sloane is a staunch advocate for students from disadvantaged communities and writes about equity issues for people who
are enrolled at two-year institutions, who often have fewer opportunities open to them than students at four-year colleges and universities.
He would track down students who stopped going to class to find out
the reasons why, and to offer his help. Professor Sloane believed in me
and thought I belonged in a four-year college. He too understood the
tendency among impoverished students to settle for less, so he encouraged me to apply to Dartmouth because of its excellence. With some
college preparation and a below-average high-school record, it took me
some time to believe I could succeed at Dartmouth. Rather than play
down my chances, for once I dared to believe that I was destined for
the best. I applied for admission to Dartmouth in winter of 2008. When
I later received an envelope from Dartmouth in the mail, with so much of
my future hanging in the balance, I remember feeling almost paralyzed
before opening it. The letter read: "We are pleased to inform you that

you have been accepted . . ." I could not believe what I was reading. After the feelings of hopelessness I experienced living on the reservation, the memories of dodging bullets during war, finally I felt I was given a break. It was truly an amazing moment.

I was excited about meeting new people and continuing my pursuit of higher education, but my transition to Dartmouth was far from easy. Dartmouth was yet another mirror forcing me to reflect on my identity, which was still a work in progress. Academically, I did great my freshman year. Still, as a much older (I matriculated when I was twenty-six), Iraq War veteran, Native American undergraduate student, I struggled to find my place within the Dartmouth community. I began to feel isolated and searched for a place to "fit in." The following year I promised myself I would make an effort to build relationships within the Native American and greater Dartmouth communities to prevent further isolation. What started as a plan to build relationships turned into one of the most tumultuous years of my Dartmouth career. I found myself losing sight of my priorities and responsibilities that I had set for myself at the outset. I began dedicating less time to doing homework and going to class, and, not surprisingly, my grades began to decline and passing my exams became a desperate battle. I had a growing and familiar sense of self-doubt and nervousness. A pattern of academic and social difficulty, similar to what I had experienced in high school, began to develop. I could feel myself reverting to those old methods of repressing my feelings. This time I was ready to tackle my issues head-on and I decided that I would no longer hide from them. So I sought help.

Through counseling I was able to slow down and take a closer look at myself. I was too worried about trying to "fit in" at Dartmouth—fitting in was something I have dealt with my whole life. In the process, I sacrificed my own values and goals. First, I was officially diagnosed as having suffered from anxiety, depression, and low self-esteem. This was another revelation shedding light on the shadows of my identity. There was a sense of relief in having the ability to name the problems I dealt with on a day-to-day basis. In high school, and somewhat at Dartmouth, my psyche translated these problems into the belief that I was defective and a failure. I thought I could never compete with the best at institutions like Dartmouth because my anxiety constantly produced self-defeating thoughts. I could never be a person capable of making change. I was broken. Because of my anxiety I had head tremors and sweaty palms while speaking in front of my classmates, and the disorder fed into further negative thoughts that I would be perceived as a fool or idiot by my peers. Second, in this cloud of self-doubt, I was forgetting why I came to Dartmouth in the first place—to help my community fight dysfunction and poverty. I began to realize that it was my own insecurities that prevented me from taking a firm hold of my identity and my goals. Counseling helped me see this and get back on track with my coursework while putting some of the pieces of my life together. Learning about my anxiety and ways to cope was liberating because I had hidden from it for too long. Slowly but steadily I gained confidence in my abilities and chances of success at Dartmouth College, and I did so with decreasing anxiety and a growing internal sense of peace. Counseling certainly helped me perform to my potential during the latter part of my undergraduate experience.

My Dartmouth experience was great and I don't regret one second of it. I will never forget walking across the stage with my diploma while my wife and her uncle, my sisters and little brother, my uncle through Lakota adoption—Albert White Hat—and his wife, and several others who have supported me along my journey looked on in the audience. During the NAD (Native Americans at Dartmouth) graduation reception, I took the opportunity to thank those who have helped me along the way, especially my late father—John Around Him Sr. My dad wanted an education for me more than anything in the world. I think he was frustrated at how difficult it was for Lakota students to get a good education. He was tired of watching students suffer from the realities of poverty, drugs and alcohol, and dysfunction on my reservation. Receiving my degree was my way of saying, "Dad, I did it. Thank you for making me who I am today. I will continue your mission of helping our people." Looking back, even though my father and I did not directly discuss identity, he showed me that I was not alone in trying to make sense of who I am. Perhaps finding our identity is a constant and evolving journey that we all take.

I am thankful that my father *showed* me the Lakota way of life. It is the Lakota way of life that I eventually intend to support using what I have learned at Dartmouth through bringing new institutions to the reservation, such as school systems that have shown elsewhere that they can produce successful college-bound students. It is my hope then that students in these schools will someday, like me, return to the reservation and help rebuild and heal our community. I also want to establish a program to preserve the Lakota culture and language by bringing more focus on language education and preservation. I intend to work to ensure that both the state and federal government recognize the serious problem of severely inadequate education systems on the reservation, and commit them to join us in improving educational opportunities for Native youth.

The trauma of my year in Iraq has loosened its hold and I am now able to look back on the richness of my early life as well as its extraordinary challenges with acceptance and a quiet mind. I am beginning to understand that growing up I was a kid who lived his entire life filled with anxiety and low self-esteem. My life on the reservation, my war experience in Iraq, and my time at an Ivy League college have made for an unpredictable journey, but one that has provided me with loving relationships and strengthened me for what lies ahead. I have overcome a lot, and in the process, I have learned to accept who I am and to truly just be myself. Finding one's identity is not always easy, but it is a journey worth taking. I will bring with me on my journey a simple axiom for living that my father taught me: "A person who cares and who takes an interest in the success of others will make a difference."

John Around Him currently lives in Baltimore, Maryland, where he teaches freshman English at Cristo Jesuit High School, a college preparatory school aimed at helping disadvantaged youth gain access to college. John lives with his wife, Deana, a recent graduate of Johns Hopkins Doctor of Public Health program. While this anthology was in production, John and Deana welcomed their son, Logan.

John continues to seek new experiences in education, hoping to build a strong application for graduate studies in the future. He maintains his goal of returning to the Pine Ridge Indian Reservation in hopes of helping Lakota students gain access to college while working to preserve Lakota culture and language. John's siblings and relatives, who have been a source of enormous support, continue to sustain the work of his late father by conducting Lakota ceremonies and traditions. John hopes that one day his own children and relatives will read of his experiences growing up and use those as a compass in finding their own identities and purpose in life. *Pilamaya Yelo* (Thank You).

PART IV

CONTINUING EDUCATION

NADs Reflect on Their Journeys

11

I Walk in Beauty   Davina Ruth Begaye Two Bears

Sleet pelted down from a steel-gray sky. It was a cold Thanksgiving Day in Winslow, Arizona, on November 28, 1968. Anita looked out her window from her bed at the Indian Hospital. The naked branches of the trees rattled in the wind, but Anita was happy. She thought again about the birth of her first child, and curled protectively around her newborn daughter. At the first sight of baby in the delivery room, Anita had cried, "Oh, look at my shiny baby!"

The name "Shiny" has stuck with me, but my real name is Davina. Like my mother twenty-six years ago, I face the ultimate challenge of childbirth and parenthood. My husband and I are happily expecting our first child this year. A family of my own is something that I've always wanted—a family free of alcohol abuse, poverty, and divorce. Our baby will be born in Wisconsin, my husband's traditional native homeland. He is Wisconsin Winnebago, or Ho-Chunk. I am Navajo, or Diné. After we graduated from Dartmouth, we traveled across the country to Arizona, where we lived and worked for four years. I was able to enjoy being with my immediate family after being away from them while back East attending college. Now it is my husband's time to enjoy his family after eight years of being away from home.

While in Arizona, my husband and I had the unique and gratifying opportunity to work for the Navajo National Archaeology Department. The contract archaeology we were exposed to instilled in us valuable, practical knowledge concerning cultural-resource management. My experience with the Navajo Nation will always be precious to me because it gave me the opportunity to work for my people and to learn to speak more of my language, and because it introduced me to the beauty of the land that makes up the Navajo reservation.

Now we are applying our education and experience to the Ho-Chunk Nation, as they begin to develop and grow in this area. It is my husband's turn to work for his people, and to learn from them.

Our interest in cultural-resource management took root while we were both students at Dartmouth. I perceive cultural-resource management as a way to maintain and preserve a group's language, culture, and traditions—a challenge facing many Native American tribes today. My interest in this area was greatly encouraged at Dartmouth and through Dartmouth's Native American Program, Native American Studies Department, and Anthropology Department, where I learned more than I could imagine about Native American culture, history, and current affairs.

Whoever thought that I would attend college back East? Not me, although I am the daughter of college-educated parents. My real dad and mother met in 1966 at Northern Arizona University, where I am currently finishing up a master's degree in anthropology. My mother graduated after eleven years of hard work; my dad never finished.

As a college student and in general, Mother did not trust any man. Although she befriended many of her male suitors, she was not interested in having a "boyfriend." Then she met my dad. He was different, and intrigued her with his intelligence, sophistication, sarcasm, and in-depth knowledge of life in the Navajo world and in the white world. He was unlike any other person she had ever met.

For the first part of my life, we lived, or tried to live, as a family—a mother, father, and four daughters, of whom I am the oldest. My father was never home like a parent should be. I remember tramping through deep snow when I was three in search of dad in the seedy bars of downtown Flagstaff. It was common for him to leave us to fend for ourselves with no money for rent, food, school supplies, whatever. Who knows what he did on his excursions? My mother rarely followed him to his "drinking get-togethers." The times he did make it home, he was often drunk out of his mind. His stays with the family varied from a few days to a few months, then he'd disappear again—no note, no warning, nothing. Often he would get a job, then take the paycheck, leaving us penniless. The whole process repeated itself again and again like a broken record. But my sisters and I were always happy to see him. I loved it when we were all together as a family.

My dad had many friends who believed in his potential—professors, coworkers, etc. Time after time they tried to support him with job opportunities, academic extensions, and numerous second chances because they saw him as an inquisitive and intelligent person. But he would always let them down by quitting and then drinking.

I ask my mom questions about him often, because my dad is no longer living. He passed away in a drinking-and-driving accident in 1985. He was never happy on this earth. The predicament of Native Americans—primarily their loss of land, language, culture, and traditions—plagued him, driving him to liquor, despair, and finally to his untimely death. To my mother, he often patiently remarked, "You are so innocent. You just don't understand." She, faced with the reality of raising four girls and the trials and tribulations of his alcoholism, found his remarks infuriating and of no practical use or help. Neither my mother nor her four daughters could rescue or change him.

However, I learned from my dad in many ways. First, he influenced me not to be what he was—an alcoholic. I'm sure that I'm not the only Indian person who experienced this life while growing up. Many children go through the same, or worse. Native Americans have the highest rate of alcoholism of any ethnic group in this country. My father's life showed me that alcohol means you can never live happily or accomplish your goals. He could not hold a job, finish school, support his family's basic needs, or even try to live life in a good way. He tried, but was not successful. Second, and more positively, my dad instilled in me a love of books and reading. My mother tells me that he began reading to my sisters and me when we were very young. I remember him reading books like *The Secret Garden* and *The Wizard of Oz* for our bedtime stories. Despite my dad's faults, I cannot stop loving him, and he will always be my dad. But, unlike my dad, I will not let myself get swallowed into a black hole of depression and drink myself to death.

My mother's example of perseverance was our saving grace and my standard to follow. Instead of giving up on her education, she went from class to class, semester to semester, and year to year. It was to our advantage that she stayed at NAU; otherwise, we would have had no place to live. She worked odd jobs and kept us clothed, well-fed, well-mannered, loved, and happy. What more could a child ask for? We didn't care that our clothes were all secondhand or from the church donation box, because deep down we knew that our mom would always be there for us. Children need love, care, and support from their parents. My mom was all of that to us. She was the person who came to all our school functions; she made sweets for our bake sales; she helped us with our homework or found someone to help us; she cooked dinner every night and made sure we went to school every day. My dad's drinking was always a problem, but she did not let it get her down, just as she doesn't let any bad news or crisis get the best of her even today. In my eyes, my mother always comes out on top with her kindness, generosity, and grace intact. She is the backbone of who I am today; if it weren't for her, how could I have survived? I remember one time, however, that my mother did briefly let go.

My teeth were chattering, I was so cold—but kept watch and tried to look calm. Cars were easily seen from the huge sledding hill that we six girls huddled on. Sledding was fun for the first hour; my two cousins and three sisters screamed and laughed at the top of our lungs as we raced down the hill, dipping crazily and sometimes crashing into snow. Our "sleds" were plastic garbage bags, but we didn't care, we were going down that hill fast. But that was an hour or so ago, when our jeans were still dry and we were warmed by the activity. Now we were pressed close together for warmth under our plastic bags against a tall ponderosa pine tree. All of us were soaking wet. Our socks for mittens weren't working anymore. We were freezing. I felt embarrassed as warmly dressed white people passed us in their stylish snowsuits, boots, mittens, hats, and scarves, asking if we were okay, or where our parents were. If they had really wanted to help, they could have taken off their snowsuits and given them to us.

One by one the cars went by, none of them my mother's blue Dodge Colt. As I listened to the girls whimper and cry, I thought of my mom's behavior over the past couple weeks. Every now and then I uttered a comforting phrase, "She'll be here soon, don't worry. The laundry should be done soon," but even I began to wonder if she had left us for good. I would never have thought this before, but it was as if she was changing into a different person. At night, I crouched next to the heater, which was connected to the living room, and listened to my aunt and mother as they partied with men I did not know. I had never been so mad or scared in my life. I hated what my mom was doing. She began smoking and drinking and, worst of all, she was doing it in our own living room! Yeah, Dad drinks, but not Mom, too! It was a nightmare coming to life. It felt like the world was being turned upside down and inside out. I felt myself begin to panic, because I realized my mom was giving up, just like my dad. Her eyes were different, she seemed like she was in a daze. My mind raced as I thought about my sisters and me. Who is going to take care of us now if both mom and dad drink? How are we going to live? Are we going to wander from family to family looking for care? How could my mother do this? Why do people have to drink? Finally, I saw the Dodge, and I watched as it inched its way up the hill, making sure it was really my mom. Yes, it was her.

I yelled, "Mom's coming!" We all ran toward the entrance of the park, and straight for the car. I looked in the back and saw the laundry was neatly folded in plastic bags. I felt so relieved that she had done what she had said she was going to do, and that she had come back for us. We were all smiling again, and crying tears of joy, as we surrounded her. "Mom, Mom, it was so cold!" "We were freezing!" "I'm tired!" "I'm hungry!" She began to cry, too, and hugged and kissed us all.

She told me later that that day brought her back to reality. We shocked her out of her depression when she saw us there frozen and looking like a bunch of drowned rats. At that point she realized that her purpose in life was her children, and that she could not give in to despair just because she felt like it. We were depending on her, and she couldn't let us down. And she didn't. After that day, she stopped acting "weird" and became "normal" again. At least that is how I thought of her, and I knew that it was a miracle. I think to myself, would I be where I am, or who I am, if she had failed to change that day? Or would I, too, be a drunk, giving up on life, because of the example set by both of my parents? I know that all of my strength is a result of my mother's love, care, respect, and encouragement. I am who I am because she chose not to give up. Many parents do.

Unfortunately, my mom and dad divorced in 1978. It was for a simple reason—my mother did not want us girls to grow up hating and disrespecting my dad. She thought that while were still very young, we should still love, care for, and have some respect for him, and she did not want us to lose that. Otherwise, she said, she could have gone on living the way we had. It was this same year that she also met my stepdad, a nuclear scientist, who lived in my home community on the Navajo reservation. He had befriended a very powerful Navajo medicine man and was living out this dying man's last request. The medicine man wanted the Navajo children of my home community to stay at home. He was tired of seeing young Navajo children bused out to boarding schools, where they would forget their Navajo teachings and be away from their loved ones. It was his dream to build a school in our home community that would not only teach the regular subjects but, more important, teach the culture and language of the Navajo. He asked my future stepdad to do this, and it was being done. My mother's home community on the reservation was having a dinner in his honor, and in a shade house, among all my mother's relatives, he and my mother fell in love.

I guess I was prejudiced, because I could not believe that my mother would replace my father with a disgusting, rude white man—and that's what I thought of him. I'll be the first to admit that I could not stand anything about him. I was the oldest and therefore knew my real dad the longest, so of course I would react this way. Before I knew what was happening, my mother and stepdad were married, and we moved to my home community of Bird Springs and began attending Little Singer School—the result of the medicine man's dream. It was and is a spectacular accomplishment—a school composed of two geodesic domes facing east, powered by wind generators and heated by solar panels from the sun. Everyone in the community pitched in and worked together to build this dream, and my sisters and I were lucky to be part of the first class.

It is ironic that it took a white man to bring my mom and us girls back to our "roots." We had lived on the reservation before, but that was in Tuba City, my dad's home community. Thus, it was my stepdad who was responsible for a very precious time in my life. In Bird Springs, we lived with our maternal relatives, which is a Navajo custom, for the first time. It was during this time that my sisters and I learned to read and write in Navajo, listened to Navajo being spoken all the time, and discovered more about what it is to be Navajo. Although my real dad was fluent in Navajo and knew the culture, he did not pass that knowledge on to us. My mother did the best she could, but she is not fluent in Navajo, although she understands it. She knows the values Navajo women hold, and that is what she passed on to my sisters and me. We were so happy during this time. I thought of my dad often, but we never saw him. He knew where we were, and we got mail from him once in a while, but he never came to visit.

Life with my stepdad, although difficult at times, was a learning experience in and of itself. He accumulated hundreds of books for our growing library, and my sisters and I always had plenty to read. My mother encouraged us as well by making sure that we visited the library in Winslow, Arizona. My stepdad was also into every electronic gadget imaginable, and worked to acquire the latest innovations in computer software and hardware. He was self-sufficient and pursued several business ventures during this time. Good came out of each one, even though they failed financially. We were always with my mom and stepdad on their business trips, and traveled to places we never thought we'd ever get to on our own. I'll admit that life with my stepdad was always interesting and a constant wonder. Although I found him extremely annoying most of the time, what he gave to my mom, my sisters, and me can never be measured or appreciated enough.

Thus I learned from and was influenced by all three of my parents—my dad, mom, and stepdad. However, at a very young age, I knew that I wanted to excel academically. Why do poorly in school, when you can just as easily do well? Why not try your best and challenge yourself to do better each time in everything, mental and physical? If you fail in one area, you may succeed gloriously in others. As I reached junior high and high school, I was further motivated to do well academically because of the negative stereotypes that I encountered. Many people believe that all Indians do is live off the government in a drunken stupor. This mentality was unfortunately passed on to their children—my classmates. I always wanted to be a good student and to challenge myself; I was always trying new and different things. I do not like to sit back and let opportunities pass me by. I may be scared to death, intimidated, and embarrassed, but I know that I can do it, and that it will be good for me. "It" can be anything. I may not win or succeed all the time, but at least I've challenged myself to do something different and new, and I've learned and matured because of the experience. Of course, to do this, or even to think this way, you need a solid foundation and someone who believes in you. For me, it was and is my mother and family, and now my husband.

I was always a good student, and by junior high knew that I wanted to graduate in the top 10 percent of my high-school class. As a high-school student, I purposely took the hardest courses offered because I knew that it would be good for me in the long run. By my senior year I was ready to go to college at any one of the three big universities in Arizona, where I had been accepted and offered scholarships. One day, however, my high-school counselor called me out of class to meet Colleen Larimore, then the Dartmouth Native American admissions recruiter. I was one of two students who my counselor thought should meet Colleen, and I remember sitting in a deserted classroom watching a video on Dartmouth. I had heard of Dartmouth in passing before, and I knew that some Navajo guy was rumored to have gone back East for his college education. I thought it was interesting that a Native woman was all the way out in Winslow recruiting Native American students for a college in New Hampshire, and that is the reason I followed through with the somewhat intimidating application process. I toiled over the essay, rewriting it several times. I chose to write about the phrase "no pain, no gain" as my personal quote. At the Flagstaff mall, my mom and stepdad ate lunch with me as I sealed the envelope to my application. We made a special trip from the reservation that day to mail my Dartmouth application by the deadline. A couple of months later, Colleen called me at home and asked if I would like to visit the college for free. I couldn't believe it! Of course I said yes—this was a big deal for me and my family. My first airplane trip ever was my visit to Dartmouth.

Leaving Flagstaff was scary, and I cried a little when I saw my family waving to me through the airport window. The little plane I was in bounced amid the fluffy white clouds; the turbulence was bad. "Are we going to crash?" I thought to myself. It reminded me of driving on the dirt roads on the reservation, with all the bumps and dips making my stomach tickle. I smiled in delight and uneasiness.

My trip to Hanover began with paranoia. I was convinced that I would get mugged and lose my ticket. So I patted it every so often in my purse to reassure myself that it was still there, safe and sound. But once in Boston, I relaxed. The people talked funny, and the air smelled like fish, but I was feeling great. I made a friend, a Mohawk student who was also participating in the admissions office fly-in program. Talking with him made the four-hour layover in Boston go quickly. While I wasn't looking, he swiped my ticket, and I never knew it until he asked me where it was. In a panic, I searched my purse frantically, and then saw him staring at me, clearly amused. "You took it! Give it back!" I shouted in relief. I felt like an imbecile, that it took no more than friendly conversation with a guy to put me off my guard.

At last we took off for Hanover. We landed in a small airport, similar in size to Flagstaff's. Right away I spotted two Indian students there to meet us. One guy was light-skinned and tall, with wavy hair and a pointy nose. The other student looked Navajo. They were laughing and snickering at something funny, and welcomed us coolly. They continued to entertain themselves with inside jokes and humor, ignoring me, as we loaded our luggage into their car and sped into the pitch-black night.

Navajo was being spoken to me out of that blackness, and it shocked me so that I didn't hear what was said at first. I blurted out, "I don't speak Navajo." I thought to myself, of all places, why the hell does this have to happen to me here in New Hampshire, two thousand miles away from home? It is highly embarrassing for me to admit that I can't understand Navajo to another Navajo who speaks it. But the students carried on with their jokes and snickering, oblivious to my embarrassment. "This is going well," I thought to myself, "what a great first impression I must be making—a Native student who can't even speak her own language. They probably think that I prefer not to speak my own language, or that I prefer not to be recognized as a Native woman." I agonized about what they were thinking about me as we drove on and then dropped off my friend.

Suddenly, the Navajo guy asked if I wanted to stop off at the Native American House, because he needed to find out where my host lived. I acquiesced. Instantly, visions of Indian students madly studying, crouched over their books and calculators, frowning in deep thought danced through my head. I imagined them in well-lit rooms, where bookshelves lined every wall. At the Native American House we descended a rickety staircase into the basement, and my vision shattered. No books? No studying? Several students lounged around a glowing TV, each casually gripping a bottle of beer. Cigarette smoke filled the air. I tried to compose myself, as I was offered a smoke and a beer. It was like a bucket of cold water had been thrown on me, and, in shock, I managed to decline their offers.

For someone who attended study hall at the BIA (Bureau of Indian Affairs) dormitory every night, and never "partied," it is not surprising that my first encounter with college life shocked me. I thought that every person would be studying their brains out, especially since this was an Ivy League school and a weeknight. Was I actually that naive? Some students do, and others don't. My first "reality check" of many during my stay at Dartmouth occurred that night at the Native American House. My host during my stay on campus was a Navajo woman from Shiprock, New Mexico. It surprised me that other Navajos were actually this far away from home and succeeding. She and her friends and roommate took me around campus and entertained me during my trip. I visited a Native American studies class with her. Only four students were present, and they were engaged in a class discussion of the film *Broken Rainbow*, which documents relocation on the Navajo and Hopi reservations and the strip-mining for coal. Never in all of my high-school education had we talked of similar subjects or current Native American issues. I was impressed and dumbstruck by this spectacular experience and discovery.

Most of the NADs (Native Americans at Dartmouth) were happy to meet me, and their enthusiasm to show me a good time was contagious. To me, the Native American students were the most sophisticated, intelligent, and outgoing Indian people I had ever met. The whole of Dartmouth radiated a seductive power. I could sense the seriousness, tradition, and prominence of this institution, as well as the pride the students held in it. I experienced a kind of intellectual ecstasy—I could feel that the whole campus was there to educate and that the students were there to learn. I knew by the end of my trip that I belonged at Dartmouth, among students who were like me. I felt motivated to learn, face new experiences and challenges, and meet new people in order to broaden my horizons and open my mind. Back at my high school in Winslow, Arizona, I wore my newly purchased Dartmouth sweatshirt with pride. A classmate asked if I would like to be interviewed about my acceptance to Dartmouth on the local radio station. I agreed, and my parents heard me in Bird Springs. I remember wondering if anyone cared or knew where or what Dartmouth was. But it was a great feeling to know that I was on my way there. I could feel it in my bones that I was going, even before I received my acceptance letter. I think of it all as a dream come true, especially since I only applied to "see what would happen."

When I returned to campus as a first-year student, I was tested like never before. I think an omen arrived in the mail before I went to Dartmouth—it was a message printed on my achievement test scores: "Based on your performance on this exam, you will represent the bottom ten percent of the student body at the college of your choice [Dartmouth]." For someone who graduated in the top 10 percent of her high-school class, this was alarming news. What a way to build a student's confidence! I wonder if they actually thought they were doing me a favor with that little bit of information. To this day, I curse the standardized-testing company that sent me that letter, because their message became lodged in the back of my mind—a constant reminder of just where I stood. At least that's what I thought.

During Freshman Week incoming students get a head start on life at Dartmouth and take placement tests. It was during this time that our undergraduate adviser (UGA) group held its first meeting. I had just finished moving into Woodward, an all-female dorm. The UGA group was designed to help freshwomen/men during their first year at college. Most of the women in my dorm belonged to my group.

We decided to meet outside, and shuffled onto the front lawn, scattered with bright red and yellow leaves. As we sat in a circle, I promptly began to freeze my ass off on the damp grass. The sun was out, but it was a chilly fall day.

Our UGA, a sophomore, smiled sweetly and began to explain a name game to us. As I looked at all the unfamiliar faces, I felt afraid, intimidated, alone, and different. I was, of course, the only Navajo or Native American person in our group. A pang of homesickness stole into my heart. Our UGA finished her instructions and we began.

The rules were to put an adjective in front of our name that described us and began with the first letter of our name. The object of the game was to introduce ourselves in a way that would help us remember everyone's name. "Musical Melody," said a proud African American woman. A friendly voice chirped, "Amiable Amy," and everyone smiled in agreement. I couldn't think of an adjective to describe me that began with *D*. I racked my brain for an adjective, anything! But it was useless. "Oh, why do I have to be here? I don't belong with all these confident women. Why can't I do this simple thing?" I remember thinking. My palms were sweating, my nose was running, and my teeth began to chatter. I looked at all their faces, so fresh, so clean and confident. It was finally my turn. I still couldn't think of an adjective. In agony, I uttered, "Dumb Davina." "Nooo!" they all protested. Amiable Amy interjected, "Why not *Divine* Davina?" I shot her a smile of gratitude, but I was horrified and embarrassed. How could I have said that and been serious? Talk about low self-esteem.

My first term at Dartmouth went well academically. I received an A, a B, and a C. But I was lonely, even though I was friends with several women in my UGA group. It was hard for me to relate to them, because I felt they did not know who I was as a Native American, and where I was coming from. They also didn't understand my insecurities. How could they, when they believed so strongly in themselves?

I look back at my first year at Dartmouth, and realize that I made it hard on myself. I took it all too seriously, but how could I have known then what I know now? It took me years to be able to think of myself in a positive light. My mother always told me, "You are no better than anybody else. Nobody is better than you." Unfortunately, at Dartmouth her gentle words were lost in my self-pity.

Going home for Christmas almost convinced me to stay home. I was so happy with my family, but I didn't want to think of myself as a quitter, nor did I want anyone else to think of me that way. I came back to an even more depressing winter term. My chemistry course overwhelmed me and I flunked it.

Chemistry was torture, and I could not keep up no matter how hard I tried. A subject that I aced in high school and actually liked did me in that term, and made me feel like a loser. What went wrong? It was just too much information too fast. I was depressed, and my heart was not really in the subject. Finally, I accepted my predicament. I'm not science material, and that's that.

Why did I do so horribly? My note-taking skills were my downfall. They were poor at best. The crux of my problem was trying to distinguish the important facts that I needed to write down from the useless verbiage quickly. By the time I got to writing things down, I'd already have forgotten what the professor had just said. In this way, valuable information slipped through my fingers. Not only were my note-taking skills poor, but so was my ability to participate in class discussion. At Dartmouth, one was expected to follow everything that was being said, think fast, take notes, ask questions, and finally deliver eloquent opinions, answers, and arguments. It was beyond my limited experience and self-confidence to do so. "*Say something!*" I screamed mentally, but it was useless. Fear paralyzed me in class. Outside of class I'd talk, but not in class amid the stares of my peers. My freshman English professor and I would have conversations in her office lasting two or three hours, but in her class, when faced with all my peers, I became mute. Once Michael Dorris, my Native American studies professor, asked me outside of class why I did not speak up in his freshman seminar on American Indian policy. I was tongue-tied. Incredibly, I felt that if I spoke up in class, I would be perceived as stupid. It did not help matters that the discussions there utterly lost me most of the time during my first couple of years at Dartmouth.

On one occasion I did speak up—in an education course, Educational Issues in Contemporary Society. It was a tough course with tons of reading. Participating in the weekly seminar was a significant part of the grade. I never talked to anyone in class. But the professor was always nice to me, saying hi whenever we ran into each other. That day was just like all the other days of the past few weeks. Seated around the oblong table were about fifteen students, the professor, and a teaching assistant. The professor did not lead the discussions; he was there as a participant just like us students, and we determined the content of the seminar. I came in, sat down, and my classmates began to express themselves, taking turns at center stage. I looked from one student to another and wondered how they made it look so easy, wishing that I could, too.

On this day I sat next to my professor, and as usual was lost. The words, ideas, arguments, and opinions whirled around me like a tornado in which I was mercilessly tossed. Too many unfamiliar words, analogies, and thoughts were being expressed for my brain to comprehend, edit, sort, pile, delete, save, etc. But this was nothing new—all of my classes at Dartmouth were confusing to me and extremely difficult.

Out of the blue, as I sat there lost in thought, my professor turned his kind face toward me and asked, "Davina, why don't you ever say anything?" His question was totally unexpected, but not malicious. Rather, it was asked in a respectful tone that invited an answer. Everyone stared me down; they wanted to know, too. I was caught off guard, but thought to myself: this is my chance to explain why I am the way I am. I began hesitantly, frightened out of my wits, but determined to let these people know who I was and where I was coming from.

"Well, I have a hard time here at Dartmouth. I went to school in Arizona. That's where I am from. I went to school in Tuba City, Flagstaff,

Bird Springs, and Winslow, Arizona. So I've gone to school both on and off the Navajo reservation. The schools on the reservation aren't that good. But in Flagstaff, I used to be a good student. Bird Springs, which is my home community, is where I learned about Navajo culture in sixth and seventh grade. I got behind though, because the school didn't have up-to-date books. I mean, we were using books from the 1950s. I really liked it though, because I learned how to sing and dance in Navajo and they taught us how to read and write the Navajo language. I learned the correct way to introduce myself in Navajo, so even though I got behind and had to catch up in the eighth grade, it was the best time of my life, and I learned a lot about my language and traditions. Then when I went to eighth grade and high school in Winslow, I had to stay in the BIA dorm away from my family, because the bus didn't come out that far. So the dorm was for all the Navajo and Hopi students who lived too far away on the reservation. Winslow was a good school, but I don't think I was prepared for an Ivy League school like Dartmouth. I mean, it's so hard being here so far away from home. I used to be in the top 10 percent of my class—now I'm at the bottom of the barrel! Do you know how that makes me feel?"

I couldn't help myself and began to sob. My words were rushing out like they had been bottled up inside for too long.

"It's awful. I feel like I can't do anything here and that the students are so much smarter than me. It seems like everyone knows so much more than me. All of you—it's so easy for you to sit there and talk. It's hard for me to do that. I envy you. I feel like I'm always lost. I hardly ever understand what you guys are talking about. It's that bad. My note-taking skills aren't that good either and it causes me a lot of problems in class, makes me get behind. I mean, we never had to take notes like this at Winslow. And it's hard for me to participate in class discussion. I mean, at Winslow we had to, but not like this. My teacher would put a check by our name after we asked one question. We didn't sit around a table and talk like we do in here. We didn't have to really get into a subject. We didn't even have to write essays. I only wrote one term paper in my junior and senior year. My English teacher would always tell us how much writing we'd have to do in college, but he never made us write! I'm barely hanging on, but here I sit, and that's why I don't participate in class discussion."

I finished my tirade. It was quiet. Nobody said a word. Then my professor leaned over and jokingly admitted, "Don't feel too bad, Davina, I don't understand what they're talking about half the time either."

We all smiled, and it was as if a great weight had been lifted off my shoulders. I'm so glad he prompted me to speak that day, and his comment helped me put it all in perspective. Not everything a Dartmouth student says is profound. It was in this class that I received a citation, which distinguishes a student's work. My professor wrote, "Courage is a sadly lacking quality in the educational world we've created. Davina dared to take steps on behalf of her own growth (and ultimately for her fellows) in an area where she could reasonably expect to be tripped by an insensitive and dominating culture. It was a privilege to accompany her." For Education 20, I received a grade of a D with an academic citation, simultaneously one of the worst and best grade reports a student can receive. "Only I would receive such an absurd grade," I thought to myself in exasperation, but I was proud despite the D. After that day in class, my self-confidence went up a notch. In my junior and senior years at Dartmouth I began to participate in class little by little. By the time I hit graduate school, you couldn't get me to shut up.

During my first year at Dartmouth, I did not find much comfort with fellow Native American students. Why was I so lonely? Isn't that what the purpose of the Native American Program was—to make students like me feel at home? Wasn't I having fun attending NAD functions and parties? To be honest, I participated, yet I did not feel accepted or comfortable among the other NAD students. It was partly due to my lack of self-confidence. Besides, it was apparent that they already had established friends and, except for a few of them, did not seem too concerned about the welfare of new students. I was an outsider, not yet a team player. Although I often talked to Bruce Duthu, the director of the Native American Program, I still felt at a loss around the students.

Finally spring term arrived after a long, dark, cold winter, and I made a new friend. This time it was different, because with Cheryl I felt at ease. She was a fellow Indian woman. We could relate to one another, and she at least had some idea of where I was coming from. However, it was the Dartmouth Powwow that really began my initiation into becoming a full-fledged NAD.

The night before the powwow was a balmy one. As Cheryl and I sat on the marble steps of Dartmouth Hall, we alternately criticized and laughed about Dartmouth life. She lit up a cigarette with a practiced hand and offered me one. I accepted and tried to be cool like her, but my lungs refused to cooperate and I coughed out the smoke. She chuckled at my pitiful attempts, but I didn't mind. I was smoking with a friend and was finally happy. At length, we got up and headed toward the Native American

House, or "the House," as it's fondly called. We entered the front door. The House was quiet and peaceful as I stepped into the study room. On my left, grocery bags full of food lay haphazardly abandoned and ignored. Where was everybody? We were supposed to be dicing up tomatoes, onions, and cheese, shredding lettuce, and, most important, making frybread dough. I knew that it would take a lot of work to do this for our Indian taco booth and powwow, so I rolled up my sleeves and began on the tomatoes. At length, a few more NADs trickled in. "Look at Davina, she's so motivated. Oh, I better get up and help, you're making me feel guilty," Bill teased. After everything was chopped, diced, and shredded, we called it quits. But the next morning, I went straight back to the House, worrying about the frybread dough. We needed to make enough to feed several hundred people, and that would take time. I began to mix the appropriate amounts of flour, baking powder, salt, and warm water, kneading the dough to the right consistency. Cheryl came down from her room upstairs at the House and joined me. After we'd been there a while, Richard, a Navajo guy, came to help. I was secretly happy that I'd beaten him to the job. Navajos are supposed to rise early, and he was late. Did I catch a look of embarrassment on his face? He lined a trash can with a garbage bag and we poured in our dough, Cheryl's Winnebago dough mixed with my Navajo dough.

After the dough was made, we rushed to the powwow grounds at Storrs Pond—a grassy camping area about a mile from campus. Already a line had formed and customers were waiting patiently for their authentic Indian food. We lit our butane stove, put on the cast-iron frying pans, and loaded them with chunks of white lard. The day steamed, and so did we, all day long. I didn't get to see much of the powwow, as the line to our popular Indian taco stand was never-ending. I slaved away and, in the process, relaxed in the familiarity of making frybread. A fellow NAD would pass me a nice cold Coke every so often to quench my thirst. We flapped dough with our hands, joked, laughed, and sweated as each golden round of frybread was snatched from us for the next hungry customer. By the end of the day, I was covered from head to toe in flour, my back and shoulders were tight, and my feet hurt, but I was at peace and happy. I sensed a feeling of camaraderie with the NADs for the first time. The day ended; I got a backrub from a NAD medical student, and it was time for the "49."

The "host drum" group and their family brought cases of beer and began to sing Kiowa 49 songs of romance and pretty Indian girls. We gathered in the picnic area and built a huge bonfire. I drank a beer, my first since coming to Dartmouth, then bravely tried a wine cooler. I visited with the family of the host drum, and we laughed loudly together under the twinkling stars. Soon the singing coaxed us into a round dance. The wine coolers took my shyness away, and my feet stepped in time to the rhythm of the drumbeat and the words of the song.

After a couple of hours my eyes and body drooped with fatigue from all the hard work, the drinks, and now the dancing. I wanted to take a hot shower, wash off the smell of grease and smoke, and sleep. A NAD asked if I'd like a ride back to my dorm, and as I was leaving, several people thanked me for my hard work. After eight months at Dartmouth, I finally felt like I belonged and was part of the Dartmouth Native American family. Never underestimate the power of frybread.

It's amazing how much my life changed after that day at the powwow. Now I couldn't wait to attend all the NAD functions, visit with the other NADs, and enjoy my time at Dartmouth. I wondered if everyone had to prove themselves to the NADs like I did. Did I prove myself? Or did I just become relaxed enough to finally have a good time? Maybe it was both.

Friction did exist in NAD, as people always complained about NAD being too much of a clique, shunning those who were not "full bloods" (full-blooded Indians). I know who I am, a Diné, even though some idiot will always say, "You don't look like an Indian." Well, excuse me for not wearing war paint, buckskin, and feathers. How someone can be ignorant and arrogant enough to know what an Indian "looks like" is beyond me. I've suffered through too damn much not to be an Indian. But I also know and understand the beauty of being Navajo—the strong matrilineal and clan ties; the lessons in my grandmother's strict admonitions; the taste of broiled mutton freshly slaughtered; the feel of dirt in my hair; and the love and wisdom of my mother. How I've lived is Navajo, even if I don't speak and understand my own language fully. How can anyone quantify what part is Navajo and what part is not? I just am. I think some people question what part of them is Indian and what part is not, and that's not healthy.

My sole problem at Dartmouth was that I did not possess self-confidence. I often looked down on myself, thinking that I wasn't good enough, smart enough, sophisticated or rich enough—whatever—to be a part of the Dartmouth family, my UGA group, or a part of NAD. That was always my problem. It took time for me to rise above my self-defeating attitude.

My sophomore year was so totally unlike my freshman year that it's comic. We had a huge and awesome class of incoming Native American freshmen and freshwomen, or '91s, as they're referred to (by the numerals of their year of graduation). All of a sudden, enthusiastic young NADs were popping up everywhere, thirsting for friendships and a good time. I promptly began befriending them and having the time of my life. Aside from the friends I had made in my UGA group, the NADs were about the only people I hung out with. Why try to make friends with people who don't seem to be interested in you? Why make that effort? I'm not sure why it works out that way, but it did in my case. I can honestly say that I never really got close to a white person, other than my roommate. Why is there such a boundary between groups? Was it just me, or was it everybody? I remember getting drunk a couple of times at frat parties, and having long conversations with white people, but then I would never talk to them again, and they weren't my friends.

In the fall of my junior year, I changed my major from visual studies to anthropology. Professor Deborah Nichols became my mentor. I enjoyed her courses on the prehistory of North America. Ever since I can remember, I wanted to go back in time to see what life was like before Columbus. Also, I loved learning about other Indian tribes. Before I came to Dartmouth, I thought that all the Indians east of the Mississippi were extinct—killed off or removed by the United States government. My eyes were opened at Dartmouth. Dartmouth gave me a strong and true sense of Indian pride. Where else could I have taken classes specifically focusing on Indian life, history, literature, and culture? Met and listened to Indian tribal chairpersons, scholars, performers, and artists, as well as traditional elders? The principal chief of the Cherokee Nation, Wilma Mankiller; Dartmouth's own Michael Dorris and Louise Erdrich '76; the Lakota educator Albert Whitehat; and members of the American Indian Dance Theatre were just a few of the people who spoke and/or performed at Dartmouth through the Native American Program, Native American Studies Department, and NAD. Dartmouth's commitment to Native people inspired me to finish my education and to develop and nurture my own growing desire to work for my people or people of other tribes.

Professor Nichols encouraged me to look into the field of archaeology. But after a summer at the field school at Wupatki National Monument in Arizona, I decided that I was uncomfortable excavating the places where Indians once lived and died—anyway, it goes against Navajo religion and teachings. As Professor Nichols did not want me to lose my interest, she presented other options in the field of anthropology. She pointed out that I could help Indians get the remains of their deceased ancestors back, as well as their sacred and ceremonial objects, which were being held in museums all over the country, or I could work on repatriation and reburial issues. Through research for a term paper, I learned more about these issues, and was instantly converted. Anthropology need not be the field most Indians love to hate. Instead of being an anthropologist who takes away from Indian people, I will be an anthropologist who gives back—through work with repatriation and reburial, or in other ways.

My interest prompted me to apply for the senior internship at Dartmouth's Hood Museum of Art. It was an intimidating prospect, but I decided to go for it anyway. I was accepted as one of only two senior interns. It was a glorious experience. I was able to handle the Hood's collections of Native American material objects as I helped transfer them from Webster Hall to a new storage annex at the Hood. I had the privilege of co-curating a major exhibit on Native North American basketry, which entailed conducting research on each and every basket in the collection.

The Native American Program was the reason I chose Dartmouth, and it was the reason I stayed. When I speak of the Native American Program, I am also including the Native Americans at Dartmouth student organization and the Native American Studies Department. NAP was the basis on which I received my education. NAP ensures that Native youth who were raised in remote areas on Indian reservations, often living in poverty, and not able to receive the best education that money can buy, are given a chance to excel at an institution such as Dartmouth. Many Native students attend Dartmouth because they know that with such an education they will be better equipped to serve their home communities or other Native communities. I am such a person.

NAP ensures that Native students are taken care of. They are not forgotten or ignored. It is hard enough getting through college, but it is even harder when you are two thousand–plus miles away from home and you hardly have contact with any other Native people, aside from students. Although I may have felt ignored by other Native students at first, that was partly my fault, as I did not reach out.

Although Dartmouth strives to keep all of its students, some do not make it. My inner strength is my family, as I mentioned, and my beliefs. I believe that we should leave the past behind us—grow from it, learn from it—but go on with your life and do the best that you can. Why not try to make life better for yourself and others? Why waste our time hurting ourselves or others? Just live your life in a good way, the way you want to live it, and be happy. Enjoy it while it lasts.

I've always felt that way. I guess that's why I try to do well in everything I do. I'm not saying that I am better than anyone else. I'm just saying, do what you want to do in beauty. My people have a saying that we use in a prayer, "Walk in beauty." I just realized that's what I always try to do: live in a beautiful way.

Davina Ruth Begaye Two Bears grew up in beautiful Arizona, a proud member of the Diné Nation. She graduated from Dartmouth in 1990 with a major in anthropology, and the following year, she was chosen as a teaching intern at Northfield Mount Hermon School in Massachusetts, where she was a teacher, student adviser, and coach. On returning to Arizona, she began working with her tribe as an archaeologist, and in subsequent years served as a student supervisor for the Navajo Nation Archaeology Department. At that time, she began taking courses toward a master's degree in anthropology at Northern Arizona University. In the future, Davina plans to continue her work in anthropology and pursue her PhD in the field.

Davina married Brady Two Bears, a member of Dartmouth's class of 1991, and together they moved to Wisconsin, where they reside with their daughter, Brenna. They are currently expecting their second child. The essay you have just read was written in 1996.

Follow Up: Shí Asdzą́ą́ Baa—I Am Warrior Woman

Ever since I was a child, I've wanted a family of my own, a home full of love and warmth and, most important, free of divorce and alcoholism. I wanted to be a mother whose first priority was her family, and to raise my children together with my husband in a beautiful house. I did accomplish having my own happy family, just not in the way I imagined.

I may as well have ended my previous essay, which you have just read, with ". . . and we lived happily ever after." I wish I could tell you that was true, that my life is one of married bliss and boundless love. Unfortunately, life is rarely so straightforward. At first everything was going according to plan: Graduate from Dartmouth, check. Get a job, check. Start graduate school, check. Marry your college boyfriend, check. Have kids, check, check, check. Buy a house, check. Get divorced? No, that was never supposed to happen.

The Birth of My First Child

One day in August 1995 I was at home in Tomah, Wisconsin. It was close to 100 degrees outside, with 100 percent humidity. Our tiny one-bedroom house was dark and quiet, as I lay uncomfortably next to my husband.[1] At nine months pregnant, it was a challenge to find a comfortable position. It didn't help that I felt as if my baby and I were being baked alive. The humidity and heat were relentless, so I finally waddled to the bathroom to take a cold shower. Finally, comfortably cool, I lay down to sleep—but just as I did my water broke and the contractions started at a regular pace. My husband, mother, and I loaded up the car and headed for the hospital an hour's drive away in the black of night.

The next day the contractions were stronger, but my baby was taking her time. I walked the halls of the delivery ward, pausing to lean against the hospital walls when the contractions intensified. I longed for my baby to come so the pain would stop. After twenty-eight hours, my body still refusing to dilate and my daughter's heartbeat slowed, the doctors made the swift decision to do a cesarean section. I was on an emotional precipice: Do I give in to my worst fears and panic, or do I agree to major surgery and calmly accept the large needle that will shoot painkillers into my spine? I knew my baby's life was at stake, so I agreed to the C-section. The surgery was quick, and my daughter was born healthy, beautiful, and hungry. When they brought her to me, I took her tiny hand in mine and greeted her in the Navajo language, *Yá'át'ééh shíyázhí*, Hello, my little one.

After my daughter's birth, I was exhausted from the extended labor and the surgery, but nevertheless I was thrust into the realities of motherhood, totally unprepared for the jarring and immediate need to be on call for my newborn daughter 24-7. Even with my mother's help, taking care of the baby was a major ordeal. My mom stayed an extra four weeks to help me out as I recovered from surgery and adjusted to motherhood. I had expected to be able to sleep once the baby was born. Hah! I soon discovered that sleep was a luxury that belonged to my past. Since I decided to breast-feed, I was the only one who could feed my daughter, and my whole life revolved around her comfort. I had to make sure that her diaper wasn't wet or soiled, that she was not hungry, not too cold or too hot, that she was bathed, moisturized, and so on and so on. I was no longer carefree and my life was no longer just about me—it was now all about my child.

I remember thinking at the time that my mother must have been insane to have seven children. My respect for my mother increased exponentially when I realized how tiring it was to care for a newborn baby. And yet I wholeheartedly embraced motherhood. Within four years I had three children, two daughters and a son. I soon realized what my mother always knew—that children are a precious gift, and they keep you motivated, grounded, and sane.

After my mother returned to Arizona, my daughter was my only company during the day, as I had no friends other than my sister-in-law. I talked and sang to my baby constantly, wrapped her tightly in a blanket each morning, then lashed her securely into the Navajo cradleboard my stepfather had sent as a gift. I propped her up in her cradleboard and she watched me do the chores, like my mother had done with me and my Navajo ancestors have done for generations. She loved it! I soon became accustomed to people gawking at my daughter in her cradleboard and tolerated the white women who would excitedly exclaim, "Oh, look at the little papoose!"

I wanted a perfect family, so I did my best to adjust to life in Wisconsin. I was willing to forgo my dreams and goals because I believed that love overcomes all problems. But one never knows the limits of love until it's tested.

My husband and I had a major problem right from the beginning. Navajo culture dictates that my husband should have moved from Wisconsin to my home in Arizona, and not the other way around. Even though I am not a strictly traditional Navajo, my "Navajo-ness" is ingrained in me, and living with the Ho-Chunks was like living in "Opposite Land." In the matrilineal Navajo culture, my children are considered Navajo and members of my mother's clan, *Tódích'íi'nii*, Bitter Water Clan. However, in my husband's patrilineal Ho-Chunk culture, our children are considered only Ho-Chunk—the exact opposite of my cultural teachings. This is just one example of our intertribal cultural conflicts. When you're young and in love, it is hard to foresee how differences in culture, worldview, philosophy, and religion will affect your marriage. You believe that love will conquer all.

The Ho-Chunk Dance

I was excited to attend my first Ho-Chunk Dance in Tomah. It took place in a wooded area around a large lodge made of saplings covered with canvas; many tents were pitched nearby. The Ho-Chunk families milled about inside the lodge and among the tents. At the time, I was an in-law to the Ho-Chunks, the "People of the Big Voice," and I wanted to attend their ceremonies and religious functions to support my husband. I went into the "cook shack," a makeshift wooden structure where dishes were washed and food was prepared and stored. People stopped to talk to my daughter, but I was ignored. My two-year-old daughter toddled happily about near the lodge and I was grateful for her presence because she gave me something to do. I was not allowed to enter the lodge where my husband's initiation was taking place. He was under strict surveillance by his Ho-Chunk kin, and I was not allowed to speak to him for several days. I felt alone and out of place wearing a traditional Ho-Chunk dress. I did everything I could to fit in, which only got me scolded by a Ho-Chunk elder. She knew I was from the Navajo tribe, but since I was a daughter-in-law, I was supposed to know their traditions and abide by them fully. My sister-in-law was not there, and I longed for her guidance. It was finally time to go home, and I was in tears as we drove away from the Ho-Chunk Dance. I thought how alone I was and how weak to be crying. The next day I vowed not to be so weepy and pathetic and thought to myself, "I am a proud Navajo woman, and I will show everyone that I am proud of who I am."

The next day, I wore my satin Navajo shirt and the skirt my mother had sewn. I piled on the Navajo "bling," a heavy silver belt from my parents, a coral necklace from my aunt Rena, and my silver and turquoise rings and bracelets. On my feet I wore the Navajo moccasins I had worn at my Dartmouth graduation. I tied my hair back tightly with white yarn and gazed at my reflection in the mirror. Damn, I looked good! I was amazed how strong I felt in my traditional Navajo clothes, and I could sense my family's love and strength permeating my very being. I held my head higher and my steps were sure when I returned to the Ho-Chunk Dance the next day. Apparently I made an impression, because I was asked to dance in the lodge that evening. I danced proudly and was grateful for the opportunity to do so.

After the Ho-Chunk Dance, I thought to myself, so what if I am sad or treated harshly? There are people on this earth who love and care about me unconditionally, like my mother and family in Arizona. There is a place on this earth where I belong, a place nestled between the four sacred mountains, *Diné Bikéyah*, the Navajo homeland, my true home, and the place where my roots are. The *Diyin Dine'é*, Navajo Holy People, in *Diné Bikéyah* will always recognize me and welcome me as one of their own. No one can take that away from me. This knowledge sustained me through many hard times in Wisconsin.

Several years later, a Ho-Chunk friend of mine told me that she remembered the day I came to the Ho-Chunk Dance dressed in my traditional Navajo clothes and assured me that she had always admired me for it. Unbeknownst to me, everyone was supposed to dress in their best that day, and my friend admired the fact that I had done so by appearing in my best Navajo clothes. However, she didn't realize that I had done so because I needed to feel the strength of my Navajo family.

The Return to Diné Bikéyah

I spent five years in Tomah. My husband and I bought a gargantuan three-bedroom house on five acres of forested land, with a two-car garage and a full basement—perfect for our three children. We had two cars, we were both employed, and we had many Ho-Chunk friends and relatives with whom we socialized often. Our lives were full, and although we were arguably living the Native "American dream," our relationship was far from the idyllic facade we presented to the world.

We both harbored personal demons, which wreaked havoc on our marriage. My demon was suppressing my Navajo identity, my career, and my personal goals. To make the transformation into a "good Ho-Chunk wife," I was expected to assimilate into the Ho-Chunk tribe and adopt the proper behavior of a daughter-in-law from a different tribe. I felt that by not being true to myself I was becoming a puppet, with my strings being yanked to and fro so I would fit into the Ho-Chunk world. All of my dreams—finishing my master's in social and cultural anthropology at Northern Arizona University (NAU), working for the Navajo Nation Archaeology Department (NNAD), and learning more of my Navajo language and culture in Arizona—fell by the wayside. I convinced myself that my dreams were not important in the larger scheme of things.

Although I kept praying that things would get better, our downward spiral was exacerbated by my spouse's struggle with alcoholism. It is ironic, or maybe predestined, that I grew up with an alcoholic father and later married an alcoholic. My spouse's alcoholism led him to commit many unforgivable acts that eventually killed my trust in him. I no longer felt safe in our own home, and my spirit began dying a slow death.

During this time, an image appeared before me often and would not go away. It was of a perfectly white square box with no openings, and I was trapped inside. I would push the walls with all my might, but it was tightly sealed and I could not get out. I soon realized that the white box represented my life in Wisconsin.

Then one day early in 2001, after yet another argument, my husband told me to go home to Arizona. He said, "I don't love you anymore." Although his words pierced my heart, I suddenly saw the top of the white box spring open. I spread my wings and fluttered into the blue sky like a butterfly, gulping in the fresh air, and I felt a tiny flame, my spirit, reignite in the depths of my soul. We had been together for fourteen years—we met at Dartmouth, the birthplace of his alcoholism. The despair I felt at leaving him and my life in Wisconsin was surreal, but I also was at peace for the first time in years. One of my sisters flew in from Arizona to collect me and my three children. On a bitter cold day in January 2001, I drove away from the icy midwestern winter with my sister and my kids to the warmth of Arizona. We had nothing but our clothes, a few toys, and diaper bags.

When we reached the outskirts of Flagstaff, where my mother lived, a thick fog limited visibility. I was anxious to see *Dook'o'oosłííd*, Abalone Shell Mountain, the Navajo's sacred mountain of the West. For an instant the fog parted, and *Dook'o'oosłííd* glittered in the sunlight. The majestic mountain was covered in blinding white snow. I felt a tingle travel from the top of my head to the tip of my toes, for I knew *Dook'o'oosłííd* was welcoming me home.

My mother's house became a halfway house for broken hearts. There I mourned the loss of my marriage as I tried to get my life back in order—for my own sake and for my children. I still longed for my husband and our familiar life in Wisconsin, and felt as if I had survived an earthquake. The seismic shift of leaving my husband was followed by tearful aftershocks for several years. They say a divorce is like a death, and this rang true for me. At the time my mother was also recovering, from the death of her husband, my stepfather, who had passed away a few years before. She understood my loss and pain, and we were kindred spirits. It hurt even more to know how dearly my children, who at the time were age five, three, and one, missed their father. Some days I felt my sanity hanging by a thread, but I refused to give in.

I faced many challenges during this time, including a dramatic child-custody battle. I would not wish that experience on anyone. The love and support of my mother and sisters saw me through that battle and through many tough years. It is probably not surprising that my life mimicked my mother's, since I was the child of an alcoholic. My priorities became finishing my degree, raising my children, and moving forward in my career, which was greatly influenced by a trip back to Dartmouth in 2001.

The Dartmouth Native American Symposium of 2001

Another significant event occurred in my life during this time: I attended the Native American Studies (NAS) symposium at Dartmouth in May

2001, which was titled "On the Threshold: Native American Archaeologist Relations in the Twenty-First Century." I felt I needed to attend,
as I had been "out of the loop" while living in Wisconsin. The many
Native American scholars who presented at the NAS symposium inspired
me deeply. I learned how tribes were using archaeology to reconnect with
their culture through their elders' recollections and explanations of their
material culture being unearthed by archaeological digs. These presentations by indigenous archaeologists, scholars, and Dartmouth alumni
cemented my decision to revive my journey to become an anthropologist/
archaeologist, and to work to strengthen Navajo identity, heritage, language, and culture.

For me the NAS symposium also ended up being a Dartmouth Native
American mini-reunion. I made new and lasting friendships, renewed old
ones, and received important updates from "the trenches." Joe Watkins, a
notable Choctaw archaeologist, became a particularly important mentor
and friend. By the end of the symposium, I not only felt I had gained a
new cohort of supportive colleagues, I also realized that Native American
archaeologists are making a lasting impact in the discipline of archaeology. I wanted to rejoin that movement.

Me, My Tribe, and Archaeology

When I returned to Arizona, I resumed my job with the NNAD at NAU,
working part-time while I finished my master's degree. In May 2002,
I finally graduated from NAU with a master's degree in sociocultural anthropology. The encouragement and support of my family and friends
were essential during this time, as were the need to provide for my children and my goal of working for my tribe, both of which kept me motivated throughout the grueling process.

After graduation, I was encouraged to apply for the position of program manager of NNAD at the NAU branch office. When I was hired
as the first Navajo to fill that position, my goal of working for my tribe
was realized at long last, but I soon discovered that I was ill prepared.
Although I was confident and experienced in supervising the Native
American college students, it was intimidating to be in charge of the
senior archaeologists, who until recently had been my supervisors. I was
grateful for the opportunity my tribe had given me, and I was comfortable
with supervising NNAD's student-training program: to train Navajo students to become educated, credentialed archaeologists. However, after my
five-year hiatus in Wisconsin, I lacked the business finesse and experience

of a fully trained archaeologist required to operate in the world of contract archaeology. Moreover, navigating the bureaucratic labyrinth of the Navajo Nation government and the Bureau of Indian Affairs was an exasperating challenge.

Our small tribal government archaeology program struggled to compete for archaeological contracts on the Navajo Reservation. Our primary competition were the for-profit cultural resource management (CRM) companies located in Flagstaff and Phoenix. CRM is a lucrative and highly competitive business in the US Southwest, and the virtually undeveloped Navajo Reservation is considered a prime business opportunity. For NNAD, competing for archaeological work was a vicious cycle: because our archaeological staff was small, we could not adequately compete, which limited our ability to generate the revenue we needed to hire more archaeologists. NNAD should have been busting at the seams with archaeological work, but instead it was going bust. My dream of conducting meaningful archaeological projects on the Navajo Reservation in collaboration with the Navajo people, remained just that—a dream.

By 2009, the stress of keeping NNAD's Navajo archaeologists employed was beginning to take its toll on my health. I developed chest pains, so I went to see a doctor. He said everything was normal and that my chest pains were likely due to emotional stress. I also began to suffer from insomnia of the strangest kind. I felt intense panic, fear, and dizziness as I lay in bed trying to sleep. My symptoms would intensify to the point where the only thing that could soothe me was taking a walk outside at night and breathing in the cold mountain air, and talking to my mother on the phone while clutching my bag of corn pollen. Navajos use corn pollen to pray with early in the morning before the sun rises, or when needed.

A new vision began to form in my mind, this time of a potted plant. The leaves had fallen off the plant and lay strewn about, leaving a single barren stem sticking up out of the soil. But the stem was still green, and I knew this plant represented me. My intellectual and spiritual growth were being stunted, and I longed to bask in the sunlight once again so I could branch out, blossom, and flourish. Something had to change, and fast, or I was going to wither away.

It was about that time that I came across an announcement for "Getting You into IU." It was an invitation for minority graduate students to visit Indiana University (IU). Two of my mentors, Dr. Wesley Thomas, a Navajo anthropologist, and Dr. Deborah Nichols, my former Dartmouth professor, had recommended IU to me, as its anthropology department offered one of the country's few PhD programs in archaeology of the social context. This is a combined anthropology and archaeology program that encourages "students . . . to develop individualized interest areas that may include, but are not limited to, cultural property, public archaeology, archaeological ethics, heritage management and repatriation"—a perfect fit for my interests. I made the trip to IU, and the professors in the Anthropology Department felt I would be a good fit for the program. My low self-esteem kicked in and I doubted I would be accepted, and even if I were, how could I afford to go back to school? What would we live on? Could I uproot my kids and leave my mom and extended family in Arizona?

I contemplated applying to IU for several months, weighing the pros and cons, and finally concluded that I probably would not have this opportunity again. I was scared, but I didn't want to spend the rest of my life regretting what could have been—it was now or never. I knew that moving to Indiana would also help my children prepare for college, so I applied to IU–Bloomington's anthropology PhD program and was accepted with full funding in the spring of 2010. My prayers had been answered.

To me, earning a PhD means I will have the freedom, and the training, to do what I could not accomplish at NNAD—researching Navajo cultural heritage topics of interest to me and my Navajo people and sharing my research. My aim is to teach anthropology, archaeology, and Navajo and Native American studies at a university or tribal college with a high percentage of Navajo and/or Native American students, while continuing my research on the Navajo Reservation. I also intend to publish works that will benefit Navajo youth and others.

My life goals are simple—to raise a family, work for my tribe, and learn more about who I am as a Navajo—and I am accomplishing what I set out to do. My road in life has not always been easy; I made wrong turns, stalled, crashed, and broke down many times along the way, but even making mistakes is valuable to one's personal growth, as long as you can learn from them, forgive yourself, and move on.

I have been able to continue my journey thanks to the support I receive from my family and friends to whom I say—*Ahéhee'*, thank you. Although life can be cruel, it can also be beautiful. I don't want to give up or be afraid, because that will stunt my growth and rob me of important life lessons and experiences. I share my story so that you, the reader, will be encouraged to follow your dreams and never give up.

T'áá 'ákódí, until next time . . .

Davina is in her fifth year at Indiana University–Bloomington in the Department of Anthropology. She is a graduate assistant for Indiana University's Native American Graves Protection and Repatriation Act (NAGPRA) Program. Davina aims to graduate by 2017 with a PhD in archaeology of the social context; and a PhD minor in Native American and Indigenous studies. She is presently in the dissertation-writing phase of her PhD program and is researching the Old Leupp Boarding School, an early twentieth-century Navajo historic archaeological site on the Navajo Reservation, which both her grandparents attended in the 1930s. She is active in educating students and others at Indiana University about her Navajo identity and heritage, archaeology on the Navajo Reservation, and other topics in Native American studies, such as Native American stereotypes and Native American contemporary and traditional music. Her passion for Native American music compelled her to become a volunteer DJ at WFHB Community Radio for "Native Spirit," Indiana's only Native American music radio show.

When she finishes her PhD, Davina plans to teach and do community-based heritage projects in the southwestern United States with the Navajo people and publish her research. She currently lives in Bloomington, Indiana, with her younger daughter and son, who are both in high school. Her older daughter is a sophomore in college.

12

The Good Ol' Days When Times Were Bad   N. Bruce Duthu

It was 1965 and I was six when Hurricane Betsy struck the Louisiana coast and all communities south of New Orleans were evacuated. We lived in Dulac, a small town seventy miles southwest of New Orleans, about as coastal a community as you can find in this part of Louisiana. It hugs the bayou and is virtually surrounded by small lakes and wetlands, flooding easily—and Betsy was no ordinary storm. People spoke in somber, almost reverential tones about this hurricane. Everybody said it was the kind of storm that changes lives forever.

The hurricane taught me my first lessons in justice—real, true, bitter justice. Storms like Betsy did not discriminate against anyone—Indian, white, or black; rich or poor; fisherman or professional. Betsy was an equal-opportunity destroyer. I recall a perverse sense of satisfaction returning to Dulac after Betsy and seeing the flooded homes of the well-to-do families, their drenched and ruined furnishings piled high on the roadside for the trash haulers. Indian families like ours hadn't suffered less, but neither had we suffered more. To me, that was significant.

I also saw the strength and love of my mother. Mom, my older brother Chuck, and I had moved in with my maternal grandfather after my mom's divorce from my father. The four of us made up what I knew as my immediate family. Since we didn't have our own car, we relied on the evacuation buses to get us out of Dulac. Our grandpa, or pépère, had helped us secure the house and then gone to help other family members. By early evening, the brooding gray skies had turned fierce and deeply black. And the wind! It howled and pressed us from all directions. The three of us waited in the front room, listening for sounds of the bus. Mom clutched us tightly. She must have been terrified. I should have been but I don't think I was.

She made me feel secure and protected. She spoke to us, but I don't remember her words. What I do remember is her calm and resolve. I never doubted we would make it through, because my mother had already willed it so.

The bus arrived just as Hurricane Betsy began to relandscape our front yard. While the storm was occupied uprooting a large tree, my mother walked us from the front porch onto the bus. The whole ground around that old tree moved up and down. It was, as my own ten-year-old son would say, "awesome"—and terrifying.

My mother calls those "the good ol' days when times were bad." Pépère and Mom had wonderful stories about those days, the hardships and the good times of life in Dulac. Most were about being Indian. Our people belong to the Houma Indian Tribe, one of two tribes indigenous to the land now called Louisiana. The tribe occupied two village sites near present-day Baton Rouge when they encountered French explorers in the late seventeenth century. There followed a pattern of southernly migration, sometimes voluntary, sometimes not. Our oral tradition establishes that the tribe settled in present-day Terrebonne and Lafourche parishes (counties) in the early nineteenth century. The seat of government in Terrebonne Parish is the city of Houma, some seventeen miles north of Dulac. Many of Houma's forty thousand residents have no knowledge of the existence, let alone the history, of the tribe for which the city is named.

Settlement patterns of the tribe tended to be kinship based, and large family clusters lived along the banks of the many bayous that meander toward the Gulf of Mexico. Leadership was informal, relying on a local patriarch to advise or help resolve disputes. The traditional language slipped away in the nineteenth century and was replaced with an archaic French, known in the vernacular as "Cajun French." Most tribal members also converted to Christianity, primarily Roman Catholicism. But the sense of identity as Indian people, as Houma, didn't erode. Despite the adaptations, the necessary taking on of a new culture, the idea of being Houma Indian persisted.

Relations between Indians and whites were never easy in Dulac, and they became more strained during the mid-twentieth century, when tribal members began aggressively campaigning for basic civil rights, including public education. The first all-Indian public school in Terrebonne Parish opened in the mid-fifties at about the same time the US Supreme Court declared "separate but equal" school systems unconstitutional.

My mother did not have access to this "separate and not-so-equal" education. Her formal education occurred in mission schools operated by various Christian churches. She attended Catholic school through the fourth grade, when she had to quit her studies and help support the family. I don't know if she would have chosen to go further. Her recollections of these mission schools are not happy ones. Religious dogma was used regularly to underscore Indian children's "unacceptability" in the sight of the Almighty. She told me how, in receiving the Eucharist, Indians had to wait until all white communicants had received the sacred Body of Christ. Seating in churches was segregated, with the "Indian section" in the back. I remember the marks left on the pews by the removal of the dividing railings. One elder Houma woman once told me that a priest tried to make her promise to withdraw her kids from the Baptist school and send them to the Catholic school as the "price" for her confessions to be heard. She punched him square in the jaw and never set foot in the Catholic church again.

Such experiences are not unusual in the history of missionization among the various tribes. From the time of first contact, religious doctrine has played an enormous role in the subjugation of Indian people. Now a law professor, I teach the evolution of federal Indian law; students read United States Supreme Court opinions openly acknowledging, and even relying on, oppression as the basis for decision. The high court's earliest major opinion on Indian land rights (*Johnson v. M'Intosh*, 1823) describes how "the character and religion of [this continent's] inhabitants afforded an apology for considering them as a people over whom the superior genius of Europe might claim an ascendancy. The potentates of the old world found no difficulty in convincing themselves that they made ample compensation to the inhabitants of the new by bestowing on them civilization and Christianity, in exchange for unlimited independence."

Given such a history, it would seem unlikely that a single Indian soul would still believe in the white man's god. And yet most of my relatives and other tribal members are Christian. Only recently have my mother and I asked ourselves why this is so. Part of it, we decided, is that we like the stories—not the ones interpreted by the priests, but the ones in the Bible, in the New Testament. For my mother, the lessons of loving your enemies and praying for those who despise you had immediate and personal significance.

The lessons became the hallmarks of a survival strategy that allowed us to go about life in a segregated community and a segregated church. They taught us how to profess love for white parishioners who visited our home to collect money and canned goods for the church fair—which we could not attend because we were Indian; how to overcome a narrow and racist interpretation of the Creator as one who would allow us into the eternal kingdom only after all the whites had safely and securely entered their glory. This was, to me, Christianity. Practicing it devoutly not only got us "soul protection" (in the event the "superior geniuses of Europe" were right about their moral and religious ascendancy), but it also helped expose the utter hypocrisy of the faith as practiced by many of those geniuses. I suppose one could say we engaged in civil disobedience by living in religious obedience.

These thoughts obviously did not preoccupy me while growing up in Dulac. As a kid, I felt wonderful and special being Indian when I was around Indian people. For my first five years of formal education, I went to the all-Indian school in Dulac. I was bright, precocious, polite, with a strong work ethic and light skin. I didn't work particularly hard at developing any of these traits—and I had no choice about skin coloring. My mixed ancestry—French and Houma Indian—is evident in my appearance, but in my community, last names and family connections tell the whole story. I identified myself and was identified as only one thing—Indian. Still, I know I received what favorable treatment could be expected. For example, my lapses into French, my first language, were typically forgiven, while other students got pretty bad whippings for the same offense.

Entering sixth grade was a big deal. It was 1969, and the elementary schools in our area were finally being integrated. Federal courts in Louisiana had ordered the public schools to desegregate in the early 1960s. In Terrebonne Parish, the high school was desegregated first, the elementary schools later. The all-Indian elementary school was dismantled and loaded by sections on large barges that were floated up the bayou six or eight miles to the site of the all-white school. There, the sections were unloaded and reassembled. For the first time, I attended school with white and black children. This was my first real opportunity to interact with non-Indians outside the church, and I made friends easily, probably for the same reasons my teachers at the Indian school had liked me. I heard that some white kids were pulled out of the school and sent into mainly white parochial schools in Houma.

Until this point I did not value formal education either for its own sake or for what it could offer in terms of a future. Education was so closely linked with religion in the minds and hearts of some families that it left bitter memories, and young Indian kids dropped out in large numbers and at an early age, often before sixteen. For other families it was difficult to imagine that education would make any difference in their children's lives. As one young friend, a distant cousin, used to tell me, "My parents ask me why I need a high-school diploma to work on a shrimp boat." We expected simply to follow in the footsteps of our parents. To think or want otherwise was unrealistic; worse, it might be perceived as a rejection of the traditional way of life. "What's the matter?" a parent would demand, "being a shrimper isn't good enough for you?"

My mother, however, pushed education. She must have thought it would give my brother and me options she never had. Perhaps she pushed education because she knew it was valued in the while culture and, like religion, if you practiced it well, even the white people would have to acknowledge you. In any event, now that we were at an integrated school, we knew we were supposed to bring home good grades. Dropping out, for us, was no longer an option.

My brother and I did well in school. Many people called us the "Duthu twins." Chuck is older by nearly a year, but we looked very much alike and even dressed alike until fourth grade. But Chuck and I have very different personalities. He's much more introverted than I am. I was more vocal in class than he was. I asked questions of everybody, while Chuck preferred to work out and quietly played his guitar. I usually tore out of the house looking for the nearest cousin or friend to play sports with. Chuck chose a vocational-technical curriculum with emphasis in marine and nautical science, and I followed the standard college-preparatory track. He seemed quite confident that his future, like most of our friends' futures, lay in working in the maritime industry. Despite our different aspirations, we were very close as brothers and as friends. I admired him for his resolve, for I still had absolutely no clue as to what I wanted to do.

I knew I wanted something different in life, even though I couldn't say exactly what it was or how I was going to go about achieving it. Much of my decision to pursue the nontraditional route of college-preparatory work stemmed from negative experiences. I remember once playing with my cousins alongside the bayou in front of our house. I must have been ten years old or so, and a white man sped by in a truck and yelled, "Get out of the way, you goddamn sabines!" "Sabines" was a derogatory term for members of our tribe. I have seen fights break out when that word got tossed around. I was angry and hurt because his comment had nothing to do with what we were doing, but with who we were. No matter what we did, in his eyes we were unalterably "sabines." The prejudice came indirectly as well. The parents of some of my Anglo girlfriends opposed our relationships because I was Indian. In one particular case, my friend was punished when her parents learned she was dating an Indian.

But my encounters with racism did not approach those experienced by older relatives. Pépère had a brother who had been tarred and nearly drowned by some white men because he had entered a "whites only" bar. I suppose it was a mark of some progress in peace relations that we had moved from blatant and physically threatening expressions to more subtle forms of racism that scarred only emotionally. But I was angry and frustrated and impatient with this glacial pace of change. I wanted to do something different, if only to demonstrate that it could be done, and could be done by an Indian.

The more positive encouragement to go to college came from my mother and other family members. Aunt Belle, one of my mom's older sisters, used to say, "An education is something no one can ever take away from you; once you've got it, it's yours for life." This was usually followed with an admonition that all the education in the world was worthless if it was not put to good use. "Never forget what was done in the past!" Aunt Belle also taught me. "That will remind you of what people are capable of doing to each other." She also used to say, "You can get angry; that's okay. But don't *just* get angry, do something about it." Aunt Belle was uncommonly blunt, and I loved that about her.

In the early '70s, I had the good fortune to meet people who had good educations and were putting them, as Aunt Belle would say, to good use. These people were transplanted Northerners, mostly white and politically and socially very liberal. Among them was James Bopp, who directed the community center in Dulac for several years. This center served tribal and nontribal families and provided a whole range of services—day care, after-school programs, a medical clinic, adult education, youth programs, etc. When I became an office aide at the center, I got to know Jim. I was inspired by his ideas for strengthening community leadership among tribal members, particularly through the tribal council. He had thoughts on economic development, on forming associations with other tribes in the state and the region, on getting young kids to stay in school and even to think about college. Some of his ideas were terrific; others were probably unrealistic. Jim had his share of critics, but in the eyes of those who mattered to me—my family—he was seen as a voice for positive change. "He's not just another white man coming in here to show us how to live our lives," said Aunt Belle.

Jim had gone to Dartmouth College, a school originally founded to educate American Indians. I'd never heard of the place, but it sounded interesting. He encouraged me to consider applying there. Jim left Dulac before I finished high school, but he stayed in contact with me and had the college send me materials and application forms. He even sent me a check made payable to Dartmouth College for the application fee, along with a glowing letter of recommendation. Eventually, I did apply to Dartmouth College, but more out of a sense of gratitude to Jim than any genuine interest in the college.

Once I had applied to Dartmouth, I was bombarded with information about its various academic and support programs. I was particularly excited about the college's Native American Program, the rich diversity of tribal backgrounds represented by the students there, and the opportunity to pursue academic study in tribal history, culture, and literature. All these impressions were confirmed when I had the opportunity to visit the college as part of a recruitment program. By now I was also familiar with the general profile of Dartmouth's student body; I knew that in more ways than one, I would not be a typical Dartmouth student.

With a high class standing, a 3.99 grade point average, and strong recommendations from two high-school teachers, I knew I could at least hope to gain admission. The only negative influence in all this came from one of the high-school guidance counselors. "Perhaps," he advised me, "you should readjust your goals, your expectations of yourself." I interpreted him to mean that maybe Dartmouth wasn't the place for someone like me, from the South, from a poor background, from an Indian background. Perhaps he was simply being a realist and saying, "Don't get your hopes up too much." Maybe. The man may have been saying, "Please be realistic, for your own good," but the attitude with which it was delivered said, "Who do you think you're kidding?" I took it as a challenge to prove him wrong.

I was accepted into Dartmouth and matriculated in the fall of 1976. The local paper actually ran a front-page story, "Duthu's Journey—from Dulac to Dartmouth." The hoopla was somewhat embarrassing but also gratifying. It provided me with fifteen minutes of fame, and it also informed the entire community that an Indian person from Dulac had done something just a little bit different.

My new success was difficult for my brother Chuck. We had graduated the same year, both with academic honors. He had gone to work on a tugboat running barges up the Mississippi River to Illinois; I was in school in Hanover, New Hampshire. We wrote frequently and shared all our new adventures. He'd always remember to list the friends who had asked about me. What I didn't know was that some of these same friends, and even some family members, had unintentionally bruised Chuck's feelings by inquiring only about me. They didn't intend to diminish what Chuck was doing, but the effect was exactly that. Yet Chuck made no mention of this in his letters.

I stayed in touch with other family members and many friends. I phoned home every weekend. Pépère always asked about the weather. When I saw my first snowfall on October 18, 1976, I phoned home immediately to tell him. Mom told me that after my calls, he made the rounds in the neighborhood to let the family know how I was doing. When asked exactly where it was I was attending college, he'd answer, "It's pretty far up the bayou." This was a humorous take on how most people give and understand directions in our community; everything is either "up the bayou" (north), "down the bayou" (south) or "across the bayou" (east or west). The bayou, at least until recently, was the main avenue of transportation and commerce, the lifeblood of the community.

Most of my friends at Dartmouth were Native American or black. I spent the summer between high school and college in Dartmouth's "bridge program," which was designed for students who came from disadvantaged backgrounds and who might, in the judgment of admissions officers, benefit from a chance to sample Dartmouth's social and academic rigors before fall term. All the students in this particular program were either black or Native American, and our friendships lasted throughout our time at Dartmouth. I also felt I had more in common with other students of color.

I credit these particular friendships and the support of the Native American Program with helping me survive my first year at Dartmouth. Without them, I would have had no outlet for expressing how I truly felt and would probably never have known that others felt exactly as I did. I could tell these friends that I felt intimidated in class and rarely spoke, fearing that I would say something stupid. The other students seemed so well-read. In an English class, it seemed that everyone had already read most of the books assigned for the class and had well-formed opinions about the author's major influences or another author's personal life. How did they all know this? Even when they were clearly wrong, according to the teacher, they sounded like they knew what they were talking about. I took an astronomy course fall term for a required science credit. It had the reputation as an easy class, but on the first day, the professor announced that the course would be different and would not likely live up to its reputation. On the second day, it seemed half the class had dropped. I should have taken the cue. The course was a monster, emphasizing aspects of physics that I had never studied before. I scraped by with a D, my lowest grade at Dartmouth. It was quite a blow to my ego and not the kind of grade I had hoped to send home in my first quarter. But I did get Bs in my other courses, so all was not lost.

The social life at Dartmouth was more difficult to manage than the academics. First, Dartmouth seemed to have traditions for everything. One particularly unfortunate tradition was the use of Indians as the school's mascot. Explanations as to why Indians were chosen for this honor were as varied as the fall colors, though hardly as brilliant. To some, this tradition commemorated Dartmouth's historic commitment to the education of Indian students. As a freshman, I was often put on the spot by students who wanted my opinion on the Indian symbol—specifically, why I found it offensive. One student wanted to know if there was a portrayal of Indian people that would be acceptable to us. In other words, "How can I still play Indian and not hurt your feelings?"

Chants of "wah-hooh-wah," "Indians on the warpath," or "Dartmouth—Indians—scalp 'em!" were accompanied by face paint and mock Indian ceremonies at athletic events to capitalize on Dartmouth's so-called Indian heritage. All the while, we real Indians were assured by students and alumni that all their displays were done to honor Native people and that we shouldn't take offense at any of it.

I, and others, did take offense. Years before I came to Hanover, Indian students recruited by Dartmouth lodged protests against the college mascot. The college administration responded in 1974 by declaring that any continued use of the Indian symbol was "inconsistent" with Dartmouth's educational and moral aspirations. By the time I arrived, the Indian symbol had become the touchstone for general debate about institutional capitulation to minority student interests. "First, they took away our Indian symbol . . . then they created all those 'victim's studies' programs . . . now there's the gay problem." The sentiments were voiced by students, alumni, and even some faculty members. In this "us versus them" atmosphere, I was made to feel responsible for all the divisiveness on campus because I was part of the Native American population that had "started the trouble."

The tradition of wealth at Dartmouth also had an impact on me. Many of my classmates came from some of America's, and the world's, wealthiest families. In itself, this was not a problem, but it did accentuate the differences between me and them. These kids used "vacation" as a verb. "We vacation in the Swiss Alps," they would say, and sometimes the differences between our lives were so vast the wealthy kids found them funny. And many times, so did I. The guy across the hall from me couldn't remember how many bathrooms were in his Tudor-style Scarsdale home. When he learned that our family had installed indoor plumbing facilities, complete with one working toilet, during my junior year in high school, he couldn't get over it. "Hey," he would say, introducing me to his friends, "this is Bruce. Did you know that his family didn't have indoor plumbing until he was in high school?"

In contrast to feeling so apart from traditional Dartmouth, I felt a special closeness to nontraditional students—mostly Indian or black—with whom I forged tight bonds. They never asked about symbols or for help in demythologizing US-Indian history. I was particularly comfortable at the Native American House, a small building that housed a few Indian students and served as a cultural center. It was an oasis on campus, where I could refresh my spirit, my mental health, my sense of humor. A couple of Native American teachers also encouraged and supported me. Professor Michael Dorris (Modoc), now a well-known novelist, headed the Native American Studies Program and was mentor, friend, and advocate to many of us. Professor Inés Talamantez (Mescalero Apache) taught a course in oral traditions my freshman year that allowed me to celebrate and share my culture with other students in the classroom.

My freshman winter term in 1977 was difficult. The Christmas break had allowed me to return to Louisiana to be with family and friends. That was alternately fun and scary. My close friends were now talking about work on the oil rigs or on boats. They had nice new cars and fairly serious girlfriends. I had no job, no car, and no girlfriend; I had a D in astronomy, had discovered how much I didn't know about Milton and Shakespeare, and had warred over symbols. High school was ancient history, and these guys were making a living. My decision to go one way while the others went another began to seem illogical. I was odd man out, and I didn't like it. Other classmates had gone on to college, but neither my closest friends nor Chuck had, and I wanted desperately to fit in. My stories of all-nighters, endless reading, and campus crises didn't compare with theirs about life out on the Gulf of Mexico or the Mississippi River. Their work was real work; it seemed like I was wasting time in la-la land.

Returning to Dartmouth—a world very different from the one I had just left—complicated things even more. I felt caught somewhere in-between. I again struggled with a supposedly easy course, Psychology I. I drew an even tighter web around the Native American House, where I spent more time than in my own dorm. I must have been scared. Feeling and thinking that I belonged nowhere, I called home, hoping that someone— Mom, my brother, or Pépère—would say, "Come home." I told my sad tale to each of them, but it was Pépère who offered the most succinct, and the most unnerving, advice: "If it gets too rough," he told me, "you'll know what to do."

That's exactly what I didn't want to hear. It already felt too rough and I didn't know what to do. Moreover, I didn't want the responsibility of figuring it out. I wanted an easy, quick, painless order to return home, where all would be forgotten, even if it meant my disparaging high-school counselor would have the last laugh. I stayed up all night trying to decipher Pépère's message. A man of few words, he was as difficult to figure out as my professors.

I concluded, somehow, that Pépère's message was actually very simple: whether I stayed or returned was up to me. It wasn't a matter of succeeding or failing, but of assuming responsibility for my decisions. I chose to stay. My "journey," as the local paper in Houma had called it, was really beginning; now I was in charge.

Soon after, in August 1977, Hilde Ojibway came to Hanover to visit her sister Therese, one of my best friends. I knew from Therese that Hilde was the fifth child of eleven and that their father was an enrolled member of the Sault Sainte Marie Band of Chippewa Indians. Like me, she had been raised Catholic, but no longer practiced.

An undergraduate at Michigan State University, Hilde was returning to the United States from a language program in Spain. The trip to Europe, I learned later, was a declaration of independence for her, an opportunity to do something just for herself. Since I was leaving for Europe myself in a few weeks, I was a good audience for her stories from overseas, and by the end of her one week in Hanover, we loved each other. I even suggested marriage. But I was only eighteen, Hilde was twenty, and we had no idea if and when we'd ever see each other again. I spent the next six months in Europe, while Hilde continued to study and work in Lansing, Michigan. We wrote constantly and ignored all the well-intentioned advice from friends and family to get on with our lives. When we began making plans for a rendezvous in London, both family and friends felt we had gone off the deep end. But it happened. Hilde met me in London and we traveled throughout Europe. We were engaged in Paris, in the spring, in front of the Arc de Triomphe.

Eventually, we decided that the best and only way for us to finish college was to do it as a married couple. We married in March 1979 during Hilde's spring break. I worked in Lansing as a high-school counselor to American Indian students while Hilde completed her studies at MSU. In the summer, we returned to Hanover and switched roles; I resumed the student life while Hilde worked in the area as a community organizer.

Neither of us knew what would happen after that. I had always felt that I wanted to return to Louisiana in some position of authority. I had once seriously considered the priesthood and had corresponded with the local Louisiana bishop while I was in Hanover. My motivations were hardly heavenly ones; priests and the church were powerful figures in my community, and several promoted social change. It was a Louisiana Catholic priest who had helped our tribal leaders pressure the local school board into opening the all-Indian school in Dulac. But a friend who was a priest in Hanover pointed out the limitations of pursuing the priesthood as a means of achieving my goal, and by the time I met Hilde, I had abandoned that idea. The story I usually tell is that love forced me to choose between God and the person I loved. It's not true, but even so, I'm glad I finished college with a degree in religion. Just in case.

I half-jokingly told Hilde that when she married me, she married Louisiana. I don't think I ever mentioned attending law school to her, because the thought never seriously entered my mind. Hilde recalls first hearing about law school at a fancy dinner party where Dartmouth alumni were feted by the college as part of the fund-raising seduction process. Selected undergraduates were invited to these events to share their observations about current life at Dartmouth to help remind the alums of their own glory years. We sat at a table with several alumni, most of whom seemed to be lawyers or the spouses of lawyers. The inevitable question for graduating seniors came my way: "Bruce, my good man—what will *you* be doing after Dartmouth?" "I'll be going to law school," I said without a moment's hesitation. The approving smiles with some audible "aahs" mixed in for effect told me I had answered appropriately. Only Hilde wasn't smiling. She was too busy dislodging her spoon from her throat. The ride back to our married-student apartment was very quiet. "So," Hilde said later, "if we had been sitting at the next table, with all the doctors, you'd be considering medical school?" Perhaps.

But getting into law school wasn't a sure thing. My grade point average was a B, but my LSAT scores were barely average. An admissions officer at Loyola University's law school in New Orleans told me my application was not promising. But I did get accepted there and at Louisiana State University's law center. Tulane waitlisted me and eventually denied me admission. I decided to attend Loyola, in part because living in New Orleans seemed attractive at the time. And because Loyola was run by Jesuits.

Hilde got a job at Loyola, which meant we were able to spend a good deal of time together. Every few weekends, we stole away to visit with my family in Dulac. Pépère died in 1979. My loss was doubly painful because he had been the only father I ever knew. The house was so different without him. Chuck married and moved to Houma, where his wife, Sandra, bore the first of their three sons. With many relatives living nearby, Mom wasn't totally alone. On Sunday mornings, Hilde slept in while Mom and I lost ourselves in stories. We talked mostly about family, about people getting married or divorced, about babies being born, and about older people dying. We talked about the community, about how things were changing so fast. Families didn't seem as close anymore; more people were moving away. There were still plenty of stories about discrimination; the old hatred was barely covered by a mask of civility.

In the early '80s, the petroleum industry suffered a downturn, which meant people in southern Louisiana had problems finding and keeping jobs. Many close friends from high school were being partly or wholly laid off. Hard times hit many of the families back in Dulac and Houma, and Hilde and I wished so often we could help, but we were still living on student loans, grants, and small incomes. Talking about law school made me uncomfortable, because it seemed like an indulgence in light of the hardships other family members were experiencing. I think now my discomfort wasn't necessary. When I graduated from law school, with honors, literally hundreds of family and friends showed up at my graduation party in Dulac. It was a community celebration. Family members had cooked and baked all kinds of food. Old friends of mine provided music. The most memorable moment came when an Indian man in his late thirties shook my hand and, with tears in his eyes, told me how proud he was. I cried too, knowing how my opportunities had come through the coincidence of time and history. What might have been for all those like this generous man, I can scarcely imagine.

Also on hand was Tom Foutz, a Tulane Law School graduate who had been a mentor to me and had been one of my best friends during my time in law school. I had had the chance to work as a summer law clerk in Tom's firm, and we spent hours talking about some of his cases, about law and legal strategies. It was a free class in trial practice, but Tom's mentoring went beyond academics and trial practice. After my first year, I called Tom for advice on how to interview for summer clerkships. He came over, and at some point during the evening he asked what I planned to wear. I hadn't given it much thought. I owned only two suits, the one I got married in and an old polyester number from college days. Tom politely suggested that I consider upgrading and updating my wardrobe, but given the late hour, and the interview in the morning, he let me borrow some of his clothes. The next morning, I walked into my interviews looking quite lawyerly. It must have helped, because I got the job.

After I graduated, my first job was in downtown New Orleans with a firm that defended corporations, mostly insurance companies. Its lawsuits involved medical malpractice, admiralty, and products liability, among others. I had somehow assumed I'd be representing injured workers, the "little guys." In fact, my clerking experience had been with firms doing just that, but these firms were not offering jobs when I graduated. Despite not being on the side I would have preferred, I liked this firm, which took training and supporting new associates seriously. The salary was nice and grew quickly. Hilde and I could now afford to splurge a little.

We continued making periodic trips to Dulac, but now the visits were different. Now that I had a law degree, lots of people, mostly family, had legal problems to talk about. My mom usually got the calls: "When is Bruce coming down the bayou? Well, when he comes, tell him I need to talk to him about a case." The calls annoyed my mom. It bothered her that so many people expected me to provide them with free legal help. The time spent counseling people about their legal issues was also time spent away from her. Given the nature of my firm's practice, I couldn't take many cases anyway and referred most people to other lawyers. Some folks felt a little betrayed when I tried to explain why I couldn't take their cases. How, they thought, could there be potential conflict of interest when we were all from the same community?

The most surprising call came from my father. He came to our firm's offices in New Orleans, like a regular client. I introduced him to my boss and showed him around the place. Except for Christmas and Easter and an occasional birthday, Chuck and I had not had much contact with our father after the divorce. He continued to live in Dulac, remarried, and had another son. His wife was always kind and generous to us—more comfortable with us during our short visits than he was. I suppose I understand why, since we were also pretty uncomfortable. He had attended our highschool graduation and my law-school graduation, and now here he was seeking my legal help. Only later did I realize how hard this must have been for him. I knew what a proud man he was. Despite our lack of intimate knowledge about each other, he came to me. I was sad that I couldn't do very much to help him on this occasion, but things eventually did work out for him.

By the summer of 1986, Hilde had completed a master's degree in public administration and was directing a large, private nonprofit agency serving plaintiffs, doing the kind of law I'd always hoped to do. We had finalized the adoption of our six-year-old niece, Lisa, and Hilde was pregnant with our second child, expected in October. Neither of us intended to make any moves professionally or geographically.

We had maintained ties to Dartmouth through the Native American Program's Visiting Committee. As a member, I returned to Hanover twice a year to evaluate and make recommendations to the college regarding Native American student support services. I learned on one of those visits that the current director of the NAP was stepping down to pursue his own legal education. When I expressed interest in the position, the dean of the college did not dismiss the suggestion out of hand. Hilde and I discussed my applying for the position. I had no formal training in student counseling or college administration, but I applied for the job. I had a background like that of many of today's Native American students, and I knew personally how difficult Dartmouth could be. I could also attest to the value of a Dartmouth education. I convinced myself and Hilde that this was a sound career move. My law partners advised otherwise, and so did some family members. Wasn't this a waste of all those years of legal training and experience?

But I needed to make my own personal contribution to the program that had supported me and had helped open so many doors. I never doubted that I had something of value to offer today's Native students, but I did worry that I might, indeed, be throwing away my legal training and experience. The prospect of developing and teaching a course in Native American law was an added incentive, but I was going to be paid much less to be an administrator than I was earning as an attorney.

Then an older gentleman in our firm, who had had a successful career as a trial attorney, warned me that his success had come at a stiff price. Like so many lawyers we both knew, he had been consumed by his practice and its material rewards. His family life had suffered. His marriage had broken up, and a teenage daughter had been tragically killed in an auto accident. He told me how he had lost the chance to spend time with his family, how he could not turn back the clock and get to know the daughter who was now gone from the world. It had to do with choices, he said. "If I had your youth and your choices, the answer would be very clear." The law degree, he reminded me, would always be mine. No one could take that away. But I wouldn't always have these choices. There was a familiar ring to this. Some of Aunt Belle's pragmatism and Pépère's wisdom was echoing.

I was offered the Dartmouth job and took it. Hilde, Lisa, and I established our new home in White River Junction, Vermont, about five minutes from the campus. Our son Joseph was born two months later. One of the hardest things about leaving Louisiana this time was knowing that our children would not grow up with family nearby. Long-distance phone calls, an occasional visit, and exchanged photos would be the primary ties to our home. But the decision felt right, difficult as it was.

I had no particular mission or agenda when I became director of Dartmouth's Native American Program. I knew that the one-on-one work with students was indispensable, but beyond that, I devoted my attention to programs to educate the larger community about the Native student population. I hoped that greater understanding might lead to greater sensitivity. It was frustrating to watch students fight the same battles that I had fought as a student, among them, still, the symbol issue. The greatest joys were to see students setting and attaining high goals for themselves and being happy being Indian. I rekindled many friendships with Native alumni now living and working throughout the country, mostly in service to their own or another tribal community.

I am still very close to my family, despite the distance. My mother visits us every year, and we've been to Louisiana a few times as a family. Once my brother visited, shortly after Christmas. Several feet of snow fell just before he arrived, and he felt he had stepped into a winter wonderland. He and I drove up to Montreal to visit a good friend of mine, another of the many good voices who have come into my life. Our time together gave us the opportunity, at last, to talk as men, as husbands, as fathers, and as brothers. We saw that though we had taken different directions, we still shared so much—respect for one another and love.

In 1991, I left Dartmouth to join the law faculty at Vermont Law School in South Royalton, Vermont. I teach first-year law courses in torts and criminal law and an upper-level seminar in federal Indian law. I also teach federal Indian law at Dartmouth as a visiting professor in Native American studies. Hilde directs a large, nonprofit agency in New Hampshire. We have a third child, a daughter named Alanna, born in January 1993.

When I think of my children and my brother's children, I think of the wonderful stories of our youth—the good ol' days when times were bad. I hope the children will all hear these stories. And I hope they will also have the good voices to teach and guide them. And I hope they will listen.

N. Bruce Duthu is enrolled with the United Houma Nation of Louisiana. He was born in Houma, Louisiana, and raised in Dulac, one of the oldest Houma Indian settlements in southeastern Louisiana. He attended an all-Indian elementary school until 1969, when local schools were integrated. After graduating fourth in a high-school class of several hundred, Bruce entered Dartmouth College, graduating in 1980 with a degree in religion and Native American studies. He received a law degree from Loyola University in New Orleans and was in private practice for several years before returning to Dartmouth to direct the Native American Program. Now a tenured faculty member at Vermont Law School, Bruce specializes in federal Indian law, a course he also teaches annually at Dartmouth. He is married to Hilde Ojibway. The couple lives in Vermont with their three children.

Follow Up: Living Life in a Posture of Humility

Approaching sixty years old is as good a time as any to reflect on the years gone by and to contemplate what to do with whatever time lies ahead of me. One thing is for certain: I don't know where I'm going and I honestly don't think I ever will (or did). One other thing is increasingly certain: I'm not as anxious about winding up someplace else as I used to be.

Years ago, my original essay for this collection of personal stories described many of the important people whose voices helped direct my path in life. Many of those people are now gone, but their voices are still with me. They help give meaning and purpose to my life by recalling the place and the people of my youth and provide examples of living life in a posture of humility toward the challenges, as well as the opportunities, that come along my journey. It is that posture of humility toward life's challenges and opportunities that I find so fascinating these days, and that offers me some measure of calmness as I step into the uncertainty of each day.

In the fall of 2007, I had the privilege of giving the convocation address at Dartmouth College to help open the new academic year. My address was titled "Reflections on Humility and Liberal Education." I confess that my immediate inspiration for that topic was frustration with the arrogance, selfishness, and insularity that had come to define the administration and policies of President George W. Bush, but I thought the message would have relevance for today's Dartmouth students and the project of liberal education generally. The relevant association between humility and liberal education, I suggested, was to approach one's education in a posture of openness, an absence of arrogance, and a spirit of deference. It's the spirit, I said, "which is not too sure that it is right," paraphrasing a famous speech by the federal judge Learned Hand (1872–1961).

The inspiration behind the inspiration was my grandfather, or pépère, Joseph Parfait, who, along with my mom, helped raise my brother Chuck and me. I was about four years old when Pépère took us into his home in

Dulac, Louisiana. This was in the early 1960s. Pépère's wife, my grand-mother, had died many years earlier while giving birth to the last of their ten children. He raised their children with the help of his siblings and the older children in the family and supported them by working as a trapper and fisherman, the work of most Houma Indian men of his generation. Except for the fish and fur economy, Pépère had little use for other white-dominated institutions in the community, including the Christian mission schools and the Catholic Church. And yet he wanted his children to have formal education and to know something about the Catholic faith. I suspect he felt this would provide them with the skills, knowledge, and perspective to make their way in an increasingly white-dominated community. He never had a day of formal schooling in his life, and I can seldom recall times when he attended church except for funerals, weddings, and an occasional holiday like Christmas or Easter. Nonetheless, I knew Pépère to be among the smartest, most intellectually curious, and most profoundly spiritual people I've ever known.

Pépère was constantly remaking himself. When the nutria and beaver fur economy ran its course owing to a declining market, he gradually shifted into carpentry and even developed a niche business in kitchen cabinet–making. This allowed him to work flexible hours indoors, away from the stifling heat and humidity of bayou country. My mom worked long, hard hours in a shrimp processing plant, which meant Pépère was often the one at home when Chuck and I returned from the Dulac Indian School. We were so accustomed to seeing Pépère cook meals for us and clean house that we assumed all men shared these responsibilities in other households. If he ever harbored resentment at becoming caretaker for another generation, we never saw or heard it. He also never intruded on Mom's role as the primary parental figure in our lives, even though we lived under his roof.

At one point in the early 1970s, Pépère decided to become a boat builder. Just like that! I saw him sketching out the design for a boat known locally as a "Lafitte skiff"—a flat-bottomed shrimp boat of about twenty to thirty feet in length and ideally suited for the shallow bays and lakes in the Louisiana marshland. I had never known Pépère to be knowledgeable about boat making, though I knew he worked on boats for a good portion of his life. With little more than a rough sketch of the design to work with, he solicited a ride to town with one of my cousins who owned a truck. They returned with a load of lumber and other supplies and the boatbuild-ing began in earnest right in our backyard under the shade of a large tree. Pépère tried to teach my brother and me the basics of carpentry over the years and I know I disappointed him. Not that he ever complained about it, but he could tell my interests lay elsewhere. He had much better luck with my brother, Chuck, who took eagerly to the trades and eventually became an accomplished handyman in his own right. With the boatbuilding, Pépère seemed determined to give me another try. I helped carry lumber for him, nailed a few boards, applied sealant between the sideboards, and generally tried not to get in the way or lose a limb. Eventually, my interest (or talent) slacked and Pépère pressed on, usually with Chuck as his right-hand man. The resulting vessels were quite remarkable. The boats had a certain stylish quality about them, were sturdily built, and proved quite durable when put into service. Pépère made fewer than half a dozen of these little fishing boats, but his venture into boatbuilding taught me a powerful lesson in ingenuity, initiative, and personal self-determination.

Right up until the time I left Dulac to attend Dartmouth in 1976, I saw Pépère continue to play his role as a respected elder within our tribal community. People from throughout our large extended family, and even a few white men, would visit to seek Pépère's counsel on certain matters. Often it was to discuss familial problems or difficulties on the job, or how to cope with the changing times. Pépère mostly listened and would occasionally nod or give a sympathetic "uh-hum." He was a man of few words and yet he spoke volumes with deep, empathic eyes, a soothing voice, and slow, measured steps. Since Pépère had taught himself basic hair-cutting skills, many of these discussions took place on our back porch, Pépère's barbershop. In my mind's eye, I see Pépère standing behind a person seated and draped in a towel, the soft buzz of the electric hair trimmer connecting and filling the unhurried exchange of voices between them.

Pépère approached these challenges and opportunities with grace and utmost humility. He never played the role of victim or sought sympathy for the hand dealt him in life. Not once did I hear him rail against white people, though I know he detested the virulent racism that pervaded our community. He could condemn the sin but not the sinner. One reason for this, I suspect, is that Pépère was one of the few people I knew who regularly interacted with whites as part of his livelihood. Whites controlled all the major industries and operations in our community, and Indians supplied the bulk of the labor or goods. Pépère sold his furs to white brokers, his shrimp and fish to white factory owners. He cut sugarcane for white farmers and built cabinets for white homeowners, but more often for Indian families. He knew the whites as individuals, and in turn, they knew him as a man, a father, a provider for a family who happened to be Indian. I have no doubt some of these folks harbored despicable opinions about Pépère's "people" generally, but even the most ardent racists had to admire Pépère's commitment to a job expertly done, his resolve to provide for his large family, and the great dignity with which he carried himself.

Among my fondest memories with Pépère were the days we'd ride the bus into the town of Houma. We had no car but had access to the big red bus that would cruise up and down the bayou in Dulac collecting passengers to bring them to town to shop, visit doctors or family. There was an early morning pickup and a noon pickup. The bus itself served as a microcosm of the social stratification in the community: blacks sat in the very back, Indians near the back or middle, and whites up front. All the drivers were white men, including one of Pépère's regular customers at his bayou barbershop. As he always did for a day in town, Pépère dressed impeccably with a pressed cotton shirt, khaki pants, and a sharp Stetson hat. Old Spice was his cologne of choice.

Shop owners were polite enough, and I don't recall an instance where we were ever denied service because we were Indian. The days of "white only" signs were over for the most part, with a few notable exceptions that were still around even during my teenage years. The big treat on these trips with Pépère was either lunch at the Woolworth counter or a twenty-five-cent chili dog at Haydel's Drug Store in the heart of downtown Houma, across the street from the bus stop. Pépère had the most disarming and gentle smile. He rarely showed his teeth when he smiled except around family. As a child, I knew how special Pépère was and I thought it quite natural that others would see him in a similar way. He always tipped his hat as he entered a store, a show of respect, and the respect was usually reciprocated.

Pépère is surely a hard act to follow! As I've stepped into roles that Pépère performed—father, grandfather, provider, guardian, counselor, teacher, and community leader—I can't help but make comparisons between the two of us. Of course, I recognize the futility of making such comparisons since our lives are separated by a gulf of time, location, and circumstances. Still, as I encounter new challenges and opportunities in my life, I often reflect on Pépère and the posture of humility with which he approached comparable circumstances. More often than not, I'm left feeling deflated since I can usually identify some flaw, some wrinkle in my conduct, words, or expression that falls short of the standard left by Pépère's legacy. And if I really want to wallow in self-pity, I can always remind myself that Pépère accomplished all that he did in his life while being functionally illiterate, a single father of ten with no formal education or capacity for English speaking (he spoke what we call "Cajun French," which is also my first language), who lived in a time and place where life for Indian people was just plain difficult.

This aspiration—or obsession—to "measure up" to Pépère's example was particularly problematic for me when my wife, Hilde, and I adopted our older daughter, Lisa, in the mid-1980s. Lisa was our niece on Hilde's side of the family, who came into our lives with her own complicated history. For my part, I tried valiantly, but in vain, to live up to Pépère's legacy as a father. I had long heard stories from my mom and her siblings how each of them felt like they were Pépère's special child. In retrospect, I know that a major part of my struggle with being a father to Lisa was that I didn't approach fatherhood with anything close to Pépère's posture of humility. I actually thought I knew what I was doing and that it had to be right. Besides the obvious differences of attempting to raise an adopted, as opposed to a biological, child I thought of fatherhood as something akin to being a potter who shapes and molds the clay to a design of his or her choosing. The better analogy is probably a gardener who readies the soil for the seed but ultimately must rely on other forces—sun, rain, nutrients, genetic makeup of the seeds—to carry the job to completion. My wife, thankfully, grasped this concept. She was the peacemaker in the household and the glue that held us all together.

I suppose that my parenting skills improved to some degree with our other children, Joe and Alanna, though there are still too many occasions when I'm more "potter" than "gardener" as a father. To be sure, our household was and is a happy one, lots of laughter, love, support, and encouragement all around. Our children work hard, appreciate the many blessings they have, respect others, and set (and achieve) meaningful goals for themselves. Only a false sense of humility would lead me to think that I've had nothing to do with that, but I recognize that I manage to make some things harder than they really need to be for our children. I must constantly remind myself that their world is far different from the one in which I grew up, and that while they may not have to struggle with poverty, overt racism, segregation, and limited opportunities, their struggles are no less real and important to them and merit my attention and respect. When I grasp and emulate Pépère's example of humility as a father, counselor, and provider, the results are far richer, more positive, and more enduring for all of us.

The same is true when I reflect on my work as an educator, teacher, and scholar. After seventeen years on the faculty at Vermont Law School,

I returned to Dartmouth in 2008 to join the faculty in Native American Studies. After all these years working in higher education, I still look forward to the start of each new academic year and especially to the start of each new class. I'm fortunate to work in an area of scholarship that is quite dynamic. The political and legal relations among tribes, states, and the federal government are in constant flux, and even old precedents have to be revisited anew in light of new developments in law and politics. Students are quite often stunned to learn how the law and legal processes were co-opted by the state and powerful private interests to help subjugate Native peoples and their lands. The language of racism and prejudice so infects many of the major case precedents in this field that I seldom need to elaborate or editorialize about the injustices done to Native peoples, and indeed to the rule of law itself. It's quite easy for a course in federal Indian law to provoke feelings of depression, frustration, anger, guilt, or some combination thereof.

Like many educators, I regularly read and try to learn from the evaluations students produce at the end of my courses. Over the years, there is a recurring sentiment expressed by many of my students about which I feel particularly gratified. According to my students, they are most surprised by my sense of optimism about the state of Native America and the prospects for justice for all Indigenous Peoples in the world. This tells me that students are in fact paying close attention to the stories I share by and about Native peoples. They know that for every narrative of domination, abuse, and violation, there was (and is) an Indigenous "counternarrative" of resilience, resistance, and resolve. The hopefulness and sense of optimism spring not from naïveté but from the legacy of survival and will to live that I saw demonstrated in my own tribal community and by my own people. Teaching from a posture of humility allows me to reach into the minds and hearts of my students, to tap into their own imaginative spaces, and to energize their impulse to do good things in the world.

And yet that optimism is tempered by the reality that the times, the people, and the very places we call home have all changed over the years. Many of my elders, including my beloved Pépère, have passed on. The French language of my youth is still widely spoken in the bayou communities of south Louisiana but mostly among the older generations. In my community of Dulac, it's a rare thing to find a child—Indian or not— whose first language is French.

In years to come, the very landscape that makes up places like Dulac may cease to exist. Massive coastal erosion of Louisiana's precious marsh and swamplands has deprived coastal communities like Dulac of an important natural buffer to rising storm surges. Flooding from hurricanes has become an almost annual feature of life on the bayou, exacerbated by rising seas brought on by global climate changes. Experts predict that low-lying regions like Dulac may be completely submerged under gulf waters in a matter of decades if nothing is done to arrest the forces—natural and man-made—that are currently remaking the landscape. I'm deeply saddened to know that the places of my youth may someday soon lie at the bottom of an expanded Gulf of Mexico.

Living in harmony with the natural environment was not a cliché for people like my grandfather; it was a way of life. His posture of humility taught that there were limits to development. I can still recall the sense of despair and anger I felt as a boy when I saw the vast ponds and marshlands behind our home in Dulac drained of water and rid of wildlife to make way for the prospectors drilling for oil and natural gas. Even then, I knew there was little that we could do about it. Complicating the picture was the fact that a growing number of Indian families came to depend on the oil and gas industry to supplement, or replace, the income that came from fishing, trapping, or hunting on the land. It therefore came as no surprise to me that a number of Houma fishermen would lend a hand in cleaning up the massive oil spill along the gulf following the 2010 explosion of BP's Deepwater Horizon oil rig.

I'll admit that it's difficult to feel optimistic about our chances to reverse these threats to the natural world. As an Indian lawyer and scholar, I often wonder whether the status of our local environment would have been enhanced had our tribe been recognized as a distinct tribal government by the federal government. Federal recognition of tribal government status is the legal mechanism that activates and gives expression to a tribe's inherent sovereign authority over their lands and people living on them. That political status would have accorded the tribe greater authority over land-use decisions, including, for example, protecting from resource development those coastal areas that sustained our people for generations. I recognize, of course, that tribal leaders might well have condoned that sort of development, but it's also possible that they might have insisted on better environmental protections and controls consistent with the tribal land and resource ethic of sustainability.

As I stated in my earlier essay for this collection of personal stories, I've tried to be attuned to the important voices that have come into my life over the years. As I've grown older, I find it helpful, even necessary, to spend time contemplating the larger lessons inspired by those voices. For me, trying to live life in a posture of humility is one of those significant lessons. I'm still working at it, but I've found that life is much more enjoyable, peaceful, and hopeful when I come closest to emulating the example set by my grandfather. I can only hope that others in our world will make similar efforts.

N. Bruce Duthu, an enrolled member of the United Houma Nation of Louisiana, continues to live in White River Junction, Vermont, with his wife, Hilde Ojibway. Their three children, Lisa, Joe, and Alanna, are grown, have completed college (and graduate school), and have begun families and careers of their own.

In 2008, Bruce left Vermont Law School to join the faculty at Dartmouth College in Native American Studies. At VLS, Bruce served as vice dean of academic affairs and was the inaugural director of the VLS–Sun Yat-sen University (Guangzhou, China) Partnership in Environmental Law. In 2009, Bruce was named to an endowed chair at Dartmouth, becoming the Samson Occom Professor in Native American Studies. In the same year, he also assumed the chairmanship of Native American Studies, a position he held until June 2015. Under his leadership, NAS launched an off-campus program in Native American Studies based in Santa Fe, New Mexico. Bruce directed the first iteration of this program in the fall of 2015. In 2016, he was named Dartmouth's associate dean for International Studies and Interdisciplinary Programs. In September 2016, President Barack Obama nominated Bruce to serve as a member of the National Council on the Humanities.

He is the author of *Shadow Nations: Tribal Sovereignty and the Limits of Legal Pluralism* (Oxford, 2013) and *American Indians and the Law* (Viking, 2008). He was also a contributing author of *Felix S. Cohen Handbook of Federal Indian Law* (2005 edition), the leading treatise in the field. He coedited a special volume of *South Atlantic Quarterly*, "Sovereignty, Indigeneity and the Law," which won the 2011 Council of Editors of Learned Journals award for Best Special Issue. He has lectured on Indigenous rights in various parts of the world, including Australia, Bolivia, Canada, China, France, Italy, New Zealand, and Russia.

13

Why Didn't You Teach Me?   Bob Bennett

Success in the white world has always been easy for me. My accomplishments never surprised me because they were enjoyable and relatively effortless. My grandmother, however, was usually more than surprised—perhaps even astounded. "And you're Indian!" she would often exclaim to express the joy, happiness, and amazement she felt for me. I did well in a white school, played varsity football, baseball, and basketball, went out with *wasicu* (white) friends, dated *wasicu* women, attended an Ivy League school, and now make a living as a professional baseball player. I was doing everything she had always hoped I would do, but because I was an Indian, she did not expect me to have so much acceptance and success in the outside world of the *wasicu*. I remember, when I was very young, going over to Gramma and Grandpa's house, only two blocks from our apartment in Rapid City, South Dakota, and listening to Gramma and her mother speak Lakota to each other. During my childhood years, she never taught me one word of Lakota; she always spoke English to me. All I knew was that they were talking "Indian" and I spoke only English.

When I came to Dartmouth as a young man, I realized that my life was not well balanced because I had never learned the Lakota language and culture from my grandmother. Before I came to New Hampshire, a former Boston schoolteacher told me that many New Englanders think that "all Indians are dead." In a frightening sense, so did I. At Dartmouth, I was shocked to realize two important truths: I am an Indian and I am indeed alive.

When I first came to New Hampshire, I was at a loss because I could not answer the questions people asked about Native American life. Hell, I could not even answer my own questions! I took a Native American studies course my sophomore year and learned more about Indians than I had in twenty years of living as one. Yet there was something ironic and troubling about the source of my newfound knowledge: I was learning about my culture and ancestors from a white professor in a white institution. That fact disturbed me and prompted me to examine why I had ended up so ignorant. That course also reminded me of a conversation I had with my grandmother.

While at her house during Christmas break, I asked her a question that caught her off guard. "Gramma, how come you never taught my brother and me to speak Lakota?" She looked surprised and sat silent for a moment. Then, with a sad, heavy voice, she said, "Oh, I really wish I had. Mom and I always talked about teaching you grandkids. I really wanted to, but I was afraid you would get made fun of by the *wasicu*." *Wasicu* was one of the few Lakota words I understood. To me it simply meant "white people," but it can also be translated as "greedy ones who take the fat."

Her reasoning is easy to understand when you consider her childhood. My grandmother was born on April 1, 1916, in Norris, South Dakota, on the Rosebud Reservation as Clara Virginia Quick Bear, the eldest of seven children. Her blood came from the Sicangu Oyate (Burned Thigh People) band of Lakota. When she was ten years old, it was decided that she should go to school. She had learned a little English from her mother, who had gone to school for a few years, but had no formal schooling. She had also learned the Lakota language and traditional tribal ways as well as Catholic spirituality from Old Gramma. The lessons she learned in Catholic mission school scarred her, and eventually those she loved, forever.

Even late in her life, many of her memories of St. Francis Mission School were still vivid. She said, "It was run by all whites. They treated us very mean and I didn't like it there much. They would punish us for speaking Indian and doing Indian things. The nuns there were really mean to us and sometimes they would lock us all in one room if someone was misbehaving. There were always a few kids who were homesick and tried to run away. It would always be just a few kids, but the nuns would take it out on all of us. My brother tried to run away a few times and they would always catch him and bring him back. One time they shaved all of his hair off. They did it so the rest of us wouldn't get any ideas of leaving."

I tried to ask her to tell more, but she did not want to continue. "No, they are all dead and gone and I don't want to talk about it anymore," she said. I never asked anything more about it. I was angry, but not at her. I understood that Gramma wanted us to learn the *wasicu* ways to keep us from experiencing her ordeal. I was angry that "civilization" had denied me the freedom to be what I was, a Lakota. I look in the mirror and there it is, my Indianness. Yet I did everything in such a "white" manner that my white friends and others would distinguish me as the "good Indian" and say, "You're not like them." This acceptance is exactly what my gramma wanted for me. According to her, being an Indian in a white world gets you "made fun of." And she was correct because I was already guilty of making fun of other Indians myself. I had fallen deep into *wasicu* ways.

I remember making fun of a Lakota boy for expressing his Indian identity. I was about ten years old when my brothers, cousins, and I first met this boy. When I asked him for his name, he lowered his head and submissively put his hands in his pockets. Then he suddenly raised his head and proudly said, "My name is Hunkpapa." We all laughed, and I said, "What?"

"My name is Hunkpapa. It's the name of my people and my parents gave it to me so I'll never forget," he replied. At this time, I was ignorant of how many bands of Lakota there were; as far as I was concerned, we were all just Sioux. The Hunkpapa, "the Campers on the End," are a northern band of the seven bands of Teton Lakota.

"Look, guys, this kid is still trying to be Indian. Hey boy, those days are over," I said as we walked away from this proud Hunkpapa.

To all of the Hunkpapas of the world, I am sorry. My grandmother's fear became a reality long before I knew it existed. I was part of that narrow-minded and twisted attitude I have grown to despise. Now I stand as twenty-two-year-old Lakota who is dissatisfied with that sense of white identity.

My mother is also a product of my grandmother's hurtful mission-school ordeal. She is shy of her Indianness and the world's perception of it. This shyness affects her thoughts and behaviors in many aspects of her life. One time last fall, we both ordered the salad bar in a Rapid City Wendy's restaurant. The restaurant provided us with plastic plates so that we could serve ourselves from the food bar. When she finished eating her first portion, she wanted to go for a return trip to the salad bar, but she was embarrassed by her messy finished plate.

"Mom, just go up and ask for another one," I said.

"Can you do that? No, I'll just wipe this one off," she said.

"What are you so worried about, Mom? Do you think that because you're Indian they won't give you one? What can they tell you other than no?" I asked sarcastically.

Her face had an apprehensive look while she pondered whether or not to get a new, clean plate. She looked around and saw another customer, who happened to be a white woman, with two plates, one messy much like hers and the other clean and full of new food. She jokingly said, "Look! She did it, but she is white." She was trying to be humorous, but there was also a sense of truth in it.

"Just go up and do it, Mom. These workers are here to help you, and if you want a clean plate, they will give it to you," I said in a fatherly tone. Then I snapped, "Even if you are Indian!" She gave a fearful laugh and headed toward the counter, nervously glancing back at me several times.

She looked like a shy little girl. She had a submissive pose, with her back slightly hunched and her neck leaning forward, as she handed the messy plate to the Wendy's worker. The young worker gave my mother a new plate.

"You see, Mom, that wasn't so hard," I said as she returned. "All you had to do was ask. Do you feel better now that *wasicu* gave you a clean plate?"

"Well, I didn't know what to expect. Now shut up and let me eat!" she snapped back. These types of incidents were not uncommon, and the way my mother perceived each one of them only served to perpetuate her shyness.

Despite the stultifying effects of her self-perception, my mother still has within her the strength of my grandparents. She worked hard to be a good provider and to discipline two wild young boys. My brother and I were raised, like many other Indian children, fatherless. As a single Indian woman with two children, my mother had a tough time making ends meet, but with much help from our grandparents and other relatives, she succeeded. Our struggle was not unique. Like many poor Indian people, we survived on federal money in the form of food stamps and welfare checks. Our grandparents also directed much of their limited resources to us. Gramma always kept us fed by cooking up a casserole, a pot of chili, a meatloaf, spaghetti, or soup. Gramma and Grandpa were always there for us on our birthday and Christmas. I think every new bike I ever got came from Gramma and Grandpa. I cannot imagine how life would have been without them in our lives.

When I was young, I shared my mother's timidity. The first racial insult I can remember being directed at me happened soon after the training wheels were removed from my bike. A maintenance man, coming down the stairs of our apartment building, did not see me approaching on my bicycle. I had to swerve to avoid hitting him. I stopped to see if he was all right and to apologize, but before I could say anything he blurted out, "You fucking Indian!" That insult scared me. I must have heard many similar comments afterward, because my mother said I came to her several times and told her that I wished I were white. She would lovingly respond, "Tell them you are proud to be an Indian."

Tell them I was proud? Proud of what? I knew nothing to be proud of, just like my mother. I was on welfare and received free lunches. I was a "savage" who killed white American settlers. I was a bogeyman, a gut eater, a dog eater. I was an exile in my own land. I wasn't aware of why my *akicita* (warrior) relatives fought and died for their ways and for the land. I did not know how my people lived, and I had no pride in my Sicangu Lakota. I didn't know the power and strength of the old stories. I didn't know how the name-calling *wasicu* had stolen my homeland and killed my ancestors. Ignorance was at the root of their misdirected bigotry, as well as my own and my mother's sense of inferiority.

Thus, during my upbringing, I made myself acceptable to nearly every white person by being just like them, *wasicu*. It was not an entirely deliberate effort on my part to fit in. These people were my friends and we had much in common and shared a similar sense of humor. I did what made me happy and really had no idea what my Indian identity was.

During high school, I was usually the only Indian in any group I was in: football, basketball, baseball, and all my social groups. I felt overly cautious when my white friends were "causing trouble." Because I was the only Indian, I was often singled out as the troublemaker. In sports, I had to be better than the non-Native players, and in social situations, I had to be more humble than others to avoid problems. As a result of this intentional and unintentional pressure, I was just as timid as my mother.

Because many Indian high-school students felt extremely unwelcome among non-Native students and teachers, they joined together for support. I am lucky that I felt comfortable with the mainstream at Central High School, but problems came from both sides of the ever-changing racial lines.

The world "apple" is a pejorative term used to describe a Native American person who has sold out the rest of the Indians and has become "red on the outside but white on the inside." Indian students who try to do well in school are often called "apples" by those who think success in the white world means you are no longer an Indian. By this definition, I fit into the apple category.

Though my behavior, social life, and school success were reason enough for other Indians to confront me, it never happened. Still, my grandmother warned me to be leery of the "bad Indians" from the reservation. "They are bad people who will stab you in the back. They are all so jealous and will try to bring you down because you are doing so good in this world," she said, very sternly. She loved Indian people, but she also remembered the teachings of the mission school.

High school never presented any major problems for me. Everything—classes, friends, teachers, sports, and dealing with other Indians—was easy. I was just like any other kid who was curious about drinking and crossing over the lines of authority. I often went to parties—Indian, non-Indian, or a mixture of both—and did my share of drinking and other stupid juvenile acts. I often drank until I got sick, but that behavior is fairly normal among high-school kids. I was involved in smashing a mailbox with a baseball bat, overturning a hotel ice machine, and other small-time crimes.

All of these little juvenile acts were gradually coming to a head when my baseball coach, Dave Ploof, confronted me. "Bobby, you have a lot of things going for you. I would hate to see your friends and other associates screw it up for you." This was the best advice anyone could have given me.

I was an investment for Coach Ploof. During the next three years, I pitched on his American Legion team. I owe much of my success to him because he taught me the discipline I needed to become a mature ball-player and to always play hard. He touted my baseball skills and maturity to the college baseball scouts.

I also played basketball. My senior year on the team remains one of the best times of my life. We finished with a great record and made it to the state tournament. I was the only Native American on the team and was very vocal on the court; I was perhaps our team's biggest cheerleader. But I was also friendly toward the opponents, which surprised many of them as well as the fans; I was supposed to be a mean, vicious, and dirty basketball player because of my Indian blood. People sitting in the stands gave "war whoops" and yelled insulting names at me during games, but I still played my heart out and enjoyed it.

Throughout my high-school sports career, opponents gave me the war whoop when I was on the field. I was an Indian beating them at their own game, and some found that hard to accept. I think their hostility was a response to their feelings of guilt at having reaped the benefits of their ancestors' taking everything we had. Yet their fear and hatred of Indians prevailed because they knew that Indian people would continually return to reclaim what had been taken from us. We threatened them when we became educated, voiced our opinions, lived next to them, or excelled at sports.

One event showed me the irony of my position as an Indian on the team. After a game, a white woman tapped me on the shoulder. As I turned toward her, she extended her hand and said, "I just wanted to say how enjoyable it was to watch you during the tournament. Good luck." I barely had time to thank her before she smiled and walked away. What did she mean? Could she have meant: "It was good to see an Indian play the way you did?" Or was it: "You are a symbol for other Indians to emulate?" I think she was surprised that I was even out there.

Both on and off the sports field, I was the "good Indian" to nearly everyone in my school. Being elected homecoming king in my senior year shows how well I fit into that image at Central High. Indians normally frightened the people of Rapid City, adults and teenagers alike. The mother of one of my better friends in junior high school, for instance, had a problem with me. Kirk's family was rich, and we liked to go to his large, immaculate house to jump on his trampoline and shoot pool. One day, as we were playing billiards, Kirk's mother asked him to go with her on an errand. She told him it would take only half an hour.

"Why don't you just wait here for me until we get back?" he suggested to me. He left the room, but quickly returned with a worried expression on his face. His mother was standing right behind him. "She doesn't want you to stay here while we're gone," he said reluctantly. I will always remember his mother standing in the doorway with an intimidating look that made me feel very unwanted. She could not wait for me to leave, so I did. That was the first time I had met her, but she only saw a strange Indian person, not her son's close friend. That memory still hurts.

I not only scared parents, but also my peers. I cannot count how many times kids moved quickly out of my way while I was walking down the halls or going through the bathrooms at school. I was an Indian and we were all supposed to be mean to the *wasicu*. When I went into stores, I always felt the eyes of the clerks on me. I hated to go into a store unless I truly had to buy something. If I were only browsing, I made a show of returning whatever product I was looking at to the shelf or rack to avoid any possible problems with the store clerks. Even now, I find myself being cautious when I go into a store back in Rapid City.

For my high-school graduation, I was chosen as one of the commencement speakers by the faculty. It must have been a good speech because it made several students cry and the audience seemed to listen intently. I wondered, was their interest in my words, or were they merely surprised to see an Indian up there? Whatever their opinion was, speaking for my fellow seniors was an honor and a privilege that I had earned.

The day before the graduation ceremony, another honor—a spotted eagle tail feather—was presented to me by Sidney and Shirley Keith, a traditional Lakota couple who live in Rapid City. Sidney is a Lakota spiritual leader. He and his wife performed an eagle feather ceremony for all of the Lakota high-school graduates. They sang to the four directions and to the sky, the earth, and finally to us. I wish I could describe how they sang because it was so powerful. Sidney and Shirley's voices calling to the spirits through the wind was something I had not heard in years. We all watched and listened silently.

In Sidney's aged hand were many spotted eagle tail feathers, all about a foot long with dark-brown plumes that had a milky-white area at the bottom near the quills. At the base of each of the quills was a leather loop attached by a twisted red porcupine quill. I knew these feathers were holy. He stopped singing for a moment and lit some sweetgrass. He "smudged" the feathers by circling them with the smoldering braid of grass in order to make them sacred and give them power before presenting them to us. He then began again with the same powerful, rhythmic singing. Though I had no idea what the words meant, I stood with my mother and listened out of deep respect. Or was it fear?

I am Lakota. Why should I have listened in fear to a Lakota eagle feather ceremony? Because I had no clue what was happening. I recognized the sweetgrass because I had seen my grandmother use it many times before when I was a boy. Seeing and smelling the burning sweetgrass in Sidney's hand brought back memories from my youth . . .

"Why are you doing that, Gramma?" I remember asking when I saw her light a thick braid of sweetgrass during a powerful thunderstorm.

"I don't want the house to get struck by lightning. This grass will help protect the house and us," she said as she walked from room to room waving the smoking braid of sweetgrass from side to side. She would mumble a prayer in Lakota at the same time. She often prayed in both sides of her life, the Lakota and the *wasicu* sides.

I remember, too, going to the Rosebud Reservation with my grandparents when I was a boy to see the powwows and hear traditional Indian songs. The constant pounding of the drums and the singing filled the air and my thoughts. I watched the "real Indians" in dance attire with their big headdresses and bustles adorned with multicolored feathers, their bells rhythmically sounding with every move, their buckskin pants and shirts with colored tassels swinging, their war clubs, eagle fans, and eagle-claw staffs in their hands, and their faces painted with red, black, and yellow clay to make them look terrifying. No one told me what any of it meant or how to learn to do it. When I was perhaps five years old, not knowing the meaning of a song didn't scare me, but as I got older it became a different story. At age eighteen, my own ignorance frightened me. I hate not knowing now, and am still frightened.

When Sidney and Shirley's song came to an end, they turned to us and he told the story of the eagle feather.

> In the old days they gave these feathers to people who did a good deed. That deed could have been anything—saving a life, doing well on the hunt, doing brave things when it came time to fight, or becoming an adult. Times have changed, but the honor in accomplishing tasks has not. You kids have done a great thing in graduating from high school and that is what the feather honors. Use it in the new world you are entering for strength and guidance.

They gave each of us a feather and shook our hands. I then had something that visibly made me more Indian than I had ever been before. The feather connected me with a part of myself that I had never known about, and I was uncomfortable with it because of my lack of understanding. That day also opened my eyes and curiosity to the spiritual world—or, in American terms, the religion—of the Lakota. Next to my Lakota blood, that feather is the most significant Indian thing I possess. It changed my perspective and attitude toward everything around me. My brother recently said to me, "When you got that feather, that's when you became an Indian. You never hung out with Indians before you got that feather." That blunt truth hit me hard. But the true significance of the feather dawned slowly on me as, indifferent to my Native American identity, I searched for my true self away from my people.

Finding friends at college was fairly easy because my ability to throw a baseball made the transition from South Dakota to Dartmouth much smoother. According to the college's baseball coach and the school paper, I was the number-one baseball recruit that year. That reputation made it very easy for me to meet people. The baseball team had guys in many fraternities who knew the ins and outs of Dartmouth College. "Yeah, this guy is cool. He's a good ballplayer," I frequently heard. Word quickly got around among the freshmen, and I soon had friends.

Without my baseball skills, I probably would not have met the people that I did. Most of the first people I met were *wasicu*, and my identity as Native American was never more than a passing issue to most of them. That I came from South Dakota was more of a revelation to people than my Indian heritage. Most of them had never met any Native Americans before, so they had some basic misconceptions about me. They assumed I could run silently through the forest and shoot an arrow well. They did not know enough to be intentionally racist, only ignorant.

But those harmless assumptions and jokes had another side to them that was insulting, racist, and full of stupidity. Under the shadow of such preconceptions, I had to shed my own cultural and personal ignorance. If I had known more about my heritage and culture, then I could have defended myself better and educated those with a distorted perspective on Indians. Many conservative people at Dartmouth have felt that my presence, or any other Native American's presence on the campus, is simply a big favor they are doing us—that we do not really belong here. Instead, we should stay on our reservations, out of the way of progress and intellectual enlightenment. To many students, and to the college in general, we are only as real as the old Dartmouth Indian symbol that many people claim is a tribute to all Native Americans. People see a symbol or a costume, but often fail to see the human being under the braids, buckskin, and paint. They do not know us or how we perceive the world; people only assume that we are out of our element and need special guidance. I think no white person can ever truly understand the thoughts and feelings of a Native American; we can only ask *wasicu* to respect the Native perspective. This was evident early during my freshman fall at Dartmouth.

When Coach Walsh recruited me for baseball he had informed me of Dartmouth and its fabled beginning as an institution to educate Native Americans. When I arrived at Dartmouth, Coach Walsh and I immediately became friendly, and we often talked openly in his office. Though he listened attentively as I talked about life in South Dakota and my Lakota background, he already had some preconceptions about me and Native Americans in general. Behind my back, Coach Walsh asked one of my teammates to watch out for me. "Don't let Bennett hang out in the fraternity basements, because his people have a big problem with alcoholism. I want you to watch out for him," he said. I was very angry when my teammates revealed this conversation to me after Coach Walsh had left the college. I acknowledge the problems with alcohol that many—but not all—Indian people face, but I did not appreciate being stereotyped.

Coach Walsh's successor, Bob Whalen, also assumed that I needed help to overcome the shackles of my Indian identity. I had filed a petition to get my sophomore summer course requirements waived so I could play in the Cape Cod Baseball League. I wrote in my petition that I had always wanted to play pro baseball and that taking part in the league would improve my chances of getting drafted by a major league team. I also stated that I intended to make up the academic work the following fall. I asked Coach Whalen to write a recommendation for me.

Coach Whalen's recommendation clearly showed that he saw me as Bob, the poor, disadvantaged Indian who needed help to join mainstream American life. The first sentences of his letter read, "I am writing on behalf of Bob Bennett. Due to his poor socioeconomic background I feel it is very necessary for him to forgo his summer residence and play baseball." The implications of this well-meant statement infuriated me.

I was so angry that I was crying and could not articulate my thoughts when I confronted Coach Whalen in his office. I told him how his letter made me appear to the registrar and explained that I had wanted reinforcement of my own arguments, not another handout from the white man. Of course, he replied that he had meant no disrespect and that he was only trying to help. I believed his sincerity, but he is typical of many white people who do not expect a Native person to succeed on his or her own merits. I have grown tired of having to justify my presence and identity to people. I was granted my request and, fortunately, Coach Whalen and I have grown since that incident to become friends.

Other incidents at Dartmouth forced me to confront my Indian identity. My freshman roommate was interested in my Native background because he was taking an environmental studies course in which he read the journal of Lewis and Clark. Lewis and Clark passed through the territory of my ancestors, and my roommate asked me to verify one observation in the journal.

"Hey, Bob, have you ever eaten dog?" he asked. "These guys said the Sioux fed them dog meat."

I replied confidently, "No, they didn't. I haven't eaten dog and they didn't eat it either. They were buffalo hunters, and wouldn't eat dogs. They used them to pull the travois and carry packs. They weren't food."

My roommate insisted that we did and even showed me the passage in the journal. How could I refute what was right in front of me in black and white? I was confused and also embarrassed because he now doubted my Indianness. I also doubted my own Indianness. That early lesson at Dartmouth about my own cultural ignorance pushed me to know more about my ancestors.

I met some other good friends through the Native American Program, although my initial involvement in the program and in the student group Native Americans at Dartmouth (NAD) was quite limited. NAD's activities didn't interest me a great deal. I just wanted to meet some other Native Americans in this strange place. I never thought too much about the political aspects associated with NAD because I had my own agenda. I was a baseball player, and that occupied most of my time and effort each term. Then I rushed a fraternity. The combination of the two shaped who my friends were and, despite my limited interaction with NAD, I came to know many of its members as well.

Academics took up most of my time during my first three years at Dartmouth. One class really opened up new doors for me. The class, Native American Studies 22, The Invasion of America, made me fully aware of something that I had been lacking all of my life—a Native American perspective on my own Lakota heritage. None of my previous classes had really touched my inner self.

The teacher, Professor Colin Calloway, had studied the Abenaki in Vermont and had learned much about the Crow people and their reservation while teaching at the University of Wyoming. I listened very attentively as he spoke of his experience with the Sioux people. "I have spent a lot of time among them and can recognize the sound of their language, but by no means can I speak it," he said. "I only learned this." He said a Lakota phrase that means "bullshit" in English. I laughed aloud as he finished because I recognized one word of the phrase, *cesli*, which means "shit." My chuckle was heard by the entire class and every pair of eyes was suddenly on me. Professor Calloway said, "I see we have a Lakota in here with us. Did that sound right?" I said yes, and he continued with his material.

I made myself the "real Indian" of the class by recognizing one word in the Lakota language. But the extent of my Indian abilities was quite limited. I became frightened of my ignorance one again. I became aware of how white I was during each of his lectures on some other tribe, and I was overwhelmed when we came to the Lakota section of the class. I did not know the Lakota were the *Titonwan*, "dwellers of the prairie," and the western people who spoke the Lakota dialect of the Siouan language. I did not know there were seven bands of Lakota or two other groups of people who were also Sioux. I did not know anything, yet Professor Calloway always looked to me for approval when he pronounced the names of one of the bands of Sioux, and I usually gave him a nod. Other people would look to me when he said something. If only they had known that I didn't know much more than they did.

In the grand scheme of Lakota knowledge, I knew nothing. After a year and a half at Dartmouth, I began to question my life as an Indian, which was really my life as a white guy who looked like an Indian. I was trying to be the person my well-meaning mother and Gramma wanted me to be: an Indian Catholic who only knew the ways of the *wasicu*.

I was searching for a personal identity before that NAS 22 class forced me to think about the path I was treading. I was trying to find my identity, but managed only to become even more lost in the blurred world of Dartmouth College. I realized how lost I was when I tried to find myself spiritually. During my first few terms at Dartmouth, my search for spirit was centered on the Campus Crusade for Christ (CCC) and the Aquinas House.

Though these groups made a great effort to treat me as a person and respected my heritage, I found it difficult to find a comfortable niche in those institutions. I can now say that my true spiritual awakening, or journey, was just beginning, and I soon abandoned white religion.

Professor Calloway's class dealt with the issue of Native religion versus Christianity. Religion was used as a tool of destruction against all tribes in the colonization of North America, and I found it difficult to accept that I was part of an institution that had destroyed so many people's cultures and lives. I did not want to be a part of that institution anymore. I wanted to learn how to be a Lakota, not a white crusader or Catholic with an entirely different culture, spirituality, language, and history.

I made the strongest attempt to regain what had been denied to me by enrolling in a Lakota language class. The professor, Elaine Jahner, had written a Lakota language book with a Lakota woman earlier in her career. She was raised in North Dakota and had a good understanding and respect for Indian culture and thinking. She knew the sound of the language and many words and pushed us patiently.

Four students, three Sioux and one Ojibwe, met weekly with her in her office. I wanted to learn Lakota very badly because I believed the language would return some of my identity. Though I learned quite a lot, Lakota was a difficult language to pick up for a twenty-year-old whose only familiarity was with Latinate languages.

In high school, I studied Spanish, and I remember writing letters to my grandmother with little Spanish phrases and sentences in them. "Gramma, I'm writing and speaking a new language," I wrote with a great sense of accomplishment. That pride now troubles me greatly because I did not even know how to speak the language of my ancestors. I could not even say "How are you?" What in the world was I doing, telling my Lakota-speaking grandmother that I could speak Spanish well? Now I'm angry with myself for being so blind.

When I told Gramma of the Lakota class and Professor Jahner, I felt proud yet nervous. I think she may have been a bit apprehensive about my reasons for learning. "Oh, you want to be Indian so much, don't you,

Bobby? But . . . ," she said. There was usually a "but" in everything she said regarding my search for identity. She did not want me to get distracted from learning the *wasicu* ways and playing their game of baseball.

Despite her warnings and hesitation, she opened up to me before I left for my junior year at Dartmouth, after doctors found that she had developed lung cancer. "Don't worry. I'm going to beat this," she told me before I returned to college. "I've been to ceremonies before and they helped me then. Just pray for me." I never knew she had gone to traditional healing ceremonies. She was even more traditional than I had thought.

I returned to school for my junior year and often thought of her. I called her to ask questions for the Lakota class, and she spoke more freely than she ever had in answering my questions despite her intermittent warnings. She started her chemotherapy treatments later that fall.

I knew the side effects of chemotherapy—weight and hair loss—so I was nervous and frightened when I came home for Christmas break to see my grandmother. However, she had changed very little. She wore a little turban and had lost weight, but her voice and eyes still had their familiar strength. We talked a lot about her childhood and how she met Grandpa. She truly opened up to me for the first time, and I think it was because she realized her time was limited. I talked to her several times about my Lakota class. She taught me how to pronounce the word "deer" in Lakota. I wish I could remember all of the Lakota conversations we had, because they were the first ever. I hated to leave her at the end of that Christmas break because I knew I would not be home until the end of the following summer. It was a long nine months without seeing her. When the time came to see her again in September, I knew the little time I had was going to pass quickly and then I would never see her again. That one week, those seven short days, we spoke of our lives together and said our final farewell. The chemotherapy and radiation treatment had failed to destroy the tumors in her lungs. She realized her time had come, and she just wanted to go home and stop the grueling cancer treatments. During that week in September, we had several great conversations about our lives. I was always on the verge of breaking down, and every time I did she would tell me to stop. "I'm old and I'm not afraid to die. I'm just so thankful that I got to see all of you kids grow up and do so well for yourself," she said in her strong voice as I was crying next to her.

She never wanted us to feel sorry for her. I was crying and feeling sorry for myself that night. She knew she was going on her last journey soon, and she wanted to be strong for me. One night, she made herself sit up, put her arm around me, and consoled me, the healthy grandson, with an amazing strength in her voice: "I'm not afraid; it's my time to go. Bobby, you be strong for everyone here and just use the blessings you got from God. Don't cry for me because I will be fine." She had such strength in her final months.

During one of our conversations, I asked her how the Lakota described "life" with their words. She thought for a moment and casually said the words in Lakota. Of course, I could not understand them, so I asked her what the words meant in English. She thought for another moment and said, "I have come this far." "I have come this far" is a literal English translation of the Lakota concept of "life." The old Lakota had a very insightful perspective on the world, and those were the most profound words I had ever heard from her.

"I have come this far." That phrase hit me that night. Ironically, my Gramma spoke the words at the end of her Lakota life. When she left this existence, my life—"how far I had come"—was just beginning. I was shedding my *wasicu* version of life and beginning to understand why my forebears had preferred to die in battle to protect their ways rather than become puppets of the *wasicu* world. Now I wish my upbringing had been as Indian as possible. I grew up solely as a *wasicu*, and that angers me greatly. My "I have come this far" is far from over, and when it does end, I want to be as content and unafraid as my grandmother was. Though she suppressed much of her Indian identity to protect herself, her children, and her grandchildren during her life, she left this world content, ready, and unafraid as a Lakota. I will follow her example.

She had gone a long way in her seventy-six years and I am thankful that I had nearly twenty-two years to spend with her. At her funeral, I put a baseball next to her body, just as I had for my grandfather years before, so she could hold it for me on the other side. That way I can play for her and Grandpa and they can give me their strength. I feel her spirit every day and I have seen her in several dreams. In her life I found strength, and her death only enhances the power we find in each other. When they closed the casket and the shadow covered her face forever, I truly realized why she did not teach me. I have to teach myself and also those who do not understand.

I am angry that a place like Dartmouth was necessary for me to figure out my identity and direction in life. The college has educated me in the *wasicu* sense, which contradicts much of the Indian knowledge I have acquired recently. Dartmouth has only licensed me as an educated Indian in the world of the *wasicu*, but that learning will be valuable in helping me help other Indians and myself. I have found more of myself, more of my spirit, and in that discovery comes knowledge. Knowledge will come to me and it will be in control. I just need to keep that in mind, relax, and allow everything that eluded me as a boy to come to me as a man.

Wanbli Wanji emaciyapi na han ma wicasa Lakota yelo.

I am One Eagle and I am a Lakota man.

My journey is far from over, and one of my yet-to-be-attained dreams is to stand on a major league pitcher's mound with my hair in a braid, knowing that I have accomplished everything I ever wanted. Standing there alone, standing as *Wanbli Wanji*, will be a testimony to the struggle of Native people and the individual battle waged within all of us. Stand proud, Indian people. *Mitakuye oyasin.*

Robert (Bob) Antoine Bennett, an enrolled member of the Rosebud Sioux (Sicangu Lakota) tribe, was born December 30, 1970, in Rapid City, South Dakota. He graduated in 1989 from Rapid City Central High School, where he participated in football and basketball. At that time, he also played baseball for the Post 22 American Legion baseball team.

Bob enrolled at Dartmouth College in 1990, finishing his coursework for a major in government and a minor in Native American studies in March 1994. This essay was written during his final year Dartmouth.

While in college, Bob played three seasons of varsity baseball, and in June 1992 he was drafted by the Oakland Athletics as a right-handed pitcher. As of the 1996 season, he was a member of the Class AA affiliate of the Oakland Athletics, the Huntsville Stars, located in Huntsville, Alabama. Bob is also a Grass Dancer, and he plans to help Native people as a lawyer, counselor, or educator after his baseball career is over.

Follow Up: To Be an Indian Is a Rough Life

As the shadow covered my Gramma Clara's face on that sad day in October 1992, my mind was blank. It was hard to look at a piece of you that is now dead, knowing you will never be able to see, hug, or talk to that person again. But even my extreme pain was outweighed by my mom's agony as we stood at the cemetery where Gramma Clara was being laid to rest. In my mind's eye I can still see the people standing around us, friends and relatives of Gramma Clara and Grampa Joe. My grandparents had a double plot on Skyline Drive, which overlooks Rapid City, South Dakota. Grampa Joe was already buried there, and Gramma Clara was to be buried next to him. The cemetery engineers had the grave neatly dug, the dark dirt piled near the hole. The Catholic priest finished the ceremony, and as everyone turned to leave, he directed them to continue to celebrate the life of Gramma Clara. My mom ran to the coffin, hugged it, and wailed. It was difficult to see her pain and she would later say it was acknowledging both of her parents were now gone. My brother and I held her until she calmed down, and then there was nothing remaining to do but let Gramma be laid to rest. Once they lowered her into the ground, we covered her, and then it was simply time to leave.

I think back to when Gramma woke me up in the middle of the night a few months earlier and told me to be strong, as the cancer was eating her from the inside. She was very brave and told me she was ready to go. That made me feel good, and still does. After her death, one of my many thoughts was, how am I going to become an Indian without Gramma Clara?

A long time ago, when we were talking about Indians, Gramma Clara told me with a laugh, *"Lakota kin otehika."* She said it meant "To be an Indian is a rough life." She was right. I have been drawn back to that phrase countless times since writing, "Why Didn't You Teach Me?" Being Indian is what? I believe my Uncle Sidney said it most simply: "Being Indian, it's a way of life. It is being a human being." The term "traditional" is applied to people from all walks of Indian life who try to maintain a connection to the historical Indians of their tribe. But what does it mean to be a traditional Indian in today's world? Our Indian ways of life have been altered drastically, and I know I would have been one of the ones to stand up to defend my way of life centuries ago, or 150 or so years from today here on the Great Plains. Even though I can tell you some stories about the Lakota I am today, I have to add that I still don't know much; however, the ancestors in the spirit world have shown themselves to me and confirmed my relationship to them.

The Indian Baseball Road

I had the good fortune to play professional baseball from June 1992 until July 1997. I put on a baseball uniform for some six hundred professional games over six seasons and got to pitch over five hundred innings in about 150 games. I was given the opportunity to play in the major leagues, but I peaked at the Double-A level—I simply was not good enough. My best chance of making the big league team was in 1996. I was working out with the Triple-A team during spring training, and I did not give up a run. If the major league team was short on pitchers, they would call up one of us minor leaguers to finish the game. One of the perks, besides the chance to play in front of thousands of people, was the amazing spread of food after the game. The minor league fare was a brown paper bag of sandwiches made of bologna, turkey, and ham, or peanut butter and jelly, washed down with a bottle of Gatorade. The big league fare was catered and beautifully arrayed in the clubhouse. When the big club was making that year's final cuts and sending the minor leaguers back to the Triple-A and Double-A teams, I was sent back to Double A when the Triple A team filled its roster.

In late 1993 I began growing my hair so I would be the pitcher with a braid standing on the Oakland Coliseum mound. At the 1994 spring training, people saw my hair long and a bit disheveled and believed I was trying to imitate Dennis Eckersley, one of the greatest long-haired closers in the game of baseball. I explained to the Oakland managers that I had received my adult Indian name and was following some new rules in my life. But they didn't care much about the hair. Their main concern was what name to put on my locker. My teammates supported my long hair, but it was funny to hear the opposing teams' fans run their mouths when they saw me pitching. My hair grew to the middle of my back and I wore it in a braid. Most people had no idea that I was a real live Indian and that my hair was a form of cultural and spiritual expression.

Playing baseball was an awesome experience, and we were treated like superstars in every city we visited. People were friendly because they thought one of us might be the next Catfish Hunter, Derek Jeter, or Reggie Jackson. I played with guys who had actually made it but were sent back to the minors for rehabilitation, or had been cut from the major league roster. Returning to the minors was a letdown for them because there were no more chartered jets or equipment assistants. For us, it was the Tin Can Express of chartered buses, and we had to carry our own equipment bags.

A Big Leaguer who came down told of his time with Oakland. The big club had just swept the Boston Red Sox in Boston and had a day off the next day. The club left on the chartered jet and the booze was flowing. By the time the jet was over Missouri all the booze was gone. A request was made to the captain to get more booze and he obliged the team. The captain radioed ahead to Kansas City and a pallet of booze was ordered for delivery to the tarmac. The plane landed, the delivery was loaded, and the party continued to Oakland. The surreal life of being on the top shelf of professional sports was what we all wanted.

I stayed at the Double-A level for three years. The fans of Huntsville, Alabama, became some of my best friends. The booster club created the "Eagle Award," named after me for being the most popular pitcher—maybe not the best, but their favorite. In fact I wasn't the best, and the writing was on the wall after three seasons in Double A. I had seen many hitters and pitchers pass through the Southern League and knew my skills had plateaued. In June 1997, I was out for a week with a forearm strain when my Uncle Sidney died. I was a wreck; my uncle was the man who made me an Indian with that feather, and now he had left this earth. Against the wishes of Oakland management, because Sidney wasn't a blood relative, I traveled home to pay my respects and say my farewell to Uncle Sidney. I missed his funeral by a few days, but I went to his grave on the Cheyenne River Reservation. I stood there feeling deeply saddened, but I could hear him laughing and see him smiling at me from the spirit world. He told me not to be so sad and to let the feather he gave me carry me. He and others were watching out for me.

Such was the road in my life, and it was about to take another turn. I returned to Huntsville, cut my hair, and a week or two later, on July 6, 1997, I got the tap on my shoulder from the assistant manager. He had a somber expression and I knew what was in store even before he said, "Q wants to see you in the office." I had outlasted most of the guys with whom the Oakland A's had drafted me in 1992. There were a few who made it to the Major League, but it was not my destiny; my talent level was not sufficient. Oakland had given me every opportunity to develop the consistency I needed to pitch in the big leagues, but again, I simply didn't have the consistent skill to play at that level. Nevertheless, those six years were awesome, and today I play catch with my son and daughters and coach other kids.

As crushing as the termination of one's professional athletic career can be, Q was actually cool and said, "I am supposed to release you after the game. We should have enough pitching to get through today and I don't want to run the risk of throwing you out there and getting you hurt. Go say good-bye to the guys and pack your stuff. You fly out Tuesday." He then asked me, "What do you want me to tell the other teams when they ask about you?"

I replied, "Tell them I am done and I am just going home to be an Indian. If they need a player come the spring, they can call."

Two days later I was back in Rapid City, unemployed but with enough money in my pocket to travel around, go to powwows, see relatives, and do nothing for several months. I got a job as a deputy sheriff in my hometown, and in November 1997 I embarked on a law-enforcement career.

I wanted to go to law school and get back all of my people's land, but I really needed a job. No call ever came from a baseball team, and in the spring of 1998 I was just another Indian guy embarking on what would be a law-enforcement career.

Regular Indian Road

Soon after returning home from Alabama, I took a deep breath, inhaling the world around me. The homelands of the Black Hills and their power surrounded me, and I had to find a new way to "make meat." *"Making meat"* is an older Lakota expression and perspective on providing for yourself, your family, your friends, and the people who call you theirs.

I never thought I would be in law enforcement, but I took the lead of my older brother Fred who began his law-enforcement career in 1992. I often think of the first "Indian Police" who worked for the reservation superintendents or the first scouts for the army. What did they think of their role? How did it fit into their 1800s psyche, when they thought in Lakota, spoke Lakota, and were as Indian as anyone could be? What would they think of me? These thoughts made me ask myself often, what is it to be an Indian? And yes, it was difficult to be Indian.

In November 1997 I was hired by the Pennington County Sheriff's Office at a wage of $12.50 an hour. For $2.50 more an hour I began to work for the Rapid City Police Department in September 1999. The Bureau of Indian Affairs then opened an office in Rapid City, and I was hired by the federal government as special agent. I more than doubled my city-police-officer salary and began to work exclusively with other Indian law-enforcement officers and among Indians who were alleged to have committed crimes. In February 2003 I was hired by the Federal Bureau of Investigation as a special agent. My application had been pending with the FBI for years but finally came through.

I was able to transfer back to South Dakota as an FBI agent in 2009. I had been away from South Dakota for six years and I was surprised to the point of having a physical reaction when I saw about eight Indian males in a detention cell at the Federal Courthouse in Pierre, South Dakota. I was taken aback because I had spent the previous three years in Amarillo, Texas, and had not arrested Native American people in a while. The word "Lakota" itself means "allies." In Lakota you acknowledge other Lakota as your relatives, and here I was in the presence of my caged relatives. The unique relationship between Lakota and the FBI in South Dakota had been defined during the turbulent 1970s with the American Indian Movement and the Leonard Peltier killing of two FBI agents, Jack Coler and Ronald Williams. I was reminded of a friend who asked, "You want to be an Indian who wants to put other Indians in jail, huh?" The canned answer of a law-enforcement officer wanting "to help people" didn't seem an appropriate response, but in so many words I said that was what I wanted to do. South Dakota has nine Lakota, Dakota, and Nakota reservations within its boundaries, and the bulk of federal criminal prosecutions come from cases on these reservations. I think I bring a unique perspective as an FBI agent.

Ironically enough, federal jurisdiction, the Major Crimes Act, on American Indian reservations came from my Rosebud Reservation after Crow Dog killed Spotted Tail in 1881. At that time there was no jurisdiction for the US government over an Indian killing another Indian. The killing was settled among the families in a traditional Lakota manner back then, but the outside non-Indian people couldn't allow savages to kill each other, thus Crow Dog was arrested. He was tried and sentenced to hang. He was given a furlough to say good-bye to his family on the Rosebud Reservation under escort of an Indian agent. Crow Dog failed to report back to the agent on the reservation but told his family to tell him he would show up in Deadwood for his hanging. Several days later Crow Dog was on time for his own hanging. However, someone appealed Crow Dog's case to the Supreme Court and he was eventually pardoned.

The formal Indian Reorganization Act and other informal practices sought to assimilate, or destroy, Lakota culture and custom, and modeled Lakota government councils, courts, police departments, and jails after the US versions of them. The irony of Indians governing, policing, incarcerating, and judging other Indians within the structure of an imposed culture is overwhelming. But that is how things are in the twenty-first century. Until a more traditional approach to law enforcement is developed, I approach my job with as traditional a Lakota mind as I can have. The nature of the crimes investigated by an FBI agent on South Dakota reservations would appall any traditional Lakota. Rapes, homicides, and serious assaults are the bulk of FBI investigations.

I thought hard about what I had learned over the past several years and how it applies to being a Lakota. I will share some stories with you.

My Lakota Path

On the path I took to learn how to be an Indian I was often met with caveats from people who knew dancing, songs, language, and ceremonies. The better teachers said humbly, "This is what was told to me, but there are other ways." Humility is perhaps the most important Lakota virtue. I am thankful for the people who understood this virtue and taught me what I wanted to learn with a quiet smile.

There also were many people who were angry, defensive, unfriendly, who would say over and over to me as I struggled to learn about my own heritage, "You're an urban Indian," "You ain't from here," "You're a half-breed" (my father was Seneca), "You are acting white," "You're not one of us." Among some there was competition to be "more Indian" than others and an atmosphere of exclusion, but that road never seemed honorable to me. I had the right to be Lakota because I was born as one, but I had to define myself within the knowledge I had given to me. So I have learned from experience that Gramma Clara was indeed right—to be an Indian is a rough life. She also was right when she warned me that many Indians would not welcome me into the way of life. On the other hand, many did.

Along my road of learning I met many who knew how to be Indian, and they welcomed those like me into their homes, lives, and families, sharing their knowledge with a smile. One instruction that was often repeated was "You have free agency to be connected with the Creator who made your people through the ceremonies He gave us." All Indians have that blood connection to a language, culture, and spirituality that the Creator gave them. Though the thousands of Indian tribes are vastly different, we are all connected to the Creator, and each of us has a vein in our heart directly connected to the one who made us. That is something millions of Indians in North, Central, and South America chose to die for—or, put another way, for which they were killed. But today, if it's in your blood, it's yours to take, and you can choose whether or not to share what you know.

"They said you were trying to become Indian, but I never knew you would become one so fast," Gramma Ella said to me with one of her special smiles. Ella was my uncle Duane's mother and of the same generation as Gramma Clara. Ella passed away several years after my gramma and was another from the generation who had their heritage suppressed. It is so sad to think of what died with Ella and Gramma Clara. It was good to see in her expression that she appreciated people coming back to learn how to be Indian. Other relatives and friends knew where I came from and chose to teach me.

My brother was a criminal investigator on the Rosebud Reservation and he got to know many of our relatives who still lived on Rosebud. We met at powwows, basketball games, through mutual friends, and other gatherings, and we chose to become friends and relatives. Aside from being related by blood, among the Lakota there is the informal "Indian way" and the formally adopted (hunka) manner of being a relative.

The Indian way method is as simple as befriending the brother of your brother's girlfriend and taking him as your brother. It is as simple as taking a teammate from any team and he or she comes to eat a few times per week with you. If you go to sweat lodge with someone, he is your brother. The water pourer is your uncle. If two guys sing at the same drum, they are brothers. At times it is as loosely arranged as being the adopted brother of the brother of this guy who let you sleep on his floor during the Founder's Day powwow.

The formal hunka ceremony is an awesome way to become a relative to someone. During one version of the ceremony the would-be relative is directed to say he/she is hungry, cold, and thirsty. After saying the words, the adopting people gather around and provide ceremonial meat and water/juice and then wrap the person in a blanket. Those gathered then sing a song and face the four directions, and after that, whatever your situation later in life, they are your relative. Relatives simply pledge to treat you well as long as you walk the earth.

Uncle Willis was an old-style man who became my relative. I used to travel up to see him in Montana on the Fort Peck Reservation. He took me in as his nephew and would tell me story after story of what he had been told in his younger days. He talked of grass dancing as a young man, taking apart an eagle for feathers or other parts, or making tobacco ties. Uncle Willis was always imparting his wisdom:

> This is what I was told. But for some the color of this direction is different. Some face the west while others face the east. It really doesn't matter, if all of your efforts are done with a good heart and mind and you do what you were taught. Don't put too much faith in a man other than yourself and what the Creator gave you for tools.

Uncle Willis was a champion old-style grass dancer. When I first met him I wasn't a dancer, but when I showed an interest he taught me the way he was taught. A large component of grass dancing comes from the many Northern Plains tribes' ceremonies to bless a new camp. It was a sacred duty to prepare the campsite, and the men would stomp the grass down to prepare the ground. Dancing told stories and brought the camps of old together. Therefore, dancing is powerfully sacred and social at the same time.

Uncle Willis drove me out to a field where an old house still barely stood. He would look over the area and say:

> Look at those trees sway in the wind. Watch that prairie chicken walk and look for food. Watch the wind move the cattails and reeds near the pond. Look at those hawks and eagles soaring above. You want to be all of that when you dance. You also have to be in Indian shape and move to the beat of the drum the singers give you for song after song. Remember to be in balance and what you do on the right side has to be done on the left. From the feathers and porcupine hair on your head to the bells on your feet, your whole body should be moving to that beat. That is a grass dancer.

He would then put on a powwow song and I would find myself dancing in a field.

I got better at dancing and started placing in the contest powwows. I took first place a few times, but usually placed lower in the cash-winning places, or not at all. The better-known dancers usually won, but for me to sneak in and get a few hundred dollars for dancing was always awesome. Getting to enjoy the company of many other good people was another benefit. Many dancers befriended me and critiqued my style. I didn't start until I was twenty-four, and that surprised many people if I got in the money at some of the bigger gatherings.

I traveled around with many people, but I became extremely close with Mike, a man from my own reservation, who was a champion grass dancer. Mike was about ten years older than me and taught me much about dancing. He also taught me more about the sweat lodge and other Lakota ceremonies. He would put together grass-dance videos for me of the dancers we would encounter. Advice from him was usually something simple: "Watch these guys and keep practicing." "Keep the beat and move your whole body at the same time." "Get your own style." I would try the others' moves and weave them into my own style. We often traveled a long way to dance.

Mike's wife, Denise, a jingle dress dancer herself who was pregnant at the time, knew the power of dancing. Mike and I were planning a trip to the Hinckley Powwow near Minneapolis in December 1995. Denise was due anytime and wanted Mike there for the birth. She and Mike were both hoping the baby would come early so we could travel. *Oskate Win* (Celebration Woman) was indeed born a few days early, and Mike and I traveled to Hinckley. *Oskate* is an older Lakota word for what is now called a powwow, or *wacipi* (they dance). This baby was a good example of how an Indian girl got her name.

My own family was initially a little concerned about my quest for Indian knowledge. Being an Indian was something most acknowledged, but none of the immediate family would participate in the older ceremonies or powwow. They felt it was strange that I, the city-white-boy-Indian, actually lived and worked on the reservation during breaks from baseball. It took some time, but all of my family came to understand the road I chose to travel.

Irony of Lateral Racism

My road has been full of people who don't smile, people who believe they are better than others, and people who are just angry or lost. My hometown of Rapid City has a population of Indians, from my tribe and others, who exemplify this. When I was working in my hometown as a deputy sheriff or policeman, I had to deal with many of my relatives and friends who were Indians. The following two stories note lateral racism from a longtime friend and from a stranger. The first story is about a friend whom I had known since elementary school, and the other is about someone I spent a few minutes with in a park and then in a courtroom.

In the first story I will call my friend "D," who was almost shot by several of us after he beat up his wife and ran away. When we caught up to him he turned to us with his hands inside his waistband, pretending he had a gun. D was lucky he didn't get shot. Once we recognized each other, he calmed down and ceased his dangerous actions as we took him into custody. On the way to jail, judgment on my level of being a real Lakota came from this longtime friend.

We were talking cordially during the ride to the jail when he became suspiciously quiet. I had a civilian observer with me in the vehicle. At one point I turned and saw my arrested friend reaching back into his pants. Unsure of what was going to happen, I thought I was about to get stabbed or shot through the safety screen. I radioed for assistance, stopped the vehicle, and went to the back seat to gain control of my longtime friend's still handcuffed hands. It turned out he was trying to dump a big baggie of marijuana. Somehow the bag was missed in his underwear when we arrested him. He said he had kids to take care of and couldn't afford the jail time and fine for possession. He begged me to just let him throw it out, but I simply could not do that.

A tirade followed of how un-Indian I was. "My aunt says you aren't Indian. All of what you do is talk and you're a fucking joke as an Indian, you do-gooder, white motherfucker," he spewed at me. (I used to give talks about education, culture, grass dancing, and baseball to various schools in

Rapid City.) When we reached the jail, he failed to calm down and continued his tirade. Several of us had to hog-tie him, carry him into the jail, and strip search him. He fought the entire time, and we had to treat him like an animal and leave him in his underwear in the cold jail cell. The jailers asked me why I had such a bothered look on my face over that "piece of shit." "I have known that guy since I was eleven," I said, "and that was hard." It is odd what an Indian will say to an Indian. His aunt might even agree.

Another incident was with a Lakota man whom I will call "M." M touted himself as a full-blood traditional Indian, and on one summer night in 2000 he was passed out drunk in a city park shelter. The park was in my patrol area in Rapid City, and I was finishing up a report on another matter at the station when the call came of a disturbance in the park. Although a fellow officer radioed in and said he would take the call, I left the station and made my way to the park. Suddenly a call for assistance came over the radio, as people had begun running from the park when the officers showed up. I quickened my pace, and as I arrived the first officer on scene radioed for someone to check on the status of the "lady" in the shelter. The officer believed the two males who ran may have been doing something to the person.

I approached the shelter with another officer, and we came upon what turned out to be a man with long black hair passed out on a picnic table. Around him were dozens of empty beer bottles. I patted him on the back and asked him to wake up. He woke up and attempted to speak, but only drunken, unintelligible garble came out. M had an angry look on his face and his speech eventually became coherent. "You fucking half-breeds are always doing this shit to me and my relatives," he said.

M stood up and then swung his right hand at me. I blocked the punch, but he had a plastic grocery bag around his wrist, which contained a cassette tape, some coins, tweezers, and a 24-ounce bottle of shampoo. The bag and its contents slammed into my left ear. I blacked out for a moment, and when I recovered my senses I was enraged and my ear was ringing badly.

I reached for M, grabbing him by the shoulder and his long Lakota hair. My fellow officer also had a hold of him and was pulling in the opposite direction. M and the other officer came flying over the table toward my direction and onto the ground. My first thought was I wanted to beat this guy. I had him by his hair, which was hanging over his face so I could not see the nose I wanted to break. I was so angry and maintained a hold of him. Other officers arrived, thank goodness—for both M's nose and my law-enforcement career. Each grabbed an appendage, and they subdued him a little before I could do something stupid. One officer, ironically one with a reputation for having a short fuse, was yelling at me to get away because he saw my rage and the hit I took. I disengaged from full-blood M.

As I was checking my injuries, the other four officers were having a tough time getting M subdued and cuffed. I noticed the commotion was still going on and M was on his stomach and fighting to keep his hands under him. So I came back, engaged M with a compliance technique, and ordered him to place his hands behind his back. I was still furious and my ear was bleeding. I began yelling at him and asked, "Do you think you're better than me, you drunk hypocrite? Shut your fucking mouth and get your hands behind your back!" I remember the look he gave me. I think I scared him and his hands went immediately behind his back. Several other officers and deputies were standing around, silently taking in this interaction between two Lakota men who were on opposite ends of the situation. Several months later he was sentenced to four years in state prison for assault on a police officer. He turned to me at the hearing and said, "Sorry bro, I didn't know they had any Indians on this police force." We actually had six.

I have undergone a transition in my life. I swore to do my duty according to the laws of the federal government and state of South Dakota, and I wanted to be a patrolman or investigator regularly on the scene of some traffic accident, homicide, or assault. If nothing happened, I would claim I was bored. Now that I am older I still uphold my duty and will run toward the sound of tragedy, gunfire, and danger, but I now know when I run that means someone is getting hurt. I like my job, but do not like seeing the hurt. The hurt I feel is amplified when I see Lakota doing bad things to other Lakota.

Domestic Indian Life

My relationship with my ex-wife could be described as one that put the cart before the horse. We had a daughter and a house before we were married, then a son, and I adopted her daughter from her previous marriage, which had left her widowed. My ex-wife and I had some significant issues and they adversely affected our ability to stay married. I am motivated now to provide the opportunity for my daughter, son, and adopted daughter to have a father. I went through most of my childhood not knowing who my dad was, not having a father-son game of catch, or just hanging out with my dad on a regular basis. It really was a difficult experience.

I have done a thousand times more with my children than my father did with me. Many of us eleven kids were angry at him. However, he eventually changed his ways and made an effort to get to know all of us, and in time we made things good between us. But it wasn't until his death in 2007 that all eleven of his children got together for the first time. I was divorced by then, and my kids were with me for their summer visit, so they traveled with me to the funeral in New York.

Remember the issues with my ex-wife? Below is an actual conversation:

> I said, "I would like to go to Rosebud and go to sweat." "You're not *that* Indian, and you don't do it often enough for me to believe that it is real for you," she said.

Life's circumstances have left a physical and literal void in what and how I can teach my kids about being Lakota. When you have a woman who has difficulty seeing you as human because of divorce angst and hurt feelings and there are hundreds of miles between households, how can I teach the kids much about a heritage that is theirs when they live as regular Americans? Sad and humorous at the same time, my kids were the white kids with the Indian dad. However, they are good kids and have had good lives to date. When they are ready, they will come to me with their desire to learn more of who they are. But most of all, they know I love them.

Final Thoughts

No old Indian person will ever say they know everything, and I have been lucky to be and become the nephew, son, brother, uncle, and friend of many wise and happy old Indians. The most humble and wisest people I have come across have said only simple things. Uncle Percy said, "Remember to shake hands with and smile at your friends because you may never see them again. The spirit of your people and the old ways are always with you. Be patient and they will show themselves to you." Percy would laugh so hard when I missed a beat on his drum during my attempts at singing and just smiled when I was getting my grass dance legs. He, like many other humble grammas and grampas, was just happy to see a person coming back to our heritage. Whenever I entered his sweat lodge, he always had a smile and a positive message. When I had a question, he would answer it as well as he could.

Nowadays, if I see something offensive being done, I call people on it and won't allow a contradiction to pass without at least telling someone an Indian perspective on it. The US government did such an excellent job of killing or isolating the Indians that the idea Indians still exist remains an afterthought among non-Indian Americans. If you don't look the way they think you should, they say you're not an Indian. In their ignorance, the average non-Indian expects a "real Indian" to look like the Washington NFL team mascot or the Indians drawn next to the Pilgrims in the Thanksgiving fantasy. Most everywhere I go I am seen as the Hawaiian, Samoan, or Korean guy.

Times have changed for people of my generation. It is still difficult to be an Indian but not close to what the generations before us had to endure. To literally be physically assaulted for speaking your own language and segregated from non-Indian Americans is hard to imagine, or to think what life was like for my great-grandmother, who was born in the 1890s and who spoke to people who witnessed buffalo hunts firsthand, who saw the first trains, or who witnessed military engagements. The Wounded Knee Massacre happened in 1890, only 120-some years ago. Children and grandchildren of survivors of that event are still alive today.

I think of a story my Aunt Rita told me of a time when she was about ten years old and took a trip to Rapid City. Rapid City can be a typical reservation border town. People of today around here never fathomed segregation existed this far north. She told me a story of being a schoolgirl who went to see the United Nations secretary general in Rapid City in the early 1950s. It was an event held at the Hotel Alex Johnson. Her school in Provo, South Dakota, had sent students to attend. She sat in the room to hear the secretary general speak and noticed a sign on the wall that read, "no indians allowed." She sat there just waiting nervously for someone to come in and take her out of the room.

Still, I am not as angry today as I was when I got to Dartmouth and had to confront my own ignorance of my own culture. I have learned much since then. When I hear a Lakota song at a powwow, a funeral, or in sweat lodge and understand the words, it is an awesome feeling. I did learn something. The power of Lakota words and lyrics is amazing when you know what they mean. When I hear fluent speakers talking around me and I understand, I know I have learned much. When people ask me a question about dancing, culture, or anything Lakota, I often have an answer. However, I have much more to learn.

So, Gramma Clara, I know how hard it must have been for you, but I now know a little more. Thanks for all that you have taught me and for giving me the will to learn more. When I think of you, I can hear you laugh and say, "You want to be an Indian so much, but it's hard to be an

Indian." Thanks for being my gramma and helping me become an Indian. I just hope to be an old Indian one day and die with my eyes closed.

Bob played professional baseball in the Oakland Athletics Organization from 1992 to 1997. After baseball he embarked on a law-enforcement career, and is currently employed as a special agent for the Federal Bureau of Investigation in his hometown of Rapid City, South Dakota. He is a father of three children, Emma, Clara, and Joe. He coaches baseball and teaches boxing.

Bob is still a grass dancer and simply tries to be a traditional Lakota in his endeavors. He was part of Dartmouth College's class of 1993 and earned a BS in government with a minor in Native American studies. He is a Sicangu Lakota enrolled with the Rosebud Sioux Tribe.

Notes

Foreword

1. Basil H. Johnston, *Indian School Days* (Norman: University of Oklahoma Press, 1988), 243.
2. K. Tsianina Lomawaima, *They Called It Prairie Light: The Story of Chilocco Indian School* (Lincoln: University of Nebraska Press, 1994).
3. Patrick Wolfe, "Settler Colonialism and the Elimination of the Native," *Journal of Genocide Research* 8, no. 4 (2006): 387–409.
4. B. M. J. Brayboy, A. J. Fann, A. E. Castagno, and J. A. Solyom, *Postsecondary Education for American Indian and Alaska Natives: Higher Education for Nation Building and Self-Determination* (San Francisco, CA: Wiley Periodicals, 2012).
5. Amanda Tachine, "Monsters and Weapons: Navajo Students' Stories as They Journey toward College" (PhD diss., University of Arizona, 2015).

Preface

1. "Undergraduate Native American Studies," Dartmouth College, http://native-american.dartmouth.edu/undergraduate.
2. Colin G. Calloway, *The Indian History of an American Institution: Native Americans and Dartmouth* (Hanover, NH: Dartmouth College Press, 2010), xiv.
3. "The Dartmouth Powwow," Dartmouth College, http://www.dartmouth.edu/~nap/powwow/.
4. "Undergraduate Native American Studies." See also "Dartmouth Powwow."
5. "Undergraduate Native American Studies."
6. "Dartmouth Powwow."
7. "Undergraduate Native American Studies."
8. "About Us," Native Americans at Dartmouth, Dartmouth College, http://sites.dartmouth.edu/nad/about-us/.
9. Calloway, *Indian History*, 152.
10. "Undergraduate Native American Studies." See also "Dartmouth Powwow."
11. "Dartmouth College Factbook, Fall Enrollments," Dartmouth College Office of Institutional Research, http://www.dartmouth.edu/~oir/pdfs/fall_enrollments.pdf.
12. "Dartmouth College Factbook: Undergraduate Admissions," Dartmouth College Office of Institutional Research, http://www.dartmouth.edu/~oir/pdfs/admissions.pdf.

13. Ibid.
14. "Graduation Rates of First-Time, Full-Time Bachelor's Degree-Seeking Students at 4-Year Postsecondary Institutions, by Race/Ethnicity, Time to Completion, Sex, and Control of Institution: Selected Cohort Entry Years, 1996 through 2006," National Center for Education Statistics, https://nces.ed.gov/programs/digest/d13/tables/dt13_326.10.asp.
15. Zac Hardwick, "Graduation Rates Differ Significantly across Race," *The Dartmouth*, November 4, 2013, http://thedartmouth.com/2013/11/04/graduation-rates-differ-significantly-across-race/. See also "Dartmouth College Facts and Figures: Fall 2014," Dartmouth College Office of Institutional Research, http://www.dartmouth.edu/~oir/FactsandFigures.html.
16. "Undergraduate Native American Studies."
17. "Dartmouth College Factbook: Degrees Awarded 2014," Dartmouth College Office of Institutional Research, http://www.dartmouth.edu/~oir/pdfs/degrees_awarded_2014.pdf.
18. Bruce Duthu, e-mail message to author, April 13, 2015.
19. "Native American Program," Dartmouth College, http://www.dartmouth.edu/~nap/.
20. "Native American House," Dartmouth College, http://www.dartmouth.edu/livinglearning/communities/nah.html; Calloway, *Indian History*, 159.
21. Annie Dillard, "To Fashion a Text," in *Inventing the Truth: The Art and Craft of Memoir*, ed. William Zinsser (Boston: Houghton Mifflin: Boston, 1997), 22.
22. Zinsser, *Inventing the Truth*, 23.

Introduction

1. In 2012, the most recent year reported by the National Center for Education Statistics, Native American students made up just 0.9% of the total college student body nationwide ("Fast Facts," National Center for Education Statistics, Institute of Education Sciences, http://nces.ed.gov/fastfacts/display.asp?id=98). At Dartmouth that same year, Native students made up 4% of the student population on campus; that number has held steady in the following years of reporting as well ("Dartmouth Facts and Figures," Office of Institutional Research, Dartmouth College, http://www.dartmouth.edu/~oir/FactsandFigures.html).
2. Colin G. Calloway, *The Indian History of an American Institution: Native Americans and Dartmouth* (Hanover, NH: University Press of New England, 2010).
3. Bill Bray, "Refuse to Kneel," in *First Person, First Peoples: Native American College Graduates Tell Their Life Stories*, ed. Andrew Garrod and Colleen Larimore (Ithaca, NY: Cornell University Press, 1997), 53.
4. Paul Chaat Smith, *Everything You Know about Indians Is Wrong* (Minneapolis: University of Minnesota Press, 2009), 26.
5. Ibid., 27.
6. Ibid., 6.
7. David Treuer, *Native American Fiction: A User's Manual* (Saint Paul: Graywolf Press, 2006), 25.
8. Demi Simi and Jonathan Matusitz, "Native American Students in U.S. Higher Education: A Look from Attachment Theory," *Interchange* 47, no. 1 (February 2016): 91–108, 97.

3. *Chahta hattak sia,* "I Am a Choctaw Man"

1. Choctaw traditional foods.
2. Tvshka Homma (meaning "Red Warrior") is the historic capital of the Choctaw Nation.

3. The Tombigbee River forms the eastern boundary of the Choctaw Nation in Mississippi, while Muddy Boggy flows through the Choctaw Nation.

4. "Blood quantum laws or Indian blood laws is legislation enacted in the United States to define membership in Native American tribes or nations. 'Blood quantum' refers to describing the degree of ancestry for an individual of a specific racial or ethnic group, for instance, 1/4 Omaha tribe" (http://en.wikipedia.org/wiki/Blood_quantum_laws).

5. CDIB is the Certificate of Degree of Indian Blood.

6. The Indian Child Welfare Act declared that Native children must be adopted by Native parents.

4. Nihalgai Bahane', A Fourth-World Story

1. Not forever on earth, only a brief time here! Even jade fractures, even gold breaks, even quetzal feathers tear. Not forever on earth, only a brief time here!

6. My Journey to Healing

1. Kerry M. Abel, *Drum Songs: Glimpses of Dene History* (Montreal: McGill-Queen's University Press, 1993), unpaginated section after the introduction.

2. Ibid., 22.

3. David Johnston, "Economic Club of Minnesota Luncheon Address on the Diplomacy of Knowledge: Innovation Exchange across Borders" (speech, Minneapolis-St. Paul, MN, April 27, 2015). The Governor General of Canada, http://www.gg.ca/document.aspx?id=16022&lan=eng.

11. I Walk in Beauty

1. I use "husband" where appropriate in my story, but we divorced in 2003.

About the Editors and Author of the Foreword

Andrew Garrod is a professor emeritus at Dartmouth College, where he previouly chaired the Department of Education, directed the Teacher Education Program, and taught courses in adolescence, moral development, and contemporary issues in US education. For a number of years, he has conducted a research project in Bosnia and Herzegovina on forgiveness, faith development, and moral reasoning. He also directed seven bilingual Shakespearean productions in Bosnia and Herzegovina that have played in Mostar and elsewhere in the Balkans; directed a trilingual production of *Romeo and Juliet* in Kigali, Rwanda; and directed numerous bilingual Shakespearean plays and Broadway musicals in the Marshall Islands. From 2000–2014 he directed a volunteer teaching program in the Marshall Islands in the Central Pacific. His recent publications include the coedited books *Mixed: Multiracial College Students Tell Their Life Stories; Growing Up Muslim: Muslim College Students in America Tell Their Life Stories*; and the chapter "Bridging the Divide with Shakespeare: Theatre as Moral Education in Bosnia and Herzegovina" in *The Reflexive Teaching Artist*. In 1991 and 2009 he was awarded Dartmouth College's Distinguished Teaching Award.

Robert Kilkenny is a clinical associate in the School of Social Work at Simmons College in Boston and a nationally recognized conference speaker on bullying. He is coeditor of *Souls Looking Back: Life Stories of Growing Up Black; Balancing Two Worlds: Asian American College Students Tell Their Life Stories; Mi Voz, Mi Vida: Latino College Students Tell Their Life Stories; Mixed: Multiracial College Students Tell Their Life Stories; Growing Up Muslim: Muslim College Students in America Tell Their Life Stories*; and *Adolescent*

Portraits: Identity, Relationships and Challenges, which is in its seventh edition. He is the founder and executive director of the Alliance for Inclusion and Prevention, a public-private partnership providing school-based mental health, special education, and after-school programs to at-risk students in the Boston public-school system.

Melanie Benson Taylor is associate professor and chair of Native American studies at Dartmouth College, where she teaches classes in literature and film. Her research focuses on the impact of economics on constructions of identity, culture, and community, particularly in the US South. She is the author of *Disturbing Calculations: The Economics of Identity in Postcolonial Southern Literature, 1912–2002* (University of Georgia Press, 2008) and *Reconstructing the Native South: American Indian Literature and the Lost Cause* (University of Georgia Press, 2012), as well as essays on William Faulkner, Louis Owens, Barry Hannah, Dawn Karima Pettigrew, and others. Her current book projects include *Indian Killers*, an exploration of violence in contemporary American literature by and about Native peoples, and *Doom: Modern American Fiction and the Ideological Indian*, a study of the Indian themes as refractions of economic anxiety in the work of US writers such as Faulkner, Ernest Hemingway, Willa Cather, and Katherine Anne Porter.

K. Tsianina Lomawaima (Mvskoke/Creek Nation) joined Arizona State University in January 2014. From 1994–2014 she served on the faculty of American Indian studies at the University of Arizona, serving as head from 2005 to 2009. From 1988 to 1994, she was a member of the Anthropology and American Indian Studies faculty at the University of Washington.

The recipient of numerous teaching honors, including the University of Washington's Distinguished Teaching Award, Dr. Lomawaima's teaching interests include US history, American Indian policy history, Indigenous knowledge systems, and research issues in American Indian education. Her research interests include the status of Native people as US citizens and Native nations as Indigenous sovereigns, the role of Native nations in shaping US federalism, and the history of American Indian education.

Many of her books have garnered national recognition, including *To Remain an Indian*, coauthored with Teresa L. McCarty (Outstanding Book Award, American Educational Research Association) and *They Called It Prairie Light* (North American Indian Prose Award, American Educational Association Critics' Choice Award). Most recent among her publications are "History without Silos, Ignorance versus

Knowledge, Education beyond Schools" in *History of Education Quarterly* 54, no. 3 (2014): 349–55; and "'All our people are building houses': The Civilization of Architecture and Space in Federal Indian Boarding Schools," in *Indian Subjects: New Directions in the History of Indigenous Education*, ed. Brenda Child and Brian Klopotek (Santa Fe: SAR Press, 2014), 148–76.

Lomawaima served as 2012–2013 president of the Native American and Indigenous Studies Association/NAISA, which she helped found in 2007, and as 2005 president of the American Society for Ethnohistory. She was awarded the Western History Association Lifetime Achievement Award for American Indian History in 2010.